ADVANCE PRAISE

"An absolutely remarkable te:
ultra-capitalism. It should be
silence at your disposal: its anaiysis is as fascinating as it is sharp."
—**Maïa Mazaurette**, *GQ France*

"Anselm Jappe describes the slow development of capitalism through the growing narcissism of the subject. The indifference and cruelty of capitalism, obsessed with quantitative value . . . is mirrored in the narcissist's indifference and cruelty to others."
—**Romaric Godin**, *Mediapart*

"Anselm Jappe has written a most insightful book. It is about the critique of value as a social practice of reified individuals. He develops narcissism as a subjective form of social indifference, cruelty, and violence. Disenchanted by its own madness, it runs amok in late capitalism."
—**Werner Bonefeld**, author of *A Critical Theory of Economic Compulsion*

"Capitalism creates a profound anthropological mutation, according to the author, by destroying all the symbolic and material limits to its expansion. . . . The globalization of capitalism being practically complete today, the modern subject ends up internalizing the 'death drive' of this fetishized world, the crucible for the outbursts of extreme violence that strike at the very heart of the most developed countries."
—**Mehdi Benallal**, *Le Monde Diplomatique*

"A stimulating work that has the merit of reminding us that it is not by small adjustments at the margin, by instilling more 'democracy' or 'sustainable development,' that the deadly and self-destructive logic of capitalism can be stopped."
—**Igor Martinache**, *Cause Commune*

"Anselm Jappe—trained in the school of the Marx of *Capital* and the *Grundrisse*, of Theodor Adorno and Guy Debord—does not do things by halves. A partial critique of the capitalist system hardly interests him."
—**Renaud Garcia**, *CQFD*

El Sereno Little Free Library
4747 Gambier Street
Los Angeles, CA 90032

The Self-Devouring Society: Capitalism, Narcissism, and Self-Destruction
Anselm Jappe
Translated by Eric-John Russell

This book is published with the support of Villa Albertine, in partnership with the French Embassy. The publisher gratefully acknowledges the support of the Hemingway Grant Program as well as the support of The French Mission for Culture and Higher Education (MCUFEU).

First published in French by Éditions La Découverte as *La société autophage: Capitalisme, démesure et autodestruction*

ISBN: 978-1-942173-79-3 | eBook ISBN: 978-1-945335-00-6
Library of Congress Number: 2023938288

10 9 8 7 6 5 4 3 2 1

Common Notions
c/o Interference Archive
314 7th St.
Brooklyn, NY 11215

Common Notions
c/o Making Worlds Bookstore
210 S. 45th St.
Philadelphia, PA 19104

www.commonnotions.org
info@commonnotions.org

Discounted bulk quantities of our books are available for organizing, educational, or fundraising purposes. Please contact Common Notions at the address above for more information.

Cover design by Josh MacPhee
Layout design and typesetting by Graciela "Chela" Vasquez | ChelitasDesign

Printed by union labor in Canada on acid-free paper

The Self-Devouring Society

The Self-Devouring Society:
Capitalism, Narcissism, and Self-Destruction

Anselm Jappe
Translated by Eric-John Russell

Brooklyn, NY
Philadelphia, PA
commonnotions.org

TABLE OF CONTENTS

PROLOGUE
A KING WHO DEVOURED HIMSELF

From the depths of time, ancient myths continue to reach us in the present, condensing into fables precise pictures of our own experiences.[1] This is no less true for little-known myths, such as the story of Erysichthon, bequeathed to us (with some variation) by the Hellenistic poet Callimachus and the Roman poet Ovid.[2] Erysichthon was the son of Triopas, who became king of Thessaly after having driven out its native inhabitants, the Pelasgians. The Pelasgians had dedicated a sacred grove to Demeter, goddess of the harvest and agriculture. In its center stood a gigantic oak tree, and the dryads, the nymphs of the forest, danced under the shade of its branches. One day, Erysichthon, eager to build a banquet hall as part of the construction of his palace, arrived at the grove accompanied by serfs armed with axes and began cutting down the trees. Demeter herself then appeared, under the guise of one of her priestesses, and called upon Erysichthon to cease. The king replied scornfully, but the serfs became frightened, wanting to avoid sacrilege. To reassert his supremacy, Erysichthon decapitated one of them. He then continued cutting down the tree, despite the blood running from its bark, as a voice emitting from within announced his punishment.

It did not take long: Demeter inflicted upon him the personification of hunger, which penetrated the body of the culprit through his breath. Erysichthon was seized with a craving that nothing could satisfy: the more he ate, the hungrier he became. He swallowed all of his provisions, his flocks, and his racehorses, but his bowels remained empty while he slowly withered away. He consumed, like a fire that devours everything in its path, what should have been enough to feed a city, an entire population. According to Callimachus, he was forced to hide away in his home, gave up going out and attending banquets, and ended up begging for food in the street after having plunged his father's kingdom into ruin. According to Ovid, Erysichthon went so far as to sell his own daughter, Mestra, to purchase more food. She managed to escape captivity thanks to the gift of shape-shifting, granted to her by Poseidon. Upon returning to the house of her father, she was sold again, several times in a row. But none of this satisfied Erysichthon's hunger: "[w]hen his terrible malady / Exhausted these provisions too, only adding / To his fatal disease, he began to take bites / Out of his own limbs, and in his misery / Fed himself by consuming his body."[3] Thus concludes Ovid's account.

Only the almost complete disappearance of familiarity with classical antiquity can explain why the metaphorical value of this little myth has thus far eluded the representatives of environmentalism. Indeed, the myth seems to encompass everything: the violation of nature at its most beautiful—and most sacred to its inhabitants—in order to extract building materials for the construction of centers of power. The bucolic pleasures of the dryads are sacrificed to those "feasts" to which the arrogant king plans explicitly to dedicate his palace. It is the powerful who turn a blind eye to the most pressing pleas to renounce such desecration, while the dominated are reluctant to lend their support (in Ovid, the serfs grumble at the misdeed even before the goddess intervenes). Their resistance, expressed in the name of respecting tradition, costs them dear, as the blind rage of contested power is unleashed against those who criticize and who would refrain from participating in the crimes. In the end, the serfs must submit and assist their master in accomplishing this misdeed. However, it is not upon them, who are merely "following orders" (Callimachus says so explicitly), that Demeter casts the flames of vengeance. She punishes Erysichthon alone, in a manner appropriate to his crime: unable to nourish himself, he lives as if the whole of nature has been transformed—for him—into a desert that refuses to lend its usual assistance to human life. Even his attempt to force a woman to remedy the damage caused by the folly of men fails, and he dies, abandoned by humanity and deprived of the fruits of nature.

This is one of those typically Greek myths that evokes *hubris*— immoderation due to blindness and ungodly vanity—which ends up provoking *nemesis*, the divine punishment suffered by Prometheus, Icarus, Bellerophon, Tantalus, Sisyphus, and Niobe, among others. One cannot help but be struck by the contemporary relevance of this myth. In particular, those who like to present the destruction of the natural environment as the transgression of an equally natural order may see it as an archetypal anticipation of their anxieties: disrespecting nature necessarily attracts the wrath of the gods, or nature itself . . .

Yet it goes much further: it is not a natural disaster that befalls the ancestor of the madmen who are today destroying the Amazon rainforest. His punishment is hunger, a hunger that grows with eating and that nothing satisfies. But hungry for what, exactly? No food can appease it. Nothing concrete, nothing real meets the need felt by Erysichthon. His hunger is unnatural and that is why nothing natural can soothe it. Instead, it is an abstract and quantitative hunger that can never be assuaged. However, the desperate attempt to allay this hunger drives him in vain to consume food, very concrete food, destroying it and thereby depriving those who need it. The myth thus anticipates, in an extraordinary manner, the logic of *value*, of the *commodity*, and of *money*:[4] while all production aimed at satisfying concrete needs finds its limits in the very nature of these needs and begins its cycle anew, the production of exchange-value, which is represented in money, is limitless. The thirst for money can never be quenched because money is not intended to satisfy a specific need. The accumulation of value, and therefore of money, is not exhausted when the "hunger" is satiated, but immediately begins again for a new, expanded cycle. The hunger of money is abstract; it is empty of content. Satisfaction is for it a means, not an end. But this abstract hunger does not take place within the realm of abstraction alone. As with Erysichthon, it destroys all the concrete "food" it finds in its path to stoke its own flame and does so on an ever-increasing scale. Yet always in vain. Its particularity is not greed as such—which is nothing new under the sun—but a kind of greed that *a priori* can never attain that which might fulfill it: "Looking for feasts in the middle of feasts," says Ovid.[5] It is not simply the wickedness of the rich that is at play here, but rather a bewitchment that acts as a screen between available resources and the possibility of enjoying them. Thus, the myth of Erysichthon has obvious parallels with the well-known myth of King Midas, who dies of starvation because everything he touches, including his food, turns to gold.

Perhaps the most notable aspect of the story of Erysichthon is its ending: the abstract rage, not calmed even by the devastation of the world, ends in self-destruction, in self-consumption. This myth tells us not only about the devastation of nature and social injustice, but also about the abstract and fetishistic character of the logic of the commodity and its destructive and self-destructive results. It can therefore be seen as an illustration of the contemporary critique of commodity fetishism, according to which "capitalism is like the sorcerer forced to throw the entire concrete world into the cauldron of commodification in order to prevent everything from coming to a halt. A solution to the environmental crisis cannot be found within the constraints of the capitalist system which always needs to grow, to consume ever more matter, for no other reason than to compensate for the shrinking mass of value."[6] This critique compares the situation of contemporary capitalism to a steamboat that continues to steer through the water only by gradually burning the planks of its deck, its hull, etc.[7] Dying of hunger in the midst of abundance: this is the situation to which capitalism leads us.

However, the troubling similarities between the lofty king of Thessaly and our situation go even further. His behavior evokes not only the logic of the inverted world of commodity fetishism, but also, more directly, the behavior of the subjects who live under its reign. The furious impulse that intensifies with every attempt to appease it and leads to the physical disintegration of the individual—who previously spent all of his resources and violated the most basic affections to the point of coercing the women around him into prostitution—recalls the journey of the addict in withdrawal. Some drug addicts thus embody the logic of capitalism, for which they serve as a sort of metaphorical figuration. More generally, Erysichthon clearly possesses the traits of the narcissist, in the clinical sense of the term. He knows only himself; he cannot establish real relations with natural objects, other human beings, or with the symbolic instances and moral principles intended to regulate human life. He denies the objectivity of the external world, which in turn denies and refuses to provide him with the most basic material relief, such as food. *Hubris*, for which Erysichthon is punished, consisted for the Greeks in challenging the gods, on the pretense of being their equals. Beyond this strictly religious dimension, the Greek condemnation of *hubris* is a warning against the desire for omnipotence against the fantasies of omnipotence that constitute the basis of narcissism.

Fetishism and narcissism: it is around these two concepts and their consequences in society today that this book will center. Erysichthon's *hubris* leads to destruction and ultimately self-destruction, a reminder of what we witness today, a situation which the category of the "interest" of "actors" can in no way help us to understand. For some time now, the impression prevails that capitalist society is on a path of suicidal drift that no one consciously wants, but to which everyone contributes. Destruction of the economic structures that ensure the reproduction of the members of society; destruction of social bonds; destruction of cultural diversity, traditions and languages; destruction of the natural foundations of life: what we are seeing everywhere is not just the end of certain ways of life and a transition to others—the "creative destruction" allegedly so common in the history of humanity—but rather a series of catastrophes at all levels, even on a planetary scale, which seem to threaten the very survival of humanity, or at least the continuation of a very large part of what gave meaning to the "human adventure," plunging human beings back into a state of "amphibians."[8]

However, the main purpose of this book is not to remind us of the countless reasons to be indignant about the state of the world in which we live, nor to add new ones. Rather than adding to the case for prosecution, this book's objective is to contribute to the *comprehension* of what is happening to us—its origins, forms, and possibilities of development—as well as to try to identify the profound *unity* of the misfortunes described, and to go back and trace what holds it all together. This is the first condition for an intervention with any chance of success.

This book extends the analyses presented in *The Adventures of the Commodity*, where I set out the essential arguments of the "critique of value."[9] It is not necessary, however, to read that book as a preliminary for reading this one, since its most important concepts are taken up here at the beginning and in various places throughout. Nevertheless, knowledge of *The Adventures of the Commodity* will undoubtedly allow for a better grasp of the stakes involved in *The Self-Devouring Society*, which follows a somewhat different path. An appendix at the end of this book summarizes the essential theses of the critique of value: we recommend this as a preliminary reading for those not yet familiar, while others can proceed straight into the first chapter.

Rather than first establishing a theoretical basis drawn from the works of Marx and then arriving at more historical, detailed and "concrete" considerations, it will be a question here of dealing with the subject-matter through various approaches, some of which are conceptual and others "empirical." The process is therefore less deductive and the focus can change from one chapter to the next: sometimes it is a matter of summarizing broad issues using fairly general concepts; other times it is a matter of examining in detail an argument, an author, or a phenomenon. This work is not a systematic treatise, but an attempt to shed new light on the modern form of the subject. The critique of value constitutes the basis of this book, but it mobilizes other approaches that have recently appeared in the humanities and social sciences and engages in a dialogue with authors who are sometimes far removed from the critique of value.

The Adventures of the Commodity provides an analysis of the essential aspects of a specific theme: the critique of value and its reading of Marx. *The Self-Devouring Society*, on the other hand, deals with much broader issues it cannot claim to have exhausted. Like the early archaeologists, I excavated intermittent shafts instead of patiently removing entire layers of the terrain. It is therefore rather a research program whose future advance can only take the form of a collective work, already begun here and there.

The insights thrown on the question of commodity subjectivity are thus varied. In the first chapter, the approach is philosophical and historical, and based on the critique of value; in the second, the discussion is engaged with psychoanalysis, the Frankfurt School, and Christopher Lasch; in the third, I utilize contemporary sociology; the fourth concentrates on the issue of violence and school shootings; finally, the epilogue takes up the concepts of "domination" and "democracy" and examines the frightening prospect of a possible anthropological regression.

As far as the mode of exposition is concerned, I hope to have avoided academic style or any other form of jargon and have managed to follow the advice of Schopenhauer: "use ordinary words and say extraordinary things"—and not the other way around.

CHAPTER 1
ON THE FETISHISM THAT RULES THIS WORLD

Is there something that binds together the seemingly disparate phenomena that form, whether we like it or not, the fabric of our lives? One of my earlier works, *The Adventures of the Commodity*, attempted to provide an initial answer to this question by describing the role of *value*, the *commodity*, *abstract labor*, and *money* in capitalist society. What was missing was an analysis of the role of the subject. This analysis is essentially based on a return to a part of the work of Karl Marx— notably the first chapter of the first volume of *Capital*—which, for a very long time, was neglected by almost all "Marxists." Here, Marx made a radical *critique* of value, the commodity, abstract labor, and money. These categories are not treated as neutral or transhistorical facts, identifiable in any mode of production regardless of its level of development. On the contrary, these are categories which, in their fully developed form, belong to capitalist society alone. When these categories completely regulate the reproduction of society and social life, they reveal their highly destructive potential and ultimately lead society, and all of its members, into a serious crisis where it becomes impossible to operate any longer within the terms of these categories. While traditional Marxism and almost all leftist movements have always limited themselves to demanding a different *distribution* of the fruits of this mode of production (the "class struggle" around, for example, the distribution of "surplus-value"), the "critique of value," on the other hand, questioned the very *mode of production* itself. This critique was developed most notably in the works of Marx; was then taken up in a fragmentary manner by the young Georg Lukács in *History and Class Consciousness* (1923), in the Frankfurt School, and the Situationists; and was elaborated systematically from the eighties onwards by the journals *Krisis* and *Exit!* in Germany and by authors like Robert Kurz and Moishe Postone. Why does a large portion of human activity take the form of *abstract labor*, which supposedly gives *value* to *commodities* and is represented in *money*? What is the true nature of these "molds" into which social life is cast?

Lessons from the Critique of Value

We will limit ourselves here to a very brief summary of the most important terms of the critique of value. In capitalist society, production does not follow any predetermined organization, but consists of separate producers who exchange their commodities, services included, on anonymous markets. In order to exchange them, it is necessary to be able to measure their products using a single metric, and their only commonality is that they are the products of human labor. However, the different labors that go into these commodities are just as incommensurable with each other as are their products. The only common denominator of all labor is the fact that it is always an expenditure of human energy, "of brains, nerves and muscles" (Marx). This expenditure is measured in duration over time. In other words, it is the sheer *amount of time* necessary for the production of commodities (and to produce their component parts and the tools needed for their production, for training workers, etc.) that determines their value. This is what Marx calls *abstract labor*: working time expended without regard to any content. Two commodities, however different they may be, and however different the concrete labor that created them, possess the same value if the same amount of time—and therefore the same amount of human energy—was required for their production. On the market, these commodities relate to each other as quantities of abstract time, that is, as values. In order to find a buyer, they also need to possess a *use-value*, which only serves to *realize* their value derived from labor. The value of a commodity, however, is invisible; what is visible is the *price* in *mon-*

ey. Money is not a social convention, a mere means of facilitating exchange, but a real commodity in which other commodities have their own value represented (for a long time, it was precious metals that assumed such a role).

Each commodity thus has a *dual character*: it is at once a concrete object that serves to satisfy a specific need and a "bearer" of a quantity of undifferentiated labor. It is labor itself that carries this dual character: concrete and abstract labor are not two different kinds of labor (nor do they have anything to do with different contents, for example, material and immaterial labor), but are the *same activity* considered both as the production of a product—material or immaterial—and as an amount of time expended. It is this dual character of the commodity and of the labor which produces it that Marx placed at the beginning of *Capital* and from which he deduced the entire functioning of capitalism.

Furthermore, these two sides do not peacefully coexist: they are in conflict, and from this conflict, the "abstract" side emerges victorious. In a commodity-capitalist society, social reproduction is organized around the exchange of quantities of labor, not around the satisfaction of needs and desires. It is enough to recall that the quantity of labor takes the form of a quantity of money to understand how much this theoretical postulate corresponds to everyday reality.

The capitalist economy is the art of turning one dollar into two and mandating that everything else conform to this singular purpose. However, this well-known fact cannot be explained by greed or the desire for pleasure. Capitalism did not invent greed, social injustice, exploitation, or domination. Instead, what constitutes its historical peculiarity is the generalization of the commodity form, and thus of the dual nature of commodities and labor, as well as its consequences.

Money is no longer an auxiliary of commodity production, but commodity production has become an auxiliary for producing money. One does not exchange a commodity for money in order to transform the money back into another commodity (that is, to exchange, through the intermediary of money, something one possesses but does not need, for something else one wishes to obtain). Rather, one purchases a commodity with money in order to resell it and obtain another sum of money. Since money, unlike commodities, is always the same, this process is meaningless if the amount of money at the end of the exchange process is not greater than the amount committed at the start. Every economic transaction in capitalism therefore serves to *increase* a sum of money. Such a system *must* necessarily grow: the growth is not a choice, but the real purpose of the process. However, this is not an increase in the "real" production (of commodities). This may or may not take place: it is only the increase in money that matters.

Yet money represents the value of commodities, and value is determined by the quantity of abstract labor. An actual increase in money is therefore not possible without a temporal increase in the labor expended. In its classic form, this increase is achieved through the exploitation of labor: the owner of a sum of money (capital) purchases the labor-power of the worker, who is forced to work longer than is necessary in order to pay their wage. This excess constitutes surplus-value, and thus ultimately the profit of the capitalist who, if he wants to remain a capitalist, will take care to reinvest part of his profit in a new, larger purchase of labor-power, since otherwise he risks being eliminated by the competitive relations with other owners of capital.

The extraction of surplus-value through the exploitation of the worker has long monopolized the attention of the labor movement and its theorists, and its denunciation was seen as the core of Marx's theory. Yet another aspect of this process remained in the shadows: such a mode of production entails a structural *indifference* towards the *contents* of production and the needs of those who have to produce and consume them. All previous forms of production, however unjust or irrational they may have been, were dedicated to the satisfaction of some need, real or imaginary, and were exhausted with its fulfillment, only to begin the same cycle over again. In other words, they *served* a purpose: to reproduce the existing society. When money itself becomes the purpose of production, no satisfied need can ever stand as the end goal. Production becomes its own purpose, and every growth only serves to resume the cycle at a higher level. Value as such has no natural limit to its growth, yet it cannot forego having a use-value, and therefore cannot relinquish being represented in a "real" object. The expansion of value cannot take place without a—necessarily much faster—growth in material production. Material growth, by consuming natural resources, ends up consuming the real world. This is what the myth of Erysichthon announces in such an astonishing manner. This growth is *tautological*—it has no content of its own and generates a dynamic of growth for the sake of growth. However, this is not just an "attitude" or "ideology": competition in the market forces each player to participate in this frenzied and insane game, or to disappear. It is easy to understand that the deep roots of the ecological disaster brought by capitalism are to be found here. But at many other levels, too, it can be observed that the need for unlimited growth in value, and the indifference to the means for achieving it, constitutes the common foundation that shapes the most diverse aspects of modernity.

The increase of money and value is only possible through the increase of *labor* performed. Modern commodity society is therefore necessarily a society of labor. In fact, it also invented the concept of "work," unknown in previous societies in the sense of a term that encompasses the most diverse activities. Building a table and playing the piano, babysitting for the neighbor, shooting a rifle at other human beings, harvesting wheat, celebrating a religious rite: these activities are totally different from each other, and no one in a pre-modern society would have thought to subsume them all under a single concept. But in the society of labor, their particularities are neglected or even cancelled out in favor solely of the expenditure of quantitatively determined labor.

We are accustomed to recognizing commodities, money, labor, and value as "economic" factors. Any discourse about them—including the one developed here—might be considered "economic" discourse. It would as such concern only one aspect of life, a particularly boring aspect that ought to be left to economists, while other areas of life would fall under the domain of psychology, sociology, anthropology, linguistics, etc. "Economism," that is, the reduction of human activity to solely economic, utilitarian, and materialistic motivations, can be called into question as a limit of any Marxist discourse, including its most heterodox variants, such as the "critique of value." According to this perspective, economism, like any other mono-causal explanation of human society, would be obsolete, and the enormous complexity of society could only be grasped through a combination of all the sciences. The "totalitarianism" of a single approach to the phenomena of human beings would even constitute one of the roots of political totalitarianism.

This view is not false if it is directed against the multiple forms of traditional Marxism, which, starting from the "base-superstructure" schema, always maintain, in one way or another, that the economy, effectively conceived as a partial domain of social life, dominates, in the final instance, other aspects of life (cultural, social, religious, symbolic, etc.), even with the qualification of a "reciprocal interaction" exerted by these domains upon one another. The critique of value, on the other hand, is not limited to underlining the imperialism of the economic sphere at the expense of other vital spheres. Rather, it analyzes commodity value as the *general form* of production and reproduction of society, activity, and consciousness. In other words: value (and thus labor, money, the commodity) is the principle of *social synthesis* in capitalist modernity. Instead of "deducing" everything from value conceived in purely economic terms, it is a question of analyzing the different expressions of the same "empty form," expressions that mediate each other but always refer to abstract labor as the "basic form" realized in everyday practice.

Every society requires a principle of synthesis: a unifying principle that allows individuals and their material and immaterial products, which are as such separate and incommensurable, to form parts of a collective that ensures the mutual satisfaction of needs. The "chain of gifts," direct political domination, and religion were among the main elements of social synthesis that prevailed in pre-modern societies, which possessed several simultaneous principles of synthesis. In capitalist society, it is *labor* that makes each individual a member of society who shares with other members a common essence, allowing them to participate in the circulation of its products. It is because their activities take the common form of a quantity of labor, represented in a quantity of money, that individuals can meet as part of a whole, that is, form a society. It suffices to imagine losing one's wallet in a foreign city to realize the extent to which one is no longer a member of society without the materialization of the principle of synthesis that connects us to others—the social bond that we always carry around in our pockets, as Marx remarked.[1]

Of course, this idea requires some important clarifications. There are activities that do not count as "labor" and are not paid, but nevertheless very important—for example, raising children, reading a book for pleasure, or having friends over for dinner. However, these activities are not free from the grip of labor; they generally play an indispensable, auxiliary role: essentially, they ensure the reproduction of labor-power. It is also true that in modern societies there is another great principle of synthesis: the status of the citizen, or member of a state or nation. But this status is in no way "alternative" to the status of laborer—an illusion characteristic of the contemporary left—but subordinate to it.

We will return to these statements for further analysis. However, it must be emphasized here that "economism" is not simply a theoretical error, but a stark reality: in commodity society, the economy has colonized all spheres of life and subjected the whole of existence to the demand of profitability. If all human activities, and thus all aspects of life, are directly or indirectly subordinated to the demands of the economy and must conform to the laws of money and the labor that produces it, then the economy—the capitalist economy—becomes coextensive with human life itself. However, this "real economism" is peculiar to commodity society and to it alone; it was completely unknown to earlier forms of social organization. It is to Moishe Postone's particular credit to have demonstrated in *Time, Labor, and Social Domination*—based on a rigorous rereading of Marx— that capitalism, far from having denied the role of labor, as traditional Marxists claim, has instead made it into a universal form of social mediation, one which directs society itself, whereas in precapitalist societies, labor was subordinated to decisions made in other social spheres on the basis of other principles of synthesis—according to feudal hierarchy, for example, which was not linked to productivity or labor.[2] Thus, two levels of "domination" must be distinguished: on the one hand, the familiar domination of certain social groups over others, which has occupied almost all of the attention of critical observers of society, from Marxists to Pierre Bourdieu; on the other hand, behind this visible domination lies the domination exercised by impersonal structures over the whole of society. This domination exerted by value, labor, money, and the commodity is more difficult to define. Marx used mysterious sounding terms to describe it, such as "automatic subject" or the "fetish-character of the commodity." Any fetishistic society is a society whose members follow rules that are the unconscious result of their own activities, but which present themselves as powers external and superior to human beings, and where the subject becomes the mere executor of fetishized laws.

The predominance of the commodity-form is not only expressed in the ever-increasing submission of life to economic tyranny. It also consists in the diffusion of a *general form* whose main characteristic is that of commodity value: devoid of all content, an empty and pure quantity without quality. The general fetishistic forms of previous cultures—totemism, religions, personal domination over slaves and serfs—had *concrete* contents, however oppressive they may have been. The value of the commodity is the only fetish form that is a pure form without content, a form indifferent to any content. This is why its effects are so destructive. To grasp the consequences of the spread of this form of social synthesis in the modern era is essential for understanding the *coherence* of the very diverse phenomena that threaten us today, but which, if considered separately, remain without any real explanation.

In most of their activities, the subjects of the commodity do not consciously sacrifice themselves to the cult of the commodity fetish. Rather, they believe they are pursuing their "interests." The question then arises as to what *form of mediation* there is between empirical consciousness and the basic social form of commodity value. In other words, it is necessary to determine the *general form of consciousness*, the form that predetermines any particular content, like a framework of perception.

Between human actions and decisions on the one hand, and the concrete, sensuous and material contents of their production (in the broadest sense) on the other, there is always a fetishistic social form that determines the fate of these concrete contents. This unconscious social form acts as a "code," giving form to activities and creating the "blind" but apparently "objective" or "natural" laws that regulate human life. In the past, it may have been "God's will"; today, it is "economic laws," "the demands of profitability," "technological imperatives," or "the need for growth." These are "laws" that clearly do not belong to "first nature" (the sphere of biology), but to "second nature," to the social environment that human beings have shaped in the course of their development. These laws are therefore undeniably the work of human beings, and yet no one has decreed them in their present form; they often lead to situations that no one consciously wants and yet to which everyone contributes.

Marx placed the pages on fetishism at the end of the first chapter of *Capital*, Vol. I as a summary of his development of the concept of value.[3] However, it is at the beginning of the second chapter that Marx gives one of the most concise definitions of fetishism, as an extension of his previous reasoning, which is often tinged with irony: "It is plain that commodities cannot go to market and make exchanges of their own account. We must, therefore, have recourse to their guardians, who are also their owners."[4] From the point of view of the logic of the commodity, commodities are self-sufficient. They are the real actors in social life. Humans enter the scene only as servants of their own products. Since commodities have no legs, they assign human beings the task of circulating them, otherwise, they could do without them altogether. And if we were to remind them that it is still human beings who produce them, would it be so surprising if they became angry?

The fetish-character of the commodity is not a false consciousness or mere mystification, but a form of total social existence that anticipates any separation between material reproduction and the psyche, since it determines the very forms of thought and activity. Commodity fetishism shares these features with other forms of fetishism, such as religious consciousness. It could thus be characterized as an "*a priori* form."

The concept of an *a priori* form obviously evokes the philosophy of Immanuel Kant. However, as considered here, the formal schema that precedes all concrete experience and in fact models it is not ontological, as in Kant, but historical and subject to development. For Kant, the forms given *a priori*, in which any content of consciousness must necessarily be represented, are time, space, and causality. He conceives these forms as innate in every human being, without society or history playing any role. It suffices to take up this question and arrive at conclusions close to the critique of commodity fetishism by removing the atemporal and anthropological character of the *a priori* categories. The fact that perceptions of time, space, and causality vary greatly in different cultures throughout the world has been noted even by some Kantians.[5] However, it is not only a question of knowledge, but also of activity. Marx's notion of the fetish-character of the commodity and Freud's notion of the unconscious are the two main forms that, after Kant, have been given to account for a level of consciousness where agents do not perceive clearly what ultimately determines them. But while the Freudian theory of the unconscious has been widely accepted, Marx's contribution to understanding the general form of consciousness has remained the most misunderstood aspect of his work.[6] With formulations such as the "fetish-character of the commodity" and "automatic subject," Marx laid the foundations for a conception of the unconscious whose form is subject to historical change, whereas Freud conceived the unconscious essentially as the receptacle of anthropological or even biological constants. For Freud, it is always a question of the relationship between the unconscious and culture in general, and for him this relationship has hardly changed since the time of the "primitive horde." In his theory, there is no room for the fetishistic form, whose development constitutes precisely the mediation between biological nature, as an almost invariable factor, and the events of historical life.

The relationship between Kant's *a priori*, Freud's unconscious and Marx's fetishism has rarely been thoroughly investigated. We will attempt to unify these approaches in a certain sense, without neglecting their differences or even their incompatibility—especially between Kant, an enthusiastic ideologue of the new form of consciousness he heralded, and Marx, who provided the first complete critique of this form.[7] Indeed, what we will be analyzing is the birth of the modern subject itself, and, without viewing it as an "epistemological error," we will nevertheless end up stripping it of many of its supposed merits. The term "subject" is often taken to mean simply that there must always be a human bearer of action and consciousness, but this generic definition explains nothing. It can be compared to the common misidentification of "labor" with any metabolism with nature—and this connection between the subject and labor is not accidental. What is usually called "subject" is not identical to the human being or the individual: it constitutes a particular historical figure that appeared quite recently, at the same time as labor. The subject is based on a split, on the expulsion of a part of oneself and on the fear of its return. One might also suspect that the subject-form—the general fact of being a subject—actually entails the erasure of all individual particularity.[8] So perhaps this subject is not necessarily the bearer of human emancipation, the "good pole" to be defended against the "bad pole" of an oppressive society. Perhaps there will be no "revolutionary subject" that puts an end to capitalist society, and that social emancipation will rather consist in the overcoming of the subject-form itself. It is therefore neither a question of "liberating the subject" nor, on the contrary, of considering its absence, via structuralism, as an ontological fact.

Marx provided an essential contribution to this debate with his concept of the "automatic subject," even if it appears only once in his work: "[Value] is constantly changing from one form into the other, without becoming lost in this movement; it thus becomes transformed into an automatic subject."[9] In a society dominated by commodity fetishism, there can be no true human subject: it is value in its metamorphoses (commodity and money) that constitutes the true subject. Human "subjects" exist in its wake, and are its executors and "functionaries"—"subjects" of the automatic subject.[10]

What then is the "subject"? What was its history? Is it possible to write a history of the constitution of the human psyche parallel to the history of forms of production, and to understand their relationship? More importantly, is it possible to write it while abandoning the old "base-superstructure" schema altogether? Not simply by overturning it, nor constructing a new admixture, but to arrive at an understanding of the "total social form."

As an example of the heuristic power of this approach, we can point to the view it allows us to cast on the birth of capitalism in the fourteenth and fifteenth centuries. There is a clear connection between the beginnings of a positive view of labor in the monasteries during the Middle Ages, the replacement of "concrete time" by "abstract time" (and the construction of the first clocks), technical innovations, and the invention of firearms—an invention that was at the origin of the enormous need for money in nascent states, which led to the transformation of subsistence economies into monetary economies. It is impossible to establish a hierarchy between "ideal" factors (conceptions of time, visions of labor) and material or technological factors; at the same time, it is not a question of a simple coincidence of independent elements. The ability to abstract and quantify seems to constitute here this *a priori* coding, this form of general consciousness without which technological innovations or geographical discoveries would not have had the same impact—and vice versa.

At this point, we can already put forward a very important element for interpreting some episodes in the history of ideas proposed in this book. We believe, of course, that forms of thought—symbolic expressions—are part of the history of the societies in which they have developed, and that they often provide the best means for understanding those societies. However, the point here is not to establish direct links between these forms of thought—for example, the great philosophical systems—and class relations, in the vein of "historical materialism." The latter invariably saw in almost all thinking from the seventeenth to the nineteenth century the expression of the "rise of the bourgeoisie" and its aspirations to free itself from feudal and clerical domination. This type of analysis is not incorrect, and it has often led to important results. But what we are proposing here concerns another level of analysis—another "geological layer"— in the history of bourgeois society. This is a level of analysis that touches on the constitution of the subject and its deep psychological dimensions, in the hope that one day a "materialist" history of the human soul might be unearthed. We do not mean "material" in the sense of presupposing an ontological preeminence of material production or "labor," but in the sense of conceiving the symbolic sphere as neither self-sufficient nor self-referential.

A Bad Subject

Narcissism is one of the characteristic features of the modern subject-form. In order to study the stages of its establishment on a social scale, a look at some philosophical works may be helpful. The work of Descartes, Kant, Sade, Schopenhauer, and many others can be seen as "symptomatic" of the establishment of a new fetishistic constitution which is at the same time "subjective" and "objective," a form of production and a form of everyday life, a deep psychic structure and a form of social bonding. Indeed, the formation of the modern subject, the spread of abstract labor, the birth of the modern state, and many other developments have taken place in parallel, or, to put it better, are only different aspects of the same process. In this process, there is no predetermined hierarchy of factors, and none unilaterally "derive" from another.

The subject-form is not always the direct emanation of the value-form in the economic sense but can also be in contradiction with it. Moreover, the subject-form contains elements from previous social formations reappropriated for new purposes (antisemitism, patriarchy, religion)—here the analogy with "geological layers" becomes obvious.

The subject is not an anthropological invariant, but a cultural construction, the result of a historical process. However, its existence is very real. It cannot therefore be attributed to a misinterpretation, as structuralism and social-systems theory would have it. A clear differentiation between the subject (of knowledge and will) and the object is not self-evident and did not exist before the birth of the modern subject-form, which established an absolute opposition between the two. This is why, in a religious universe, the subject is not considered the autonomous creator of its world, but is largely determined by external subjects, such as God or spirits. The subject thus partly shares in the status of the object. At the same time, nature is not conceived as mere objectivity, obeying invariable laws, but viewed as a kind of subject endowed with its own inscrutable will. The term "subject" can, moreover, indicate both an individual subject and a collective subject, such as a people or social class. The subject-form implies that the agent is always identical to itself, totally autonomous and in a relationship of exteriority to its social context.

Our approach is to think together the concepts of "narcissism" and "commodity fetishism" and to indicate their simultaneous development; or, more precisely, to demonstrate that they are two sides of the same social form. As we will see in more detail in the next chapter, the narcissist, following Freud, is essentially a person who remains, despite appearances, at a primitive stage of their psychic development: they perceive, like the newborn, the whole world as an extension of their own ego. Or, to put it better, narcissists do not conceive of a separation between the self and the world—since they cannot accept the original separation from the maternal figure. In order to "magically" deny this painful separation, and the feelings of impotence and distress it entails, the narcissist experiences the entire world, including their fellow human beings, as an extension of their ego. Obviously, this is accomplished unconsciously. Behind an appearance of normality, the adult narcissist hides the inability of recognizing "objects," in the broadest sense, in their autonomy and accepting their separation. The egocentrism of the narcissist— its most visible aspect—is only a consequence of this process. The external world is perceived as a *projection*: objects and people are not perceived for what they are, but as extensions of the subject's inner world. Faced with the feeling of omnipotence of the narcissistic ego—which resorts, if necessary, at least in the case of a small child, to forms of hallucinatory satisfaction of its desires—the world is only an object to be manipulated, or even an obstacle for the effective realization of desires so easily to satisfied within the sphere of the imagination. The physical body of the narcissistic subject is also part of this potentially hostile and refractory external world. In the division between the narcissistic self and the world, the boundaries of the external world begin with one's own body. The latter can resist the self and painfully remind it of its limits, as well as the irreducibility of the external world to its desires. As for the ego, it does not immediately identify with the body and its sensations, but only with the inner world and the subject's impulses—what Freud called the "primary process."

Of course, the narcissism referred to here does not consist merely in an excess of self-love, vanity, and the cult of the body, nor even in the cult of the ego or in egoism, as the more common use of the term suggests. Narcissism, in the psychoanalytic sense, is on the contrary a weakness of the ego: the individual remains confined to a primitive phase of psychic development. It does not even reach the stage of Oedipal conflict, which gives access to "object relations." It is the opposite of a strong and glorified self: impoverished and empty because it is unable to flourish in true relations with external objects and people. It limits itself to reliving the same primitive impulses over and over again.

It's Descartes' Fault

The subject-form was gradually configured from the Renaissance onwards, and especially during the Enlightenment. Yet it did not simply appear alongside the rise of capitalism, but is consubstantial with it. There is general agreement on the point of departure of this development: the subject is the result of "secularization." Somewhere between Pico della Mirandola and Nietzsche, the human being declared its independence from God. It emerged from its "minority" (Kant), from its filial relationship to the higher powers, to become an adult and understand that it itself constitutes and governs its world.[11] But has "secularized" man really left metaphysics behind? Has it really outgrown its need for religion, as one does an infantile stage? Or has metaphysics only changed its appearance while continuing to determine our lives? Is the modern subject not the result of the transformation of past forms of social fetishism? In many ways, the famous *disenchantment* of the world has turned out to be a *re-enchantment* of the world. Metaphysics is no longer limited to the beyond, but has infiltrated the here and now. In so doing, it ceased to be recognizable as such, because instead of constituting a separate realm, it burrowed within the everyday relationships of human beings, in the production and reproduction of their lives. From the beginning, the historical formation of the subject did not occur as a break with Christianity, but as its continuation by other means.

The decline of the traditional Christian worldview after the Middle Ages meant that humanity ceased to appear as the mediator between divinity and nature, halfway between the two. The human being became partly God itself, powerful like him, and partly mere nature, belonging to the science of biology, or even mechanics and machinery. The imperial relationship to "external nature" has become the same as that to "internal nature." The human body became regarded as a physical body like other objects, with the difference between the living and the non-living fading from view.

On the other hand, according to the Christian worldview, the body can give rise not only to sin, but also to salvation. As the adversary of the soul, it is also very real. It is therefore not the mere incarnation of the spirit and is entitled to future resurrection. This conception does not render the concrete the mere representational form of the abstract. The concrete is not the simple accident of a substance. From the fourteenth century onwards, Europeans discovered the earthly dimension of existence; they then ceased to consider life as preparation for the afterlife. Exemplary here are the paintings of Giotto (died 1337), or the beginnings of fashion that emphasized the body rather than veiling it (trousers and leotards became widespread at the end of the fourteenth century). The vision of modernity as an increasing secularization and emancipation from religion and its devaluation of the earthly dimension, however, is only one part of the story: at the same time, the secular subject of the economy began to devalue the material world, transforming it into a representation of the abstract and rendering the concrete into an accidental embodiment of the substance of value.

Without presenting here a detailed history of the genesis of the subject-form, let us examine at least two of the main founders of modernity: Descartes and Kant. If read slightly differently than the usual heroic legend would have it, some troubling conclusions can be drawn about modernity.

Textbooks on the history of philosophy commonly describe Descartes as having made a profound break in the history of thought. He is even said to be the true founder of modern philosophy, along with Galileo, Francis Bacon, and Thomas Hobbes. This assertion does not seem exaggerated: compared to the scholastic tradition, which always consisted of interpreting a sacred or canonical text such as the Bible, Aristotle, or the Church Fathers, and even compared to the abundant forest of Renaissance naturalist philosophy, Descartes appears—and presented himself—as the first thinker since the Greeks to construct a metaphysical and epistemological discourse from scratch, without any presuppositions, as if no one had thought before him. Although the details of his arguments are imbued with scholastic procedures and content, and he invariably refers to God the moment a flaw appears in his argument, his basic concepts are indeed revolutionary. As a result, he must also shoulder all the praise and blame that modernity has attracted since. Opinions about Descartes have developed in line with judgments made about modernity itself. For anti-modernist traditionalists, he represented the subversive force of Reason, undermining the throne and the altar, and was even said to have been the cause of the French Revolution. The Church initially blacklisted him. Then, during the age of triumphant scientific progress, Descartes was seen as a hero, the embodiment of "French genius." The rise of mistrust towards instrumental reason during the twentieth century has again made him a favored target. Thus, his proposal to "make us masters and possessors of nature," which met with widespread approval during the nineteenth century, now appears, at a time of ecological catastrophe, as the root of all evil—even its paradigmatic formulation, leading us straight into the abyss! Those who continue to transform the human being and the world into a machine no longer need any theory. But those who oppose it often start by criticizing Descartes— while, of course, Hobbes, Bacon, Locke, Leibniz, Mandeville, and Adam Smith also take a portion of the blame. Descartes is often "the one we love to hate," from Martin Heidegger to Karl Jaspers and Hannah Arendt, to Dany-Robert Dufour today. It may therefore seem too convenient to account once again for the misdeeds of modernity by criticizing him, but it can hardly be avoided. He lends himself too easily to it, and each generation can find new faults in his work, new reasons for criticism, unnoticed by earlier critics.

The same applies to the history of the constitution of the subject. It is not a question of attributing to Descartes something like an initial approximate formulation of the status of this subject. On the contrary, the narcissism and "absence of the world" characteristic of the modern subject are already found there in such a pure form that it can be said that the successive centuries have only developed, little by little, everything that was already contained in this initial intuition. In this regard, it is a bit like money: capital is contained in its "concept" ("money as money," in the words of Marx), as well as all of its possible developments, but it took more than half a millennium for money to become completely *in actu* what it always was *in potentia*.

Descartes is the representative of the bourgeois revolution par excellence. His intention was to demolish the existing world down to its foundations in order to rebuild it according to the laws of the rational subject. At the same time, he confined himself to a strict conservatism with regard to morality and the political and social order. On the one hand, certain concessions to Church dogmas were purely opportunistic or fearful; yet on the other, his abhorrence of any questioning of the social order is undoubtedly part of the very essence of his program. Descartes paradigmatically announces what the innovations of bourgeois society will consist of: splitting the atom down to its nucleus, creating the "vortex" (not by chance a central concept of Cartesian physics) of a permanent destruction and restructuring of forms of life and the ideologies that accompany them. It is a question of subverting nature in order to safeguard the structures of social domination, not of subverting society: in short, a kind of "conservative revolution." Nothing is accepted as natural except what is produced by man. As such, Descartes foresaw an infinite progress of the sciences, but he did not conceive this as a broadening or joy of knowledge, but rather with a view to its practical applications—something he advocated for above all in medicine, which he predicted to have a promising future.

Descartes expresses his horror of "those troublemaking and restless personalities who, called neither by their birth nor by their fortune to manage public affairs, are forever coming up with an idea for some new reform in this matter."[12] If his "provisional code of morals" is intended to be stoic, it is not far from the flattest conformism: he proposes to follow the most moderate and popular opinions and laws of his country, "commonly accepted in practice," to resign himself to misfortune and to "try to conquer myself rather than fortune, and to change my desires rather than the order of the world," because only our thoughts are under our complete control.[13] Consequently, he even abandoned Galileo's heliocentric hypothesis after its condemnation by the Church of Rome, even though he believed it to have been solidly proven and, moreover, completely harmless from the point of view of the authorities. He declares that he wishes to avoid anything that he could "imagine to be prejudicial either to religion or to the state."[14] Indeed, if everyone were allowed to invent new customs, and not only "those God has established as rulers over his peoples or even those to whom he has given sufficient grace and zeal to be prophets," there would be "as many reformers as heads."[15] Yet his point of departure appears to be very revolutionary: "as regards all the opinions to which I had until now given credence, I could not do better than to try to get rid of them once and for all . . . in destroying all those opinions of mine that I judged to be poorly founded."[16] However, he ends up reintroducing through the window what he kicked out through the front door, most notably the ontological proof of the existence of God, the keystone of the scholastic edifice he claimed to detest.

It was during the era of Descartes that the unification of the world under the sole principle of value, labor, and money took a great leap forward. Descartes was the reflection of this *reductio ad unum* and, at the same time, contributed to it, reducing the multiplicity of details to only two principles: matter and motion, *res extensa* and *res cogitans*.[17] With this rigid distinction, Descartes radicalized the separation between the subject, identified with thought alone, and the rest of the universe, including even the body of the thinking subject, reduced to the status of a mere object. Man is a subject only insofar as he thinks; human faculties that are not required for this activity, such as the imagination, fall outside the circle of subjectivity *stricto sensu*. The boundary between the knowing subject and the known object, between mind and body, between subject and object in general, now passed through man himself, who was beginning his modern ascent through splits and separations.[18] Knowledge and the foundation of understanding now found their source in the *self*, although an abstract "self," a "self" that was the result of a process of reduction that stripped it of all concrete and individual qualities. Thus, this "self" was endowed with only two qualities: to exist and to think, in a completely formal sense and empty of concrete determinations.

Putting an end to the agonizing plunge into the abyss of methodical doubt, the *cogito ergo sum*—I think, therefore I am—was achieved with the radical bracketing of the body, matter, the senses, and space:

> Then, examining with attention what I was, and seeing that I could pretend that I had no body and that there was no world nor any place where I was, I could not pretend, on that account, that I did not exist at all, and that, on the contrary, from the very fact that I thought of doubting the truth of other things, it followed very evidently and very certainly that I existed; whereas, on the other hand, had I simply stopped thinking, even if all the rest of what I had ever imagined had been true, I would have had no reason to believe that I had existed. From this I knew that I was a substance the whole essence or nature of which is simply to think, and which, in order to exist, has no need of any place nor depends on any material thing.[19]

This presupposes an absolute distinction between the soul and the body and implies that the soul is easier to know than the body, or even that it could exist without it. Neither the imagination nor the senses can assure us of things without the aid of the understanding; whereas it is possible to know things through the understanding alone, without the aid of the senses. Descartes thus challenged the doctrine of the materialists: "everything unimaginable seems to them unintelligible."[20] Consequently, as Descartes assures us: "if there are still men who have not been sufficiently persuaded of the existence of God and of their soul by means of the reasons I have brought forward, I very much want them to know that all the other things of which they think themselves perhaps more assured, such as having a body, that there are stars and an earth, and the like, are less certain."[21]

For Descartes, it is quite consistent that the body is nothing more than a machine before the soul, from its divine origins, intervenes. Even the work of God is compared to that of a craftsman who builds "a very perfect machine."[22] Descartes often uses this analogy: that the animal is a machine and that the human body, before divine intervention, is both an animal (an assertion in keeping with a certain Christian tradition) and a machine (decidedly more modern). In his theory of blood circulation, Descartes explains that it derives as necessarily from the disposition of the organs as the movement of a clock from its mechanical wheels.[23] A machine imitating an animal without reason would be indistinguishable from a real animal, he asserts, whereas a human-like automaton could never have a true language or sufficient reason to respond to the most diverse situations.[24] It is exclusively thinking—the mind, language—that makes one human. The rational soul cannot thus be derived from matter and is expressly created by God and housed in a very special way within the body. Our soul has nothing to do with the beasts; it is of "a nature entirely independent of the body" and does not die with it.

The body and the sensations it engenders are of no assistance in establishing the slightest certainty about the world. Everything— body, space, time—could be a fiction. Descartes states that it is even difficult, in principle, to distinguish between waking and dreaming. But if, in spite of all doubts, he could find at least one indubitable thing, he would have a point from which, like Archimedes, to "move the entire earth." It cannot be the body or sense-certainty, he insists: "Am I so tied to a body and to the sense that I cannot exist without them?"[25] But no deceptive mind can make it such that "I" do not exist. I cannot feel without a body, he says, but I can think without one. I am "nothing but a thinking thing; that is, a mind, or intellect, or understanding, or reason. . . . I am not that concatenation of members we call the human body. Neither am I even some subtle air infused into these members, nor a wind, nor a fire, nor a vapor, nor a breath, nor anything I devise for myself. For I have supposed these things to be nothing. The assumption still stands; yet nevertheless I am something."[26] The perception of external objects is devalued in the Cartesian approach because they might not exist or because their apprehension through the senses or thought might be erroneous; these objects only serve to confirm the existence of the perceiving or thinking mind. The fact of receiving impressions from the outside is inadequate for proving that these objects really exist. Thus the impression of the sun is very different from what reason says about it. The conclusion is distressing: "All these points demonstrate sufficiently that up to this point it was not a well-founded judgment but only a blind impulse that formed the basis of my belief that things existing outside me send ideas or images of themselves to me through the sense organs or by some other means."[27]

It is clear here that the Archimedean point discovered by Descartes comes with a very high price. The soul is entirely distinct from the body and can exist without it: this is the foundation of his metaphysics. But, after having demonstrated this, he must undertake enormous efforts to reassemble what he had previously taken apart and prove the existence of the external world after having placed it "in brackets." The body is part of this external world and should be distrusted because its existence is *a priori* as uncertain as that of a chimera. Descartes therefore had to demonstrate that his body was indeed his body in order to arrive at a more reassuring conclusion: "Not without reason did I judge that this body, which by a certain special right I called 'mine,' belongs more to me than did any other. For I could never be separated from it in the same way I could be from other bodies."[28]

It is especially in his late treatise, *The Passions of the Soul*, that Descartes goes to great lengths to demonstrate that the soul and body, despite everything, do influence each other. All his explanations, including of tears, pallor, or sighs, are presented as strictly physical phenomena; and if a frightening impression produces fear or courage, this is due, he says, to the "disposition of the brain," that is, its structure. The self does not have the same substance as the world, the *res extensa*, which obliges Descartes to resort to an almost comical auxiliary construction: the "pineal gland" is considered as an "interface" (as we would say today) that bridges the gap between the subject and the world of objects, which would otherwise risk being forever separated.

The split between subject and object, thought and the physical world, soul and body, quickly emerged as the core and central problem of Cartesian philosophy. It occupied his immediate successors and returned in the twentieth century to haunt the debate on early modernity and the role of science. The importance of Descartes in understanding the rise of capitalism has also been noted, as has his contribution to the definition of the modern individual. What we want to emphasize here more specifically is his early formulation of the phenomenon we now call "narcissism."

Given the definition of narcissism provided above, it is easy to see that the Cartesian approach anticipates the narcissistic constitution of the contemporary subject. Its systemic doubt, its step-by-step abandonment of all certainties until it arrives at the only absolute, the *cogito*, has the appearance of a controlled regression to early childhood—as is the case in certain psychotherapies. The external world exists here only as part of the internal world and must be constructed from the sole reality of the certainty of existence.

The subject is thus historically born with the risk of radical solipsism, where the existence of an external world, and even of other people or sensuous bodies, is hardly self-evident. Most of the characteristics of the modern subject are already gathered in Descartes: solitary and narcissistic, unable to have real "object relations," and in permanent antagonism with the external world. Moreover, the subject is structurally white and masculine, as this model of "disembodied" rationality is precisely that which the white man has based his claim of superiority over the rest of the world.[29] The oscillation between feelings of impotence and omnipotence, a characteristic element of narcissism, is found in the Cartesian vision of a "self" that is at once nothing, a pure idea without extension, and yet also the origin of the whole world. His assertion that "I can know the self—the mind—without knowing the world, but not the world without the self," indicates a kind of priority of the self that comes from a feeling of omnipotence: without me, without my mind, the world would not exist.[30]

The numerous comparisons in Descartes of the human body, but also of the universe and of divine action itself, to a "machine" or "automaton" can, from a Marxist perspective, lead to two different interpretations. According to traditional Marxism, they "reflect" the introduction of manufacturing and the rise of the bourgeoisie which derives its wealth from that manufacturing. This is not wrong, but the critique of fetishism can also point here to an almost visionary anticipation of the Marxian concept of the "automatic subject."

The book by French philosopher and physician La Mettrie, *Man a Machine* (1748), and then, a century and a half later, Frederick Winslow Taylor's invention of the "scientific management" of human body movement to increase productivity, as well as eugenics (with its economic aspects), the optimization of "human material" or "human resources" in industry, the current economic use of the body in the "market of the living" (organs, genes, uterus, etc.), and of the cadaver for "artistic" purposes (exhibitions of plasticized cadavers by the German doctor and artist Günther von Hagen) —all of these could be viewed as further stages in this reduction of the body to a machine.[31]

The division between subject and object makes man into a radical stranger to the world. Faced with the grandeur of the mind, the world is no more than a material in which the mind seeks to realize itself. The resistance, whether natural or human, that this material opposes to the subject's purposes drives the subject to subjugate, dominate, mistreat, or even reduce it to dust if necessary. The division does not oppose "man" against the natural world, as is often claimed. It is much more radical: it opposes a disembodied mind to everything else that constitutes the human being, other people, and the body itself. Thus, this body, if it is not productive enough, if it does not work enough or sleeps too much, or expresses too many physical desires, appears more and more, throughout the development of capitalism, as an enemy, a resistance to be overcome—which is what Taylorism, diets, or techniques aimed at reducing the need for sleep, have all sought to accomplish.[32]

The external world is thus perceived as hostile *a priori*, as a limitation of the self. This represents a major difference from older conceptions of the human being as part of a "chain of beings" or a structured cosmology where each person receives their rank through participation in a higher essence. For Descartes, the *res extensa* does not even exist, or has at best only a very limited ontological dignity. Instead of a sense of belonging to a shared universe, modern man is confronted with a permanent hostility that is not only the result of particular situations or individuals, but often of the "world" as such.[33] Relentless competition is the cause and consequence of this hostility. Undifferentiated *resentment* is often its expression, as we shall see below, while the most extreme consequence is the desire to do away with this oppressive world altogether, to *annihilate* it. It is interesting to note that Edmund Husserl, founder of phenomenology and admirer of Descartes, wrote in 1913 that Descartes, in order to establish his philosophy, first had to carry out an "annihilation of the world" in thought.[34] But at that time, this annihilation was still a purely mental experience in the head of the thinker dozing by his fireplace. Descartes certainly could not have foreseen that the serial killer, the one *running amok*, would be the latest incarnation of a subject-form he helped to formulate.

Excursus: Descartes the Musicologist and the Acceleration of History

With regard to the place of Descartes' philosophy in the context of his era, a new and rather interesting approach for our analysis has been proposed in Germany by philologist Eske Bockelmann in his book *Im Takt des Geldes. Zur Genese modernen Denkens*[35] and essay "Die Synthese am Geld: Natur der Neuzeit."[36] Bockelmann notes that "beat" in poetry and music, that is, the habit of perceiving a sequence of sounds in terms of "accentuated/unaccentuated" ("high tempo" and "low tempo"), is not as "natural" as is generally believed. The beat does not correspond to biological rhythms, such as the heartbeat. Ancient poetry was based on long and short syllables, while music was set to very different rhythmic forms from the modern. Around 1620, the situation changed, almost overnight, with the introduction of specific beat. This is exemplified by the work of the German poet Martin Opitz, who at the time theorized the need for beat in poetry and rewrote his own verses according to his new rules. A parallel development occurred in the field of music, with Descartes himself playing a role: his very first work, written in 1618 at the age of twenty-two, well before his philosophical or scientific works, is a *Compendium musicae* in which he describes, for the first time, musical listening according to beat. This curious coincidence powerfully demonstrates how the irruption of modernity had repercussions at various levels at this particular historical moment.

Soon enough, interpreting each sequence of sound in terms of "accentuated/unaccentuated" alteration became so ingrained in the deepest unconscious—a conditioned reflex—that people could not even imagine listening differently or even having done so. Today, we even interpret the sound of a dripping water tap through this pattern—and we see in this example that no sound is "inherently" accentuated but is simply in opposition to another posited as "unaccentuated." Bockelmann defines beat as a "pure relationship without content," where each element is not defined by its own quality, but by its opposition to another element. His considerations, however, go far beyond metrics: in the philosophical, mathematical, and scientific revolution of the seventeenth century, we find the same *relationship without content*. Galileo was the first to think of pure motion without a moving object. All content, every quality in nature became a variable defined only by its relation to a function, and finally a pure number. Everything that was concrete was limited to this abstract quality: to vary according to function. This was the first basis for the 1:0 binary code that now dominates the world through digitalization.

Descartes, Bockelmann asserts, did the same in the field of thought: he conceived the world as a purely functional relationship between subject and object, between the function and content of knowledge. He then filled it with surreptitiously introduced content. Faced with the subject of knowledge, all objects became equal. This subject-object relation could then be applied to anything: parts were always thought of as absolutely separate, and yet existing only in their reciprocal relationship.

But why did this revolution in perception take place at this particular time? According to Bockelmann, the reason was that *money* had begun to penetrate everyday life for several decades. Not pre-modern money, but "money as money," as Marx called it. This money is a pure representation of all commodities, all values. It became a universal relationship that mediated all human activities. It was in this moment that the first "global economy" was born and that a social synthesis through money began to unfold: everything was referred to money, everything was measured in money. For the first time in history, value did not consist of a precious thing, like metals, residing *within* money, but could be detached from any such anchor. It existed as "absolute value," "value purely for itself." This value was no longer the unity of something concrete, but a pure unity, without specific content, which existed only as a pure reference to the totality of commodities. It became the reference to content detached from content, from any possible content, as in the case of a movement of thinking without reference to any object. Value became the pure act of referring, and commodities constituted, in this relationship between two poles, the pure "reference," that to which value referred. It was not the reference of a determined content to an abstract form it might have taken, but the reference to the very activity of referring: money does not contain value, but constitutes the mediation with everything that is conceived as containing value. Between monetary value and money there is a pure relationship of exclusion and contradiction, and this relationship is asymmetrical. It is the relation between function and the content of function, between content as such (the world of commodities) and that which has absolutely no content and is a unity by virtue of that (value). By handling money on an everyday basis, by satisfying more and more needs through money, human beings learned at that time, without realizing it, to organize their perception of the world, from numbers to music, from science to poetry, according to the polarity between "pure reference" and "pure referenced object."

Bockelmann wants to shed light on the genesis of the modern subject by demonstrating the role money has played therein. What he analyzes is the social and mental *a priori*, the "filter" of which we are no longer even aware. His book has met with objections to the details of his argument, but the main criticism is that he conceives of money only as a medium of exchange, situated in the sphere of circulation, and not as a representation of abstract labor. It must be emphasized that the genesis of the social synthesis not only resides in *circulation*, where everyone has, more or less, the same status as buyer and seller, but is essentially found in *abstract labor*. In this sphere, not everyone has the same standing. For example, women are traditionally excluded from abstract labor; their domestic activities do not count as work, do not create value, and are not represented in money.

When Descartes states that "I manifestly know that nothing can be perceived more easily and more evidently than my own mind," he already announces the Kantian turn, the definitive passage from "naïve realism" to subjectivism, to the examination of subjective faculties rather than the ontological structure of the world.[37] It might be worthwhile to reread the history of modern philosophy as an intellectual expression of human "psycho-history." Yet for now, we will limit ourselves here to observing that in all post-Cartesian philosophy, the relationship between mind and body, thought and extension, once separated, has been the main problem. This proved so difficult that the solutions proposed, if one looks at them with a bit of hindsight, often present aspects that are truly delusional. The "occasionalism" of Nicolas Malebranche and Arnold Geulincx, in the generation following Descartes, denied any possible action of the soul on the body. It seriously conceived human action according to an analogy of two clocks, wound by God at the beginning of time and constantly striking the same hour. In this way, the soul acts at the same time as the body, which obeys only mechanical laws. When the desire to eat causes the mouth to open, it is not a question of interaction, but of synchrony triggered by God. Gottfried

Wilhelm Leibniz later developed this approach within his theory of "monadology" and "pre-established harmony." Preposterous as a philosophical conception, it appears significant to us today as a prophetic (and unintended) vision of capitalist society and its "social synthesis." Each monad, according to Leibniz, is "windowless," deaf and blind, alone in the world, without any *a priori* connection to other monads. However, regulated according to an automatism external to them, the monads unite and form bodies and actions in the world. The monads only relate to each other through the mediation of the instance that establishes this harmony. How can we not see in this a prefiguration of the commodity subject, a social atom linked to others only by an anonymous mechanism, namely, the state and the market?[38] If, in Leibniz, it is God who establishes harmony, a few decades later, it will be, in Adam Smith, the "invisible hand" of the market that will more or less fulfill the same function of harmonization between social actors, who only pursue their own selfish interests without any "window" towards other actors.

The relationship of this subject to the world is indirect and undifferentiated. In its emptiness and absolute poverty, the monad-subject knows only competition as a social relationship; self-affirmation, whether individual or collective, becomes the essential content of human existence. Since a direct agreement between monads is impossible, the only way out is through mediations turned autonomous, such as money and the state (law). The more the subject settles into its active role, the more it degrades the world into a passive material that must remain at its disposal—which is not at all the case, remember, in ancient, medieval, or non-European worldviews.[39]

The subject developed in the era between Descartes and Kant is a pure subject of knowledge, and therefore an individual subject. In parallel, between Hobbes and Rousseau, the political and public dimension of the modern subject-form was developed. The work of Hobbes corresponds to that of Descartes, and not only in terms of a mechanistic vision of the world. Hobbes asserted politically the same radical separation between the social atom and a world alien to it as Descartes did epistemologically. His theory is truly the "mother of all bourgeois theories" because it considers the isolated individual and its drive for self-preservation and self-affirmation to be the basis of any form of society. Almost all political theories formulated after, including those hostile to the consequences Hobbes drew, would take this statement as a given. Yet in truth, this is hardly the case, as many anthropological works have shown—notably the theories of Marcel Mauss and his school of thought on the social bonds created by the gift, where the individual has always existed as a member in a chain or network.

Another fundamental stage in the formation of the subject was the development of the notion of *homo economicus*. This took place mainly in Great Britain between the end of the seventeenth and the beginning of the nineteenth centuries, through the work of Locke, Mandeville, Hume, Smith, Malthus, and others. Their "economic" theories were based on a completely new anthropological concept: for the first time in history, material gain was affirmed as an end in itself. According to this view, the vocation of human beings is not to be virtuous but to accumulate wealth. When traditional virtues are an obstacle to the creation of material wealth, they must be abandoned and replaced by others. The definition of a science of economics and its autonomization from other fields of knowledge went hand in hand with an effective autonomization of the economy itself: rather than providing society with the material basis for what it considered truly important (service to God, glory, civic life, contemplation, etc.), the economy became the supreme end to which the other spheres of life were called upon to contribute and to submit.

This historical and philosophical moment was crucial for the transition to a "modern" society.[40] However, other aspects of this so-called "Enlightenment" period must also be emphasized. According to Michel Foucault, this was the period of the transition to the "disciplinary society," well exemplified in Bentham's infamous "panopticon." But this analysis must be extended to the role of the subject. The violence exerted on individuals from outside was then transformed into *self-discipline*. Everything that the dominant had previously imposed on the dominated through coercive means now began to be internalized by the latter, who executed it upon themselves. The modern subject is precisely the result of this internalization of social constraints. One is all the more disciplined when one accepts these constraints and succeeds in imposing them on oneself against the resistance that arises from one's own body, feelings, needs, and desires. It is violence against oneself that first defines the subject: on this point the philosophers of the Enlightenment are very clear. Women, "negroes," children, servants, and generally members of the lower classes were deemed inferior precisely insofar as they proved unable to internalize these constraints in a sufficient manner. Servants would allegedly cease working as soon as they were left unattended, while women were supposedly governed by their "emotions." At the same time, the subject-form actually went beyond the bounds of the feudal system, since it was not strictly linked to birth, as it was, for example, with the nobility. In modern society, those excluded from the status of the subject could still, at least individually, lay claim to it, but only if they demonstrated an internalization of social constraints at least equal to that produced by white, adult males. This is the "democratic" dimension of the subject-form: the virtual right for everyone to participate in the same form of internalized submission. It is difficult to see anything "emancipatory" in this gradual spread of the subject-form, which, conversely, indicates the extent to which capitalism has overcome any truly external opposition. The history of "democratization" over the last two centuries can be summarized essentially as efforts to allow even wider categories of the population to gain access to the status of the subject (workers, the poor, women, immigrants, the disabled, ethnic minorities, "sexual minorities"), but without being able to prevent others from being ejected from it, at least in the full sense of the word—for example, the unemployed or migrants, and in general all those who are "superfluous" from the capitalist point of view.[41] Even the heir to a great fortune can have their status of subject revoked, even to the point of a legal disenfranchisement, if he is not "disciplined" and spends his inheritance merely satisfying his own desires.

The question of who is and who is not a subject no longer depends only on whether one belongs to one group or another, but also on the capacity of each individual to *submit* to the demands of production and to silence everything that opposes it. In this context, one need only recall that the word "subject" etymologically means "submissive" [*sub-jectus*].[42] One becomes a subject by accepting submission and renewing it daily.

Since the Enlightenment, the subject has been defined as a *worker*—from Rousseau, who wrote that "work is . . . an indispensable duty for social man. Rich or poor, powerful or weak, every idle citizen is a rascal," to Beaumarchais, who reproached the nobility: "You took the trouble to be born, nothing more." However, this definition does not encompass only workers in the strict sense, but anyone who has subjected their life to the demands of production—not the production of objects of use, but the production of "value"—and to the demands of the accumulation of "dead" labor, represented in the money that accumulates into capital. In other words, the subject is the other side of commodity value, its living "bearer." It has internalized not only the "necessity" of work, but also the same indifference to the concrete, to the external world, to content, an indifference that constitutes the essence of abstract labor. An empty form, a will without content, an indifference to the outside world— this is the profound isomorphism between the modern subject and abstract labor. The eventual refusal of this absurdity, this denial of any real relationship with the world, can only *disqualify* an individual in the society of subjects and render him unworthy of participating in the status of subject.

The modern subject is characterized by a *false universalism*. On the surface, being a subject is a purely formal quality that characterizes everyone in society. But closer inspection reveals that it is a deeply contradictory form with an inner fracturing: the subject is necessarily partial. It is only the Western, white man who is a modern subject, in the full sense of the term. It is a question of an individual existing essentially as a bearer of their labor-power and succeeding in subordinating it to all other considerations, beginning with those relating to the body. Anything that does not fit into this schema is expelled from the subject and attributed to others. Consequently, the latter are not considered subjects—at least not in the full sense of the term—because the qualities attributed to them are incompatible with the status of the subject. These minor subjects, or non-subjects, have historically been primarily women and non-white populations. Eventually, the above-mentioned changes have broadened the scope of "subjecthood" without breaking the fundamental separation between subjects and non-subjects. "Subjects" establish ambiguous relationships with non-subjects, or minor subjects, ranging from repulsion—which can go as far as the desire to annihilate them—to attraction, since they represent everything that the subject has had to expel from itself in order to attain the status of subject. From the beginning, the subject was thus founded, in both the logical and historical sense, on an *internal split*. Only a part of humanity is defined as a subject, and even within this restricted framework, only a portion of possible human qualities makes the individual into a subject. Everything else—starting with nature—forms the "dark side" of the subject, where the repressed part arouses fear because of its separate existence. The subject constantly feels threatened by this external or even internal non-subject, which is nevertheless its own creation and which, in turn, justifies its existence. This dissociation is constitutive of the subject and defines its very essence. It is not something that occurs later, an accident that could be detached from the substance. It is an illusion to believe that one could just as easily create a subject that does not share this defect.

Everything that triumphant rationality had to expel from the subject, to "separate" from itself, such as its own "irrational" impulses, has become threatening, formless, and obscure and has to be attributed to an "other" in order to be dominated. Thus, the white, masculine bourgeois subject projected an unbridled sensuality onto the working classes, people of color, women, gypsies, and Jews in turn. Seeing everywhere homosexuals ready to assail him and corrupt swindlers after his money, he attributes to others what he cannot admit as part of himself.

What is driven out of the modern subject in order to enable its constitution is, in particular, everything that cannot assume the form of "labor" and, consequently, the form of "value," which can be represented as money. The most important part of this process of expulsion—or "dissociation"—is constituted by the many activities that aim to ensure the everyday reproduction of the working subject and its perpetuation, but which do not enter directly into the production of value, nor are they found on the market or expressed in money. These activities are traditionally those assigned to women. The structure of the modern subject therefore necessarily includes their subordination. Women obviously have their place in the production of value, and are even indispensable to it, but only as auxiliaries. If many of them have (apparently) succeeded in extricating themselves from this condition, it is because others have taken their place; thus women coming from countries of the South, for example, are increasingly taking on the household chores or childcare of families in the countries of the North. Indeed, the mechanism of separation between subjects and non-subjects is an objective logic, which can be largely detached from its historical bearers and transferred to new agents. Many women have obtained access to the subject-form in the economic sphere, although it remains to be seen whether this is also true in other domains.

Men, too, are forced to expel their culturally "feminine" aspects (their feelings, for example, when they are at work), and they too can find themselves in the condition of "woman" (for example, by having to perform certain domestic work considered "feminine," or by not working at all). For the masculine subject, the closest, primary non-subject has always been women. The subject-form is of masculine origin and developed on the model of the hierarchical relationship between soul and body, mind and nature, form and matter—as evidenced by the Latin etymology of the word "matter": "mater"/"mother." This hierarchical relationship corresponds to the relationship between men and women, where it is realized in the everyday, beyond any philosophical theory.

Kant, a Theorist of Freedom?

One exceptional witness to this birth of the modern subject was Immanuel Kant. The Königsberg philosopher described this new master of the world openly and without false modesty, which has, curiously, earned him a reputation as a "philosopher of freedom."[43] He radically announced—and not critically, but affirmatively!—the complete separation of the form and content of consciousness and the expulsion of "all inclination" and "all emotion" (his words) from the subject. The subject was reduced to an empty will desiring nothing but itself. Indeed, for Kant, the will is only free when it is not conditioned by anything external. The "autonomy" of the subject is achieved at the cost of expelling everything that is not derived from "pure reason"—starting with its own "inclinations." In reality, this autonomy is a deceptive autonomy because, faced with a totally separated objectivity, the subject oscillates between a feeling of omnipotence and a feeling of impotence. The centrality of "freedom" in Kant's theoretical architecture has dazzled generations of enthusiastic commentators, which sometimes lead one to wonder if they have really read him. For Kant, "freedom" is only valuable when it is identical with emptiness and does not apply to anything concrete. In the empirical world, governed by time, space, and causality, there can be no freedom: the subject's actions are subordinate to natural laws and their rigid causality. Freedom can therefore only consist in emancipation from this alien and oppressive world, which the subject must escape by taking refuge in the spheres of pure reason and morality. At the same time, it is precisely the subject who "creates" the objective world, for it is with its *a priori* categories—namely, time, space, and causality—that it gives order to the world of sensations, without which the latter would only be a "formless chaos." What becomes common to individuals that empirically differ from each other is the "unity of apperception" that carries out this synthesis of the diverse.

Thus, for the rational subject, reality exists only insofar as it is apprehended through the categories of this subject—the rest is forever unknowable, and thus basically non-existent. The subject thereby remains radically separated from reality. The "purer" reason is in separating itself from the sensuous world, the more it is haunted by the sensuous, and the more it is afraid of this "amorphous chaos," which it must try to control by resorting to even more reason. Here we see the link between Kantian "displacement" [*refoulement*] and the Freudian unconscious. Yet with one major difference: Kantian reason is not only a *reaction* to the disturbing sphere of the sensuous world, but it itself produces this sphere as a separate and disturbing sphere. Modern "irrationality" was thus the product of modern "rationality," which projected its "irrational" dimension onto empirical beings.[44] For Kant, as long as the will remains within the sphere of pure reason, it is omnipotent and not subject to external conditioning. But as soon as it wants to become "practical," it encounters in the moral sphere—the world of human actions—the same heteronomy as in nature—and, according to Kant, being conditioned by a world outside the subject is incompatible with freedom. The Kantian response is to retreat into a sphere of pure morality. The "pure" will must not desire anything concrete, because then it would be dependent on this object of desire and no longer free. The "faculty of desire" appears in Kant as slavery, a submission to the heteronomy of natural laws, which painfully belies the omnipotence that the subject has been attributed in the sphere of pure reason. From the point of view of the *"higher power of desire"*—which obeys reason alone—no object is ever worthy of the subject.[45] Objects are mere substitutes, unimportant as such, from which the will must seek "purity." To really desire them—whether health, fame, wealth, etc.—would lead to dependency that prevents the will from being free. This would constitute an unbearable offence to the subject, who experiences any dependence on other people or on nature as a total negation of its autonomy.

What, then, according to Kant, is true freedom, and indeed its only possible form? Voluntary obedience to laws, and especially to the moral law as such, to its pure form—this is the famous "categorical imperative." It must be the simple fulfillment of a duty, without any pleasure.[46] This Kantian morality has been much criticized, even ridiculed,[47] but the sinister character of the injunction to obey the mere form of the law—its "majesty" or "legality" as such—regardless of the content of these laws, must be emphasized. Kant claims that these are empty of any particular content; but in truth, he surreptitiously introduces concrete and far from "pure" content (e.g., respect for private property in his famous example of the "deposit").[48] We see once again that the universalism of the empty form is fictitious and that in truth it contains concrete content that is not admitted as such. The sensuous world, chased out the front door, returns through the window. Naturally, within this framework, any form of "sensuousness"—the "lower power of desire"—must be suppressed as severely as possible. Kant himself set a good example: although he enjoyed coffee, he almost always refused it and found a thousand other masochistic ways to impoverish his life while calling them "exercises in virtue."[49] This is not anecdotal, but symptomatic of his philosophy. Kant spoke in this regard of "*self-satisfaction*, which in its proper meaning always implies only a negative liking for one's existence, a liking in which one is conscious of needing nothing."[50]

This will to become independent of the sensuous world—of any need or desire—in order to enjoy total stillness has similarities with the "death drive," which Freud defines as an attempt to return to the inorganic calm that preceded life. According to Kant, "inner tranquility . . . is the effect of a respect for something entirely different from life [namely, the moral law], something in comparison and contrast to which life with all its agreeableness has, rather, no worth at all. He now lives only because it is his duty, not because he has the slightest taste for living. This is how the genuine incentive of pure practical reason is constituted. This incentive is none other than the pure moral law itself insofar as this law allows us to discern the sublimity of our own supranatural existence."[51] By considering human freedom as defined by its opposition to all sensuousness, Kant marks the culmination of the long struggle to separate the subject from the sensuous and empirical world, and to make it, precisely, the "transcendental" subject, radically distinct from the "empirical" subject. The "automatic subject" which, according to Marx, governs the fetishistic society of capital is thus not a negation of Kant's "autonomous subject," but its fulfillment.

This interpretation of Kant's work focuses mainly on his ethics, as he developed it after the publication of the *Critique of Pure Reason* (1781), as an "application" of the principles established therein. However, it would be wrong to distinguish between the "good Kant" of the *Critique of Pure Reason* and the overly rigorous moralism of his later writings. The *Critique of Pure Reason* already presupposes an abstract individual in opposition to an indifferent, distant world, reduced to what the subject, equipped with its categorical "instrument," can make of it.[52]

However, the Kantian subject is not simply the creation of a particular philosopher, however important he may be. It is the philosophical representation of a real development. The presumed autonomy of the Kantian subject is in truth acquired at the price of a painful internalization of the constraints of a nascent capitalism; it results in contempt for everything outside the subject, and hatred for everything that the subject has had to expel from itself in order to attribute to others. Ultimately, this hatred can turn into self-hatred. The extreme result of the subject-form Kant described so well is the death drive: the desire to be done with the world, which condemns subjects to alternating feelings of impotence and omnipotence, through which the subject itself suffers from its inner emptiness and inability to develop a real relationship with the world.[53]

The Marquis de Sade and the Moral Law

In the same era as Kant, the Marquis de Sade, who could not differ more from the German philosopher, also provided an apologetic description of the new subject-form and its destructive tendencies. Although they begin from opposing points of view, their ideas are in fact complementary.

Sade was in many ways a defender of capitalism at a time when it was in the process of unraveling all the limits that had previously been in force, in perfect accord with the liberal theories of the time. He can even be considered the brother-enemy of Kant—the one who expressed the dark side of the Enlightenment.[54] Like Kant, Sade demanded the subordination of all spontaneity to rigorous machine-like laws, a system of regulating every aspect of individual life. For Kant, as for Sade, pleasure consists only in submission to a rigid rationality.[55] The Marquis de Sade is one of the philosophical founders of capitalist modernity, based on the rationalization of life, permanent economic warfare, and the severing of the traditional links between man and the world. He is also one of its most concentrated and cynical expressions. His works sing the praise of modernity and its boundlessness, of a furious and endless desire in the face of a world devoid of meaning, a desire that can only be gratified with destruction since nothing concrete can satisfy it—as is the case with the commodity-form.[56] In the same way that the commodity-form must consume the world down to its last remnant in order to affirm itself, Sade's "libertines" must consume their victims down to the last ounce of flesh. They are confronted with the impossibility of satisfaction in a world that they themselves have already transformed into a desert, faced with the need to constantly increase the doses of the ersatz imitations that replace pleasure.

The extreme egoism preached by Sade in his work corresponds exactly to what takes place in a society where the only social ties lie in the exchange of commodities between isolated producers. The irremediable solitude of the human being articulated by Sade, in which he indulges, is not ontological or eternal—it is being actualized as he writes. Sade undoubtedly possesses the merit of having drawn out all of the consequences of what Kant called "asocial sociality," where social atoms meet only to satisfy their needs according to their strength on the market. A world where there is no "other" is not at all archaic—it is a very modern world. For Sade, satisfaction is only complete when it is "despotic," when it is not shared with others—the same modern solipsism as found in Descartes.[57] George Bataille was right when he said that Sade promises to bestow upon readers the complete sovereignty once reserved for kings.[58]

The desires described by Sade, born precisely during his epoch—the desire for limitlessness, the narcissistic negation of the world, the rupture of social ties, the war of all against all, the desire to see humanity or the world as a whole disappear[59]—are akin to a hatred of the object, whose mere existence limits the narcissism of the desiring subject.[60] In fact, Sade derives a negation of all limits from his radical atheism. This refusal of limits is first of all, at the subjective level, the highly narcissistic project of the fulfillment of all desires, as well as of contrary desires.[61] As Bataille rightly comments: "The man subject to no restraints of any kind falls on his victims with the devouring fury of a vicious hound."[62] Once again we return to the myth of Erysichthon. . .

Thus, Sade anticipated some of the most characteristic features of our limitless society. With regard to recent school shootings and other massacres in public places, where senseless killing—carried out with the "apathy" so dear to Sade—almost always ends in suicide, one might consider the following reflection on Sade by Bataille:

> If we start from the principle of denying others posited by de Sade it is strange to observe that at the very peak of unlimited denial of others is a denial of oneself. . . . Free in the eyes of other people he is no less the victim of his own sovereignty. . . . Denying others becomes in the end denying oneself. In the violence of this progression personal enjoyment ceases to count, the crime is the only thing that counts and whether one is the victim or not no matter; all that matters is that the crime should reach the pinnacle of crime. These exigencies lie outside the individual, or at least they set a higher value on the process begun by him but now detached from him and transcending him, than on the individual himself. De Sade cannot help bringing into play beyond the personal variety an almost impersonal egotism. . . . What can be more disturbing than the prospect of selfishness becoming the will to perish in the furnace lit by selfishness?[63]

Here, crime, especially that of the "crazed killer," becomes real work. And if this suicide is not individual, but collective, even better: "Do you know, Dolmancé, that by means of this system you are going to be led to prove that totally to extinguish the human race would be nothing but to render Nature a service?—Who doubts of it, Madame?"[64] Such a desire to do away with humanity as such, too rebellious against the individual's desire for omnipotence, had perhaps never before appeared prior to Sade.

Enough Philosophy, Time for Action

According to Ernst Lohoff, a German author writing in the tradition of the critique of value whose essay on the "enchantment of the world" we are partly adopting here, the history of the seventeenth and eighteenth centuries could be described as the stage of the "formal subsumption" of individuals under the subject-form, and that of the nineteenth and twentieth centuries as the stage of "real subsumption."[65] These categories run parallel to the two moments distinguished by Marx in the subsumption of labor under capital, to which correspond to the extraction of absolute and relative surplus-value, respectively. The first phase is one of disembodiment, the creation of a subject as pure spirit, culminating with Kant. Here the subject loses all substance and becomes a pure form. As a universal legislator, the subject replaces God, but it must become "transcendental" and situated in the "pure law," beyond all empirical reality. With Kant's successors, a seemingly opposite movement began: this disembodied, otherworldly spirit is incarnated within pseudo-concrete entities—such as the "people"—that set out to conquer reality in order to make it equal to themselves. It is only in this way that the identification of individuals with the subject-form and its internalization could become a mass phenomenon and penetrate into the depths of social life.

Kant's philosophy pushed the separation between pure form and the realm of the sensuous to its extreme, but it also marked a turning point. Thinkers later began to work in the opposite direction, aiming to bridge the gap. However, this was not carried out as a reconciliation or free union—an aspiration that belongs to the "utopian" programs of Friedrich Schiller and the Romantics, through to Herbert Marcuse and the artistic avant-gardes—but as the annexation of the realm of the sensuous to disembodied reason. Kantian dualism, with its "pure," intelligible form on the one hand and the realm of the sensuous and empirical on the other, nevertheless entails a certain recognition of the existence of the latter, however inferior it may be. It must be dominated and controlled, but without disappearing. Thus, the struggle always begins anew. According to post-Kantian philosophers, the sphere of the sensuous is a representation or emanation of the subject in which the sensuous world has no independent existence.

This process corresponds entirely to the basic logic of value: the "concrete"—use-value, concrete labor—only serves to represent the abstract (value, abstract labor).[66] A bomb and a toy are thus only transient and interchangeable representations, basically undifferentiated, of a common substance: a quantity of labor represented in a quantity of value, in turn represented in a quantity of money. Similarly, for Kant's successors, who proposed a "monistic" vision of the world, abstraction invades the sensuous world, and the sensible is reconstructed insofar as it is "posited" by the abstract.

In Hegel, history and nature are rehabilitated—but only as figures of Spirit, whose true essence lies elsewhere. As such, the subject becomes *substance*. It is not "given" *a priori* as in Kant, where the subject-form is part of the original baggage of every human being. Henceforth, the subject must be conquered, or constructed—it exists only as the result of a development. However, in Hegel himself, this process is presented as *already accomplished*, since within world Spirit (which Hegel, as is well known, believed to have been achieved with the advent of his own philosophy), subject and substance coincide—it is only a matter of contemplating retrospectively the path that has led there.

This contemplative attitude did not satisfy his successors, nor even his own disciples. In order to make the subject act in the empirical world, it was necessary to change the perspective again. The realization of the subject had to become a program yet to be accomplished—which implied the possibility that some individuals or groups of people would not participate, or only in a limited capacity. This perspective also made it possible to conceive of the subject as a collective entity, and above all to move from thought—that is, from the theory of knowledge—to action and will. Reason as a universal subject was replaced by practical activity: labor. This is what Marxists did with the Hegelian heritage (but the turn was already underway in some of Hegel's early writings). In order to move from contemplation to struggle, it was also necessary to replace the single subject of knowledge (which did not need an adversary) with a conflict between two or even more subjects. In the words of Lohoff,

> [a] subject of real metaphysics who desires and acts needs an antagonist against whom it can direct its will and actions, and it is through victory over such an adversary that it can demonstrate and realize its own status as a subject. Marxism has also taken this necessity into account by evoking a frontal opposition between classes. The introduction of the bourgeoisie as an anti-class in relation to the working class, however, does not mean a real abandonment of the idea of a universal subject, but only a temporary diversion.

The proletariat is indeed faced with an anti-subject: the capitalist class. But the two antagonists do not possess the same degree of ontological dignity. The working class is, we are told, 'more real' than the capitalist class. Only it, as the embodiment of the universal principle of labor, possesses the status of a universal subject *in potentia*, which can be universalized. This difference also predetermines the outcome of class conflict. The triumph of labor and its class has not yet been realized historically, but it is certain to occur.[67]

Two collective subjects—often, but not always, in competition with each other—took center stage from the second half of the nineteenth century, at the latest, and remained there for at least a century: class and nation (the latter also in the form of "people" or "race"). "These new world-historical actors are characterized by an utterly imperial claim. They are no longer satisfied with erecting a kingdom opposed to the depths of the sensuous, but want to *immediately* assert a universal principle within sensuous reality. It is this claim to omnipotence and total conquest, a true secular religion—that is, the promise to completely transform even everyday life according to their glory as demiurges—that transforms these new mega-subjects into the most important school for integrating the masses into the subject-form."[68] Up until that point, eighteenth-century political theorists such as Rousseau had contrasted the heroic citizen, concerned only with the common good, against the vile interests of the particular individual who followed only their own sensuous inclinations—each man was called upon to make, in his heart, the "citizen" prevail over the shopkeeper. As Lohoff explains:

> the workers' movement continued the relationship to nature established by commodity society, while introducing new actors for key roles. According to the socialists, humanity detaches itself from the animal condition and becomes a subject through the confrontation with nature, not only by using reason, but also and above all by practically transforming nature by means of labor. While conforming to the form of activity characteristic of commodity society broadened the basis for the constitution of the subject, it came at a high and historically unprecedented price. To make labor the practice constituting the subject meant linking the process of becoming a subject to its submission, to a praxis rigorously stripped of all the qualities that could it make it a specifically human activity. It is precisely this activity purged of all concrete, sensuous, or material characteristics, abstracted

into a pure, self-referential expenditure of 'brains, nerves, and muscles' that is now supposed to elevate the human being to the rank of subject. Far from mobilizing the potential multiplicity of humanity's relationship to nature against the capitalist regime, the socialist religion of labor has replaced disembodied "pure reason" with humanity reduced to a physiological substrate.[69]

The workers' movement carried with it a critique of the false universalism of the Enlightenment: in the figure of the "citizen," the real inequalities of living conditions, especially economic ones, disappeared behind political participation and equal rights for all. These social conditions constituted the "bourgeois" side of the modern individual, which the young Marx contrasted to the "citizen" in "On the Jewish Question" (1844). Labor, which could be defined in sociological as well as ontological terms, transformed those who had previously been excluded and despised into subjects of higher dignity. Making labor the basis for everyone's participation in collective life and in the status of subject was to allow a true universalism to flourish. However, this necessarily implied hierarchies and exclusions at the expense of those who could not or would not conform to the regime of labor.[70]

At the opposite end of the political spectrum, the right focused on the mega-subject of "nation," which it interpreted in an increasingly biological manner. The biological foundations of competition—often in the form of "social Darwinism"—could not only be applied to individuals acting on the market, but also to nations, imagined as engaged in a permanent struggle for survival. Thus, war played the same central role for accessing the subject-form as labor did in the other—even if, in the first half of the twentieth century, the two forms often merged, especially in totalitarian regimes. The exclusion of a part of humanity from the status of subject, on the other hand, was *implicit* in the theories of the workers' movement, where it was conceived as temporary and capable of being overcome: the rebellious could be "educated" and transformed into good workers. History, from this perspective, would necessarily lead to a future scenario where everyone would work in harmony. In contrast, the reactionary version of the diffusion of the subject-form, whether nationalist or racist, made exclusion the very principle of the subject and considered the inferiority of the non-subject as definitive. The nationalist or racist did not want to turn those who belonged to another nation or race into members of their own; on the contrary, they had to be either dominated or eliminated.

If subjecthood was acquired through the use of reason, as the Enlightenment claimed, or by working, as the labor movement would have it, it required a certain amount of effort, which, at least in theory, also had to be constantly repeated. The "right wing" of the religion of the subject, on the other hand, offered much easier access to this status: one entered it by birthright, which, without any further effort, allowed one to enjoy a feeling of ontological superiority over non-subjects who were unlucky enough to be born in the wrong place, or never had the possibility of changing their circumstances.

Being a subject by virtue of belonging to a community by birthright, as proposed by "anti-Enlightenment" theories, offered another attractive possibility: it made it possible to mobilize—and therewith reap the benefits of the subject-form—its own irrational side (its "dark side," the importance of which the proponents of the Enlightenment had to deny or diminish). The suffering and fear aroused by submission to the value-form are still mobilized today in defense of the subject-form: racism and antisemitism, sexism and homophobia, chauvinism and populism all bear witness to this. This kind of subject believes itself to be constantly surrounded by enemies and imagines itself leading the fight to prevent the "decline of the West." The subject-form in its "birth-subject" version draws considerable energy from this recourse to resentment, which is an expression of feelings of helplessness. This offers a great advantage over the version of the subject-form based on "labor" or "reason," which is necessarily more "laborious" and invites a struggle to overcome the dark side of the subject-form.

Nation and class lost much of their importance in the second half of the twentieth century—especially after 1968, at least in the so-called "developed" countries—in favor of an "individualization" of the subject-form and narcissism. Historically, the narcissism of the collective subject preceded that of the individual subject, and it constituted a kind of "school" of the subject-form.[71] However, there has been a spectacular return of the "nation" in the last few decades all over the world, which does not contradict the previous analysis, but confirms it.[72] The subject can never consist of the mere performance of systemic functions. Its irrational side, starting with hatred of others and of itself, however useless or counterproductive it may be from the point of view of the simple reproduction of the system, does not disappear, but rather increases in times of crisis.[73] The monsters it produces, often by rearranging old and new elements, can become autonomous and eventually interfere with the smooth running of the system. "With the deepening of the crisis, the role of the subject-form as a mere instance of the execution of an objectified and subject-less domination diminishes, and the religion of the subject begins to maraud and develop a destructive force of its own in its new variants as a result of its decomposition. As a continuation of the critique of religion by other means, the critique of fetishism must take note of the importance of the apotheosis of the subject as a magical and murderous force."[74]

Narcissism as a Consolation for Impotence

Two German thinkers of the first half of the nineteenth century did much to elevate narcissism upon the terrain of philosophy, in quite opposite ways. Arthur Schopenhauer, the "philosopher of pessimism," was one of the first to thematize the suffering of modern life, particularly the isolation and atomization of the individual. However, far from making the connection to the new bourgeois society, Schopenhauer saw it as an ontological fact, an expression of an eternal, even cosmic, human condition. In his view, it was the *principium individuationis* that made life miserable, and in order to escape it, one had to go beyond the "will to live" and merge into the flow of the universe, attaining a form of nirvana—Schopenhauer was one of the first European authors to explicitly refer to Buddhism.

Schopenhauer's thinking thus aims at the blurring of the boundaries between the self and the world and is characterized by fantasies of fusion and regressive desires for a return to an original union. For him, the primary ontological principle is not reason, as with Kant, but the *will*. However, unlike later bourgeois philosophies, especially in Germany, he does not preach the triumph of the will, but rather its annihilation. In the oscillation between feelings of powerlessness and omnipotence that haunts the narcissist, Schopenhauer clearly represents the depressive and impotent end of the spectrum. The feeling of being a stranger to the world begins with the subject's own body: "the body is already an object, and, from this point of view, we call it too a representation. This is because the body is an object among objects, and must obey the laws of objects."[75] The metaphysics of the will is based on the same subalternization of the body and the same reduction of the human being to a disembodied spirit, while nevertheless amounting to an antithesis of Descartes' rationalist philosophy. In his popular writings, collected in *Parerga and Paralipomena* (1851), Schopenhauer also revealed himself to be the champion of an attitude closely linked to narcissism: resentment.[76] This may explain the riddle of why the writings of this philosopher of resignation became the bedside reading of the triumphant bourgeoisie of his time.

If this Frankfurt rentier formulated the bourgeois and conservative variant of narcissism, a contemporaneous author, who died in poverty, provided the omnipotent version. The thought of Max Stirner, curiously, appealed to certain dedicated opponents of the bourgeoisie. He provided such an extreme formulation of narcissism in *The Unique and Its Property* (1845) that bourgeois society refused to recognize itself therein. Stirner thus became the "father" of individualist anarchism.[77] Like Sade, he advocated the absolute sovereignty of the individual. In a historically unprecedented manner, he radically posited the concrete individual as the sole parameter and aim of the universe, refusing to sacrifice itself for anything. His "every man for himself" was intended to be a radical negation, as radical as possible, of the bourgeois world of his time, based on the fatherland, religion, morality, and the cult of labor. Yet he was merely anticipating the next stage of capitalist society, which was already underway. As the title of the book put it, having a "property" was the primary characteristic of this "unique." However, Stirner pushed narcissism to properly psychotic levels in the denial of natural reality: "Since I cannot grasp the moon, is it therefore supposed to be 'sacred' to me, an Astarte? If I could only grasp you, I surely would, and if I find a way to come up to you, you shall not frighten me!" After the moon, he attacked the sun with impotent rage: "How little the human being is able to conquer! He must let the sun run its course, the sea swell its waves, the mountains rise to the sky. So he stands powerless before the *unconquerable*. Can he resist the impression that is he *helpless* against this gigantic world?"[78]

Industrial capitalist society subsequently demonstrated its capacity to level mountains and dry up seas. If it did not recognize itself in Stirner, it was because he, like Sade, developed the egoism of bourgeois society to the point where it became counterproductive and incompatible with that very society.[79]

CHAPTER 2
NARCISSISM AND CAPITALISM

The previous chapter outlined a preliminary definition of narcissism. Let us now revisit and deepen it. This is not an easy task. The very meaning and definition of the term narcissism evokes confusion in a way unmatched by many other terms of psychoanalytic origin. Its origin, however, is well known: starting in 1910, Freud took up the concept, which had been introduced by other authors a few years earlier, and in 1914 devoted an essay to it. He refers to it in many of his successive writings, but always in a rather fragmentary manner.

What is Narcissism?

Recourse to the divine word of the founding father is of limited assistance here. As soon as Freud used the term, it received the most diverse interpretations in psychoanalytic circles. Béla Grunberger noted in 1971, at the beginning of his important study entitled *Narcissism: Psychoanalytic Essays*, that "anyone who addresses the problem of narcissism comes up against the paradoxical polysemy of the concept," and that from the beginning, the definitions given by Freud himself "seem to form a heterogeneous and sometimes contradictory whole."[1] In the decades that followed this observation, there was a veritable explosion in the use of the word, which went far beyond the circles of psychotherapists and entered popular discourse, to the point of regularly making the front pages of psychology and self-help magazines. Books such as *Le Pervers narcissique et son complice*,[2] *Stalking the Soul: Emotional Abuse and the Erosion of Identity*,[3] *La Manipulation affective dans le couple. Faire face à un pervers narcissique*,[4] etc., focused mainly on the "narcissistic pervert" and its effects on working and romantic relationships. They identify narcissism with excessive self-affirmation and selfishness, relating its effects to those of harassment and manipulation in everyday relationships.

In the popular use of the term, a narcissist is someone who is in a permanent state of self-admiration and is especially concerned with their physical appearance; it refers to a person who spends their time strutting in front of the mirror or trying to attract attention. This usage parallels the word "fetishism," which, for example, can be used to describe automobile or fashion "fetishes." This isn't necessarily wrong, but it encompasses only a small part of the phenomenon— its most conspicuous aspect.

Even in the so-called "specialist" literature, the word narcissism is used in many different ways. A closer look reveals that these are not, or not only, divergent or contrary interpretations of the same phenomenon, between which one has to choose. Rather, it is the use of the same word for describing different phenomena.

Roughly speaking, a "negative" and a "positive" use of the term can be distinguished when it comes to the question of "secondary narcissism"; as far as "primary narcissism" (to be discussed shortly) is concerned, its very existence is subject to debate.

For Freud, narcissism clearly indicates a *pathology*. He first uses the word in his 1910 writing on Leonardo da Vinci, which deals mostly with the genesis of homosexuality, to characterize an individual "in love with himself and his body." Narcissism appears as a "perversion" of the libido.[5] In his later writings, such as *Totem and Taboo* (1912–1913), Freud occasionally mentions narcissism by connecting it to the "ego as libidinal object," but also to the feeling of "omnipotence" that appears in magic and animism. Thus narcissism is tied to the belief in the magical omnipotence of thought, gesture, and language, which would characterize both the "savage" and the psychotic.

In 1914, Freud published "On Narcissism: An Introduction," a more systematic essay of a few dozen pages. Here, narcissism is no longer a perversion, but a necessary component of the human psyche; it is the equivalent of egoism among the drives of the self.[6]

Freud introduces a distinction between an "ego-libido" and "object-libido" (or "objectal"), depending on whether it is directed towards oneself or towards objects (in the broadest sense: people, things, or actions, real or fantasized). It should be remembered that, according to Freud, the amount of libido present in the subject is constant, but that a "conversion" between the different forms of libido is constantly operative.[7] Throughout life, the ego is the "great reservoir of libido," from which the latter can flow to objects but also withdraw back towards the self. Freud draws a comparison with "the body of an amoeba [as] related to the pseudopodia which it puts out." The more one loves oneself, the less one loves "objects" (others), and vice versa. But at the beginning of life, there is no ego, and each drive is autonomous. The libidinal drives and the drives of the ego (which are those of self-preservation, the other major group of drives) are inseparable:[8] this is what Freud more specifically calls "primary narcissism" (the distinction between primary narcissism and secondary narcissism, which is only sketched out in the 1914 essay, gained major importance in his subsequent writings).[9] In this first Freudian conception of narcissism, being one's own object of love constitutes an intermediate stage between auto-erotism (the search for erogenous zones) and object-love.[10] This first identification, in which the ego chooses itself as an object of love, also constitutes the first entry into a "total object" as a unification of partial sexual drives. Thus, primary narcissism contributes to the formation of the self. Its progression is absolutely necessary for the child's psychological development and can later give rise to the necessary balance between loving and being loved. On the other hand, a stasis or excessive accumulation of the libido in the individual (when the libido cannot exteriorize) creates a tension experienced as painful, because the psychic apparatus always aims at reducing tensions and excesses of arousal (external and internal). Thus, the excessive or total reflux of the libido towards the ego produces what Freud at that time called "narcissistic neuroses," which include psychoses such as paranoia, megalomania, and melancholy—whereas today we more often speak of "chronic depression." Illness, sleep, and hypochondria are other modes—normal or harmful—of returning to the initial narcissism and refocusing the libido on the self.

In this context, Freud introduces, for the first time, the concept of the "ego ideal."[11] This extends narcissism into adulthood, as much in self-idealization as in the idealization of the object, as often occurs in the domain of love.[12] Human beings retain a lifelong nostalgia for originary perfection and omnipotence:

> The development of the ego consists in a departure from prima-ry narcissism and gives rise to a vigorous attempt to recover that state. This departure is brought about by means of the displace-ment of libido onto an ego ideal imposed from without; and sat-isfaction is brought about from fulfilling this ideal. At the same time the ego has sent out the libidinal object-cathexes. It becomes impoverished in favor of these cathexes, just as it does in favor of the ego ideal, and it enriches itself once more from its satisfac-tions in respect of the object, just as it does by fulfilling its ideal. One part of self-regard is primary—the residue of infantile nar-cissism; another part arises out of the omnipotence which is cor-roborated by experience (the fulfillment of the ego ideal), whilst a third part proceeds from the satisfaction of object-libido.[13]

We envy or admire the narcissism of others, especially children (but also cats or criminals, says Freud!) because the renunciation of pri-mary narcissism, imposed by the reality principle, leaves the memo-ry of a painful loss for the rest of one's life.

The "ego ideal" should not be confused with an "ethical" ideal; it corresponds with what the individual would like to be. Depending on the context, this ideal can also consist of always striving to be the "toughest," the meanest one in the gang, the one who responds with a punch to every sideways glance, or the one most capable of earn-ing money by any means and having the flashiest car, or even being the most beautiful woman in the country thanks to cosmetic surgery. Freud emphasizes that the ego ideal is far from necessarily involving a sublimation of the drives: "The formation of an ego ideal is often confused with the sublimation of instinct, to the detriment of our understanding of the facts. A man who has exchanged his narcissism for homage to a high ego ideal has not necessarily on that account succeeded in sublimating his libidinal instincts."[14]

Freud repeats much of this content in number twenty-six of his *Introductory Lectures on Psycho-Analysis* (1917), adding that the possibility of auto-erotism renders sexuality less adaptable to the reality principle than the drives of self-preservation, and that object-love derives from primary narcissism.

After 1920, within the framework of his "second conception" of the psychic apparatus, centered on the distinction between the "id," the "ego," and the "superego," Freud opposes the primary narcissistic state (which would be non-objectal, thus without the presence of an object external to the ego) to object relations. Narcissism then consists of being unable to differentiate between the ego and the id, with an intrauterine life as the prototypical example. It would therefore be prior to the formation of the ego, without knowing any divide between the subject and the world; it would be the original state of the human being after birth, when the pleasure principle reigns supreme. In *Group Psychology and the Analysis of the Ego* (1921), he writes: "Thus, by being born we have made the step from an absolutely self-sufficient narcissism to the perception of a changing external world and the beginnings of the discovery of objects. And with this is associated the fact that we cannot endure the new state of things for long, that we periodically revert from it, in our sleep, to our former condition of absence of stimulation and avoidance of objects."[15] The adaptation of the ego to the reality principle imposes renunciations that are very difficult to live with; it is only bearable at the cost of a more or less frequent and profound return to forms of primary narcissism, re-establishing the original unity as the most pleasant state for the individual. Festivals and other forms of traditional celebration thus have the function of enabling a momentary reunification between the ego and its ideal:

> It is quite conceivable that the separation of the ego ideal from the ego cannot be borne for long either, and has to be temporarily undone. In all renunciations and limitations imposed upon the ego a periodical infringement of the prohibition is the rule; this indeed is shown by the institution of festivals. . . . But the ego ideal comprises the sum of all the limitations in which the ego has to acquiesce, and for that reason the abrogation of the ideal would necessarily be a magnificent festival for the ego, which might then once again feel satisfied with itself.[16]

In reality, there are many other forms of narcissistic regression, often much more harmful than festivals. In general, secondary narcissism refers, as here, to a momentary regression, but it can also denote a lasting structure.

In his later writings, Freud further emphasizes the distinction between primary and secondary narcissism, leaving an important theoretical problem for his successors: can there be a totally non-objectal initial phase, a kind of prolongation of the intrauterine state, without distinction between the ego and the id? And, if it exists, how can the child overcome it? Melanie Klein and her school rejected, or strongly reformulated, the concept of primary narcissism. According to Klein, there are only "narcissistic 'states' characterized by a turning round of libido onto internalized objects," and so there is necessarily some form of object relation after birth.[17] But just as the concept of narcissism never played a central role in Freud's thought, it remained of modest importance in psychoanalysis until the seventies.

Recently, French psychiatrist and psychoanalyst Patrick Juignet summarized his rejection—which he seems to share with many contemporary psychotherapists—of the Freudian conception of "primary narcissism": "Contrary to the Freudian tradition, we do not consider the primitive phase of undifferentiation as 'narcissistic.' . . . We therefore strongly disagree with the characterization of this phase as 'primary narcissism'. If we stick to the definition of narcissism as the concept of the constitution and development of the ego, it is [in the case of the primitive stage of undifferentiation] a phase preceding narcissism. It is not desirable, in our opinion, to call two different aspects of psychic evolution by the same name."[18] For Juignet, there are two "lines of development" of the individual, "that of narcissistic development (the construction of identity and the cathexis of the ego) and that of libidinal development (the construction of the object and its cathexis), both of which have a relative autonomy in relation to the other."[19] He calls "pre-narcissistic" the stage corresponding to the absence of individuation and which "manifests itself in what Freud called the 'oceanic feeling' that continues the feeling of fetal life."[20] However, Juignet insists, so little is known about the traces left by intrauterine experience that it is better not to base theories on such unverifiable speculation.[21] The fusional stage of the first six months of life would therefore be "pre-narcissistic" and would be followed by the first forms of individuation that Juignet calls "primary narcissism." This would be the beginning of the formation of the ego, but with still unstable cathexes. The phase of autonomization is said to be followed, around the age of four, by "narcissistic consolidation" and then, in adolescence, by a new phase of "narcissistic instability."

Juignet's perspective is an example of the significant shift that has taken place over the decades in psychoanalytic discourse: narcissism has increasingly been considered as a normal aspect of life—as long as it does not cross the line and become "malignant" or "perverse." It has gone from being considered negative to positive in the eyes of many authors: a "narcissistic balance" must be maintained and the "narcissistic wounds" suffered by subjects must be avoided or treated. Narcissism thus plays an important role in the formation of individual and collective identity, akin to a form of "self-esteem" considered indispensable for the health of the individual, provided that it does not expand to the point of becoming a threat to others.

For Grunberger, whose 1971 book on narcissism heralded the surge in the use of the term in the media, narcissism is the "guardian" or "motor" of life. In the beginning, all libido is narcissistic, existing at birth and remaining the source of all happiness. Narcissism is a psychic instance in the same manner as the id, the ego, and the superego, and is irreducible to and even precedes them. Early relationships should stimulate the narcissism of the small child, otherwise the child might not develop a sufficient will to live. There is an original conflict between narcissistic self-sufficiency and the anti-narcissistic objectal push, and psychic balance depends on their harmonious alliance. Other authors, such as Michael Balint, speak of a primary love and an original tendency to divest oneself of narcissism. If completely narcissistic, the child would not aspire to anything.[22] In order to invest in its mother as an object, the child must distinguish her from the original narcissistic unity formed with her. According to others, it is the ego ideal—differentiated from the ego, which is born from the first object relations—that pushes one to escape the original fusion with the mother and to abandon narcissistic omnipotence. For Janine Chasseguet-Smirgel, the ego ideal is a "pivotal concept that stands between absolute narcissism and objectality, between the pleasure principle and the reality principle, since it results from the split between the ego and the object."[23] It is the ego ideal that drives the individual to seek something other than impulse satisfaction. For all of life, Grunberger says, human beings seek to reduce the gap between their ego and their ego ideal, and to regain the lost perfection, the paradise of the original fusional state.

According to Heinz Kohut, author of another well-received book on narcissism published in 1971, destructiveness is not a primary drive, "but a set of behaviors which derive from an attack on narcissism by greatly compromising it."[24] "Chronic narcissistic rage" is said to be "one of the most pernicious disorders of the human psyche."[25] It must be distinguished from ordinary aggression because it is directed against an object that is part of the inner world of the "ego" (or "self") and helps to maintain its inner equilibrium—Kohut calls it "self-object." When this object fails and removes its support for the "self"—for example, when the subject believes itself to be loved by someone who has withdrawn their love, or when a subordinate refuses to obey and damages the claim of superiority—narcissistic rage aims at restoring the absolute power of the grandiose self. Narcissism thus appears as an excessive reaction to the loss of self-esteem. What concerns Kohut is the weakness of this self-esteem in many contemporary subjects and the corresponding need to compensate for this weakness with pathological narcissism. He analyzes the conditions that give rise to self-esteem in childhood, above all through his renowned considerations on the "gaze of the mother," which, by meeting the child's gaze, gives the child self-confidence; we shall return to this aspect later. However, his conception of narcissism has very different bases from Freudian theory, of which Kohut notably rejects the theory of the instincts and the threefold division of the psychic apparatus (id, ego, superego). This demonstrates once again that the concept of narcissism can be used in different theoretical contexts and with very different meanings.

In recent decades, attention has increasingly shifted to "narcissistic perversion" as opposed to "object-love." This debate does not deal much with libido theory at the individual level, but emphasizes the sociological dimension of the phenomenon—the narcissistic pervert is defined as a "sociopath"—as well as aspects of interpersonal interaction. The descriptions of the phenomenon are similar: narcissists have a "grandiose ego" and do not experience gratitude; everything exists for and because of them. Self-assertion at the expense of others is here paramount. The narcissistic pervert must actively belittle the self of the other and enjoy triumphing over and humiliating them, especially in public. Yet this does not provide any real satisfaction and so the process must always repeat itself: the narcissist therewith exhibits compulsive traits. All of this takes place because the narcissist falls short of Oedipal sexual satisfaction. Paul Denis summarizes the explanations of Paul-Claude Racamier, author of the concept of "narcissistic perversion" (which essentially belongs to French discourse, whereas the rest of the world speaks instead of "narcissistic personality disorders"): the origin of narcissism is to be found in the mother's narcissistic, non-sexual, seduction of the child: "The Oedipal prohibition allows tenderness because it prevents direct sexuality with the parents while designating other possible sexual objects: companions for sexual games, objects of future love. On the contrary, narcissistic seduction eliminates third parties and prevents the development of the Oedipal complex and fantasy life in favor of the development of an imagoic mode of thought—in which a phallic maternal imago dominates psychic functioning for the benefit of a narcissistic affirmation of completeness and omnipotence."[26] The narcissist avoids the encounter with the "other" and seeks to deny the limitation of its own power that results from the very recognition of the other, beginning from the constitution of the "Oedipal triangle."

For others, such as Grunberger, narcissism, as a nostalgia for the prenatal state, is opposed to the drives and the tensions they generate. Narcissism itself contains an aggressive component and is not opposed to a death drive—whose existence Grunberger denies. Thus, for some, narcissism is deadly, while for others, it is identified with life itself and is what allows the death drive to be overcome. In meta-psychological terms, narcissism can just as easily be identified with Eros as with Thanatos, with the force that wants to destroy everything in order to return to an "inorganic calm" as with that which builds by binding living beings together. The more the concept of narcissism is explored, the more astonishing it becomes for its extreme ambiguity.

Narcissism and Fear of Separation

Rather than take a position in the face of this proliferating and confusing debate, we will use our own concept of narcissism—which owes much to Christopher Lasch—in a broader sense than that of narcissistic perversion. Even behavior that does not appear to be "narcissistic"—such as "New Age" thinking, for example—will be considered. The "narcissistic pervert" is generally aware of his actions and takes pleasure from the treatment inflicted on his victims. The narcissist, in a broader sense, may, on the contrary, be completely unaware of their narcissism and not behave in any way that is usually described as "narcissistic."

Intrauterine life clearly consists of a situation of complete fusion, in which there is no distinction between the self and the world, subject and object, interior and exterior. Any need is immediately satisfied. For the rest, we can only speculate on what the fetus experiences. It is quite tempting to imagine that this is a life without tension or pain, in uninterrupted bliss. We can equally imagine that ideas of paradise and the golden age—so present in different cultures and always situated at the beginning of time or, to put it better, before the beginning of historical time—are mythological transfigurations of that paradisiacal state that every human being has known, or of which they keep a vague memory after their brutal expulsion from the maternal womb. It can even be argued that much human behavior, from the preference for small and protective places to the mystical search for union with God, corresponds to a desire to return *in utero*.

Nevertheless, all of this is pure speculation. What appears much more plausible is that birth constitutes a sudden transition to a completely different state. The satisfaction of needs is no longer immediate or guaranteed, but may or may not occur, or may occur with delay. It seems quite obvious that every delay in satisfying needs is experienced by the newborn as a threat to its own survival and triggers anxiety attacks. In truth—and this is surely one of the great paradoxes of human existence—it is easier for us to know what is happening in the most distant galaxies than to understand what we felt at the beginning of our lives, or what babies experience as we hold them in our arms. However, there is every indication that the newborn experiences the pain of being "thrown into the world" [*Geworfenheit*][27] and being completely dependent on the outside world, including the mother's care.[28] This is what Freud called the *Hilflosigkeit* of the baby, i.e., its impotence, its "distress," or its "state of helplessness."[29]

This helplessness is greatly increased by one of the defining features of the human condition, the importance of which is not always recognized: premature birth. Compared to most animals, even those closest in evolutionary terms, baby *Homo sapiens* are born in a much less complete state. They must, so to speak, accomplish much of their development after birth—unlike other animals. During its first months, the human being remains in some respects in a fetal condition. Freud was one of the first to highlight this particularity of human ontogeny as one of the most profound reasons—and a kind of ultimate explanation—for the distinction between nature and culture, man and animal.[30] Human beings detach themselves from their parents much more slowly than any other animal—and this prolonged dependence, combined with the weakness of innate instincts, is a decisively human feature. According to some authors, a "second birth," a "psychological birth" (Margaret Mahler) takes place from about the fifth month: it is only at this moment that the human infant reaches approximately the degree of maturation that other primates possess at birth. Only then does the child realize that it exists as distinct from its surroundings and gradually leave the "symbiotic" relationship with the mother.

In fact, the newborn's feeling of helplessness in the face of a world whose stimuli exceed its capacity for development and reaction must be so strong that it closes in on itself during the first months of life, preserving its fusional experience. Feeling united with the all-powerful mother, it feels all-powerful itself: its real and total impotence is compensated for by an imaginary omnipotence, which nevertheless has a real basis in the lack of distinction from the mother. The child relies on substitute or even hallucinatory satisfactions in the absence of real satisfactions—thumb sucking is the paradigmatic example. It cannot yet accept the fact that objects—the first of which is the mother's breast—are independent and can deny its desires. It sees them as an extension of itself. Or, to put it better, in no way does it experience the separation between itself and the mother, itself and objects, itself and the surrounding world. The first months of life are therefore a kind of transitional phase that possesses the characteristics of both intra- and post-uterine existence. The essential element, the symbiotic relationship with the mother, no longer really exists, but is reconstituted "as if" it did—especially in the long moments of sleep. While it is speculative to attribute our nostalgia for a golden age of fusion to the uterine phase, it is very likely that similar postnatal states leave traces in our memory. If this entry into life is likely to be accompanied by great anxiety—it is understandable why all babies, even those who receive the greatest attention, bawl at times with great ferocity—it also includes moments of extreme euphoria and blissful fusion with the environment.[31]

Little by little, the child opens up to the world and to the "reality principle." The separation from the mother is not without problems and pain, but from about the fifth month onwards, the child gradually establishes genuine relationships with objects and finally "accepts" their autonomy—in primus that of the mother herself. What the child loses in fusion, it gains in autonomy. An important stage in this process of autonomization is the famous Oedipus complex, the keystone of Freudian psychoanalysis. As everyone knows, in its original formulation, from between the ages of three and five, the young boy sexually desires his mother and imagines killing his father, who prevents him from fulfilling his desire. The father then threatens his son with castration, and (if all goes well, according to Freud) the son ends up submitting and renouncing his desires. The son then identifies with his father and assumes the latter's role, which later allows him to gain real access to genital sexuality, but also to the father's social role and to social authority in general. The internalization of the paternal prohibition is at the center of what Freud later calls the "superego": an inner voice that imposes—among other things—the rules of the society in which we live.

The Oedipus complex has been discussed endlessly: is it universal or not, how does it present itself in the female child, at what age does it occur, etc. For the purposes of this discussion, however, we can limit ourselves to this minimal definition: from the second year onwards, the parents (or the environment in general) progressively limit the child's "polymorphic perversion," i.e., their spontaneous tendency to obtain libidinal satisfaction, involving their entire body, from people of all ages, sexes, and kinship, as well as from animals and inanimate objects. This limitation occurs in all cultures and contexts—examples include the universal taboo on incest and excrement. The ban on playing with one's own excrement or genitals is as much a part of this limitation as the most visible repression: that of the child's attraction to the parent of the opposite sex and their aggressive attitude towards the parent of their own sex. From the orthodox psychoanalytic perspective, this is, at the same time, the beginning of the child's moral conscience and social behavior. According to other points of view more critical of the bourgeois family and the society of which this family is the nucleus, the father's victory[32] in the Oedipal conflict constitutes, on the contrary, the beginning of the internalization of the authoritarian and patriarchal order and thus of the reproduction of a repressive society opposed to pleasure and hostile to the feminine.

The Oedipal conflict ends with the defeat of the child, who must abandon his incestuous desires. This is a harsh victory of the reality principle over the pleasure principle, but the defeat paves the way, according to psychoanalytic orthodoxy, for psychological maturation. With the real entry of the father on the scene, the "third party" or "triangulation" appears: the child is forced to abandon the dual relationship with the mother, exposed to the danger of being "devoured" in a symbiotic relationship. Until then, the father, even if he is present and takes care of the child, is not really perceived by the child. Once the father becomes a key figure, he shows the child the possibility of living with the mother in a manner other than fusion. He forces the child out of this perfect union and, through the relationship with the father, to open up to the world of "others," both people and objects.[33] By renouncing excessive but unattainable desires, the child manages to obtain minor but real satisfactions until, as an adult, it can finally assume the role—sexual and social—previously envied in the father (or the mother, in the case of a girl). The limitations imposed on the pleasure principle, which originally reigns supreme, pave the way to effective gratifications derived from accepting the reality principle—an acceptance that ultimately always serves to obtain pleasure, but through channels that are longer and more indirect but safer. The reality principle itself, so unpleasant for human beings, is ultimately recognized, says Freud, only to better serve the pleasure principle.

This is the ideal evolution according to Freudian psychoanalysis—we will discuss later whether it is "ideal" from a point of view less committed to the perpetuation of bourgeois society. It allows the individual, as Freud himself admits, not a perfect happiness, but an acceptable compromise with reality—in the final analysis, a compromise between "nature" and "culture." However, a harmonious solution to these conflicts in the individual represents the exception and not the rule. Many factors can disrupt the success of the developing human being in this succession of events: constitutional or innate factors (what today would be called "genetic"), to which Freud attributes notable importance, as well as failures on the part of the maternal figure and other people who take care of the child. Above all, however, there is the resistance the individual itself opposes to this limitation of its original omnipotence and its polymorphic perversion. Especially in the first iteration of his theoretical edifice—until about 1920—Freud essentially attributes neuroses to conflicts in the Oedipal phase: the transformation of primal desires has not been completely successful and the individual, even as an adult, remains nostalgic for these desires (incestuous, perverse, aggressive), and often in completely transformed forms. This results in feelings of guilt, which are expressed in the form of neuroses. Just like dreams and missteps, these serve essentially to partly satisfy the desires that the individual has had to renounce.

Freud largely concentrated on the study of neuroses and hysteria, leaving aside psychoses, just as he privileged the Oedipal phase over the so-called "pre-Oedipal" phase, on which he focused more towards the end of his life, notably in *Inhibition, Symptoms and Anxiety* (1926). Thereafter, Melanie Klein and her school focused their attention on the early years of life, suggesting that an essential part of the development of the individual is already at work. Of course, the difficulties of producing knowledge about this early phase are immense, yet a certain consensus among psychoanalysts has nonetheless emerged, notably on the importance of the fusional phase, whether it is named "primary narcissism" or "pre-narcissism."

Freud was the first to state that "narcissistic neuroses" (i.e., psychoses) are more serious than obsessional neuroses and can be traced back to "libido fixation points" from much earlier phases. They are also much more difficult to cure, because narcissistic neurotics refuse transference: "It is very remarkable that in the case of all the narcissistic neuroses we have to assume fixation points for the libido going back to far earlier phases of development than in hysteria or obsessional neurosis."[34] It is known that a disorder in childhood development generally has more serious consequences the earlier it occurs. To put it schematically, if disturbances in the Oedipal phase often lead to neuroses, problems in an earlier phase can lead to psychoses or other serious "personality disorders" such as "borderline personality." It must therefore be assumed that the overcoming of primary narcissism is a particularly delicate process susceptible to causing serious consequences—all the more so as it coincides, in a way, with the most difficult of all separations: the separation from the mother and the awareness of existing as a being distinct from the world, a world that is not always at our disposal. As has been mentioned, the gains in pleasure brought by the recognition of reality in a second phase—and above all the Oedipal prohibition—typically make the child accept the limitations imposed upon them. They transform their imaginary omnipotence—which does not stand the test of reality—into a limited but real power. In order to do so, they must admit their dependence on the outside world and their state of separation from it, so that they can then successfully reap the benefits of learning its rules.

However, there is another way of reacting to this problem: the child recognizes separation and dependence only in appearance, while inwardly safeguarding the illusion of omnipotence and a state of fusion.[35] This can occur without any obvious disorder, since the child adopts the behavior that adults expect of them. But the acceptance of reality remains superficial and as if accompanied by a "mental reserve." The individual in question continues to maintain archaic aspirations, often throughout their life and normally without any clear awareness. He does not recognize the barrier between child and adult and still hopes to fulfill his incestuous desires, often in a way unrecognizable because of their displacement. He denies sexual difference in his unconscious in order to deny castration—and this applies to both men and women. Similarly, they are reluctant to truly recognize the existence of the other, of the world, of objects that are external to them and that only grant them power—always partial—after they have admitted his impotence. This can be too painful to accept. Phantasmagorical constructions then compensate for the unwilling concessions made to the reality principle, making it possible to return from time to time to the original state of bliss—this is called a "regression."

While primary narcissism is a normal and indispensable stage of the individual's development, secondary narcissism is a pathological attempt to deny, or revoke, the release from primary narcissism. It is defined by a lack of libidinal cathexis in the external world. "Objects" (including people) are obviously perceived, but without the subject investing its libido in them, or rather very little. The libido instead remains excessively concentrated in the subject itself. A balance between the libido of the ego and the libido of objects is, however, essential for psychological well-being—that is what, after Freud, others have called the "narcissistic balance." When the libido, says Freud in "On Narcissism: An Introduction," flows entirely towards objects, there is an impoverishment of the self, which may be acceptable and pleasant in the momentary and highest state of amorous passion, but which usually reveals itself to be unpleasant for the individual.[36] The contrary situation consists of too much libido concentrated in the individual, or too much returning to it. According to Freud, this occurs especially in the case of rather visible pathologies, such as megalomania or melancholy.

What has been better understood since Freud—because the phenomenon itself has greatly increased—is the important place occupied by secondary narcissism in psychic life, even and especially in its less easily detectible forms. The narcissist maintains only pseudo-relationships with other people and "objects"—and of course, there are different degrees of secondary narcissism. He does not recognize, in his unconscious, the existence of objects outside of himself; they are experienced as parts of his self. For him, these objects are projections of his inner world, extensions of his own being, just like the very small child who cannot yet bear its state of total dependence. In secondary narcissism, the subject continues throughout their life to deny this dependence by "annexing" external objects and denying them any autonomy. This denial of separation is a more essential feature than the "self-love" usually attributed to narcissism. In Ovid, Narcissus is not really in love with himself, but with his image; he ends up drowning while attempting to embrace it since he does not recognize the dividing line between his self and the world (the water).[37]

Despite its excessive ego and the fact that it "swallows" the world, the narcissist's personality is neither rich nor happy. Above all, it lacks the essential capacity to enrich itself through contact with objects and to truly integrate them into its self. People and things both remain external to it. They are experienced only as projections, extensions and confirmations of itself, its self always remaining self-same without experiencing anything real and without development. It remains confined to a kind of "mirror stage," merely reflecting itself everywhere *as it is*. This is why the narcissist is unbearable for those around it; it also feels, at least at times and confusedly, its inner emptiness and lack of a real personality. Its extreme need for confirmation from others only exposes it to frustrations that lead to "narcissistic wounds" and ultimately to "narcissistic rage." Its lack of inner resources means that its internal equilibrium collapses quite easily, or that it is permanently on the run to avoid these frustrations. In the end, the narcissist is not a triumphant personality, but a miserable wretch.

The narcissist may have a very demanding ego ideal (or an "ideal self," the two terms are more or less equivalent in Freud), but it does not have, or only partially, a superego of Oedipal origin. It has not internalized moral laws and it is typical of the narcissist to respect social rules only outwardly, while thinking that they do not really apply to itself and that the most skillful conduct in life consists in avoiding the rules as soon as they are disadvantageous. But this does not prevent it from suffering the effects of what is called an "archaic superego," a concept developed above all by Melanie Klein, formed in the pre-Oedipal phase and which is much more ferocious and irrational than the Oedipal superego. Indeed, this superego is particularly punitive; it does not attack the subject in the name of moral principles, but from an insufficiency in relation to the ego ideal. As has been mentioned, not being handsome or "cool" enough, not being successful enough and earning too little money, putting on a few extra pounds, or owning an obsolete mobile phone; all of this can cause feelings of inadequacy and anguish in the narcissist, at least equal to the remorse inflicted by the classic superego.

Psychoanalysis and Revolution: Erich Fromm and Herbert Marcuse

The psychoanalysis of Freud was a major challenge to thought when it emerged at the beginning of the twentieth century—and it remains so today.[38] Few theories have been so hotly debated for more than a century, and on the frontlines of both its supporters and opponents, there has always been a wide range of participants, including those with very different political approaches. Psychoanalysis has also represented a challenge to the field of the critique of capitalism. The most "orthodox" Marxism rejected it. Thus, in *The Destruction of Reason* (1954), Georg Lukács (whose trajectory carried him from Marxist heterodoxy to orthodoxy) paints a broad picture of the currents of bourgeois thought, which he describes as "irrational," and goes so far as to align Freud with fascism.

Psychoanalysis was prohibited in the Soviet Union in the thirties, after initially arousing interest, expressed particularly in Mikhail Bakhtin's book on "Freudianism," published in 1927 under the name of Valentin Voloshinov.[39] Pavlov's behaviorism, the official psychological doctrine in the Soviet Union, was obviously more useful for the manipulation of the masses. Freud was always a liberal (or "enlightened conservative") and opponent of "Bolshevism." He never encouraged attempts to draw revolutionary social and political consequences from psychoanalysis; indeed, writings such as *Civilization and Its Discontents* were often regarded as "reactionary." Part of the left was convinced that psychoanalysis was irreconcilable with the program of social emancipation, or, in any case, that it made no contribution to it and could be ignored. This distrust is still alive, and while not always stated overtly, it can reveal real problems in psychoanalytic theory. At a vulgar level, the more "classist" currents of the left tended to denigrate sexual themes as "petty-bourgeois" and, more generally, to consider neuroses as a problem of the bourgeoisie and of those who do not work.

Psychoanalysis has always had a great weakness in its claims about a "human nature," a supposedly immutable anthropological and biological substratum. Yet reference to "nature" is generally characteristic of the "right": in reactionary discourse, at least in its classical version, it is nature that has made men unequal and established hierarchies between races, classes, and sexes. Human beings are born different, this discourse proclaims, in intelligence and talent, and competition and the pursuit of individual self-interest are "natural." Human beings are by nature selfish and seek only personal advantage for themselves and their families. Others add that human beings "by nature" need religion, or even a "master," or assert that homosexuality, or a working woman who wants equality with men, is "unnatural." Any attempt to change human "nature" would thus only lead to violence and totalitarianism. It is easy to understand that Hobbes, with his *homo homini lupus* (man is a wolf to other men), is the true founder of this naturalization of social relations, which led to social Darwinism and eugenics.

For the left, on the other hand, culture, society, and education trump any hypothetical human nature. This asserted pre-eminence of culture over nature in human beings then becomes the basis for the assertion that humanity, by acting collectively, can take its destiny into its own hands—the linchpin of any revolutionary theory. Almost all suffering becomes the consequence of class society, not of humanity as such. It is therefore possible to overcome these problems or even to create a "new human being" who, for example, would no longer know selfishness.[40] Freud's theory, however, does not admit this Promethean enthusiasm.[41] For him, the unconscious, whose structure is fairly fixed, imposes narrow limits to the variability of human behavior. The drives, of somatic origin, cannot be modified and are at most controllable. The major role Freud attributed to childhood, the least "social" part of life and the one where individuals are least differentiated by cultural and social factors, necessarily limits the possibility of a conscious self-creation of society. The conceptions of collective life developed by Freud, especially in *Totem and Taboo* (1913) onwards, reinforced the "anti-utopian" character of psychoanalysis: society appears only as the multiplied version of the individual and its drive structure. It repeats an archaic structure and re-enacts the drama of the "primitive horde": thus, ontogeny repeats phylogeny (the evolution of the individual repeats the evolution of the species), including in the psychic field.

Civilization and Its Discontents (1930) seems to complete this disillusioned, even reactionary, observation: Freud holds happiness to be impossible at both the individual and social levels. It is only possible to limit unhappiness—for example, with a slightly more permissive sexual morality, even if Freud never goes so far as the idea of "sexual liberation." He also introduced the concept of the "death drive," which had been formulated since 1919: war, aggression, destructiveness, and sadism are not just the consequences of a sick society but part of our constitution as humans. It seems very difficult to put such a conception of life in the service of the profound social transformation that the left believed possible. However, the power of Freud's ideas was such that, even on the left, some were quick to try and use them to promote social emancipation. Otto Gross and Wilhelm Reich were the first, followed by Georg Groddeck, Sándor Ferenczi,

Otto Fenichel, Géza Róheim, and others, each in their own way.[42]

We will examine this development from a particular angle: Christopher Lasch's criticisms, circa 1980, of Herbert Marcuse, author of *Eros and Civilization* (1955), and Norman Brown, author of *Life Against Death* (1955).[43] These authors criticized the neo-Freudian revisionists (notably Erich Fromm) for their critique of certain aspects of Freud's work. What is remarkable about this game of "Russian dolls" is that all of them—except Freud himself—argued in the name of some form of social emancipation and critique of capitalism, but in different, even opposed ways. All of them assumed the point of view of a fundamental critique of consumerist capitalism and accused their predecessors of making only a pseudo-critique, or a critique that remained inscribed, unbeknownst to them, within the framework of the society it claimed to overcome.[44]

The Institute for Social Research—usually referred to as the "Frankfurt School"—was, from the moment Max Horkheimer took over its directorship in 1931, at the heart of a major project of uniting the tools of Marxist materialism with psychoanalysis. Indeed, for the authors of the Institute, psychoanalysis is "materialist," but in a rather broad sense, going beyond economism. In the beginning, this approach was taken up by Erich Fromm in his *Studies on Authority and the Family* (1936). Writers associated with the Institute mainly tried to link psychological "characters"—"types"—to the social classes created by capitalism: for example, by demonstrating the "anal" character of the bourgeois class, which was fixated on accumulation and saving. These accumulative behaviors are not neuroses for the bourgeoisie, but form the basis of their social role and drive them to blind obedience, leaving them susceptible to the transformation into an "authoritarian personality," full of prejudice and resentment, ideal prey for fascist propaganda.

In the 1940s, members of the Institute who had emigrated to the United States continued this research—half theoretical, half empirical—on the "authoritarian personality," published under an eponymous title in 1950. However, the way in which those who now constituted the core of the Institute—that is, Horkheimer, Adorno, and Marcuse—viewed Freud had changed significantly in the meantime.

Erich Fromm, who had gradually come into conflict with them—and especially with Adorno—from 1937 onwards, became the target of their attacks and was labeled a "neo-Freudian revisionist."[45] The Institute, on the other hand, wanted to make a return to the "real" Freud, including those aspects of his thought that were apparently the most difficult to integrate into a critical theory of capitalist society.[46] Freud's later writings, neglected by the revisionists, seemed on the contrary very important to the future authors of *Dialectic of Enlightenment*, who sought to understand the rise of fascism through the internalization of social constraints and necessarily violent character of any civilization.

The neo-Freudians (mainly Fromm, Karen Horney, and Harry Stack Sullivan), on the other hand, diminished the importance attributed by Freud to the drives, especially the sexual ones; they insisted on the role of education, social factors, and culture and sought links with anthropology and sociology. Their theory de-emphasized the role of childhood in an individual's history as well as that of the Oedipus complex, whose universal character they disputed. They also denied *a fortiori* the existence of the death drive. In general, they did not admit the existence of insurmountable conflicts within the human being. For them, it was a question of "humanizing" Freud, freeing him from the baggage of biology, from the pessimism of his late works, and from the despairing concept of the "death drive" in order to discover the grounds of individual happiness and social harmony.

According to the neo-Freudians, Freud was wrong in postulating an incompatibility between the drives and civilization; it would be enough to abolish excessive repression in order to achieve an individual and collective equilibrium—a kind of psychic social democracy, a corollary of the welfare state. But, at least in Fromm, this is always accompanied by a very critical vision of capitalist society that seems to leave open the possibility of an emancipatory self-transformation of society, in contrast to Freud's Hobbesian pessimism.[47] What Fromm had abandoned around 1941 was the Freudian theory of the libido, which seemed to him incompatible with a Marxist reading of the socio-economic origins of the psychic characteristics of the different social classes.[48] If the anal character is typical of the bourgeoisie, why explain it with rituals of cleanliness in early childhood, which can be identical amongst different classes? For Fromm, it is the social relations corresponding to the socio-economic conditions that directly form character from childhood onwards, without passing through the phases of the libido.

Adorno made the first public attack on Fromm in a 1946 lecture to the San Francisco Psychoanalytical Society.[49] His main target was Karen Horney, a German psychoanalyst who had also emigrated to the United States and who had been close to Fromm for a time. But Adorno's critique was actually directed at Fromm. In it he anticipates the essence of the critique expressed almost ten years later by Marcuse. According to Adorno, Freud's atomism expresses a social reality: the split between the individual and society. Revisionists want to treat "the inhumane relationships as if they were already human"; they thereby "lend an inhumane reality a glance at the humane" and "are angry at the reactionary Freud . . . while his irreconcilable pessimism testifies to the truth about the conditions, of which he does not speak."[50]

Adorno's argument, like Marcuse's later on, seems paradoxical at first sight: why do these two authors, who are not primarily interested in the clinical, therapeutic value of psychoanalysis, but in its possible contribution to the project of "progress beyond the 'patricentric-acquisitive' culture,"[51] accuse Fromm of "sociologism" and defend Freud's theory of the drives, which considers intersubjective relations—and thus society—as secondary to a largely innate drive structure that exists only at the individual level? The insistence of the "culturalists" on the importance of the "environment" and interpersonal relations from the beginning of individual life seems much closer to Marxist theory. The latter emphasizes the social dimensions of existence, whereas the Freudian vision of the human being seems close to bourgeois liberalism, for which the only true reality is the individual and its *pursuit of happiness*, and which shares the openly proclaimed view of Margaret Thatcher: "There is no such thing as society!"

In order to understand the position of Adorno and Marcuse,

some clarifications are needed. Marcuse formulated the essence of his critique of Fromm in an article from 1955, published the same year as an epilogue to *Eros and Civilization*. He first explains the initially honorable rationale for neo-Freudian revisionism: "The psychoanalytic conception of man, with its belief in the basic unchangeability of human nature, appeared as 'reactionary'; Freudian theory seemed to imply that the humanitarian ideals of socialism were humanly unattainable. Then the revision of psychoanalysis began to gain momentum."[52] For Freud, even the "highest values of Western civilization" presuppose alienation and suffering. "The Neo-Freudian schools promote the very same values as cure against unfreedom and suffering—as the triumph over repression."[53]

Revisionists give priority to inter-individual relations between adults, and thus to social reality, whereas Freud, "focusing on the vicissitudes of the primary instincts, discovered society in the most concealed layer of the genus and individual man."[54] Marcuse admits that Fromm, at the beginning of his career, was trying to free Freud's theory from its identification with contemporary society. In his articles of the thirties, published in the Institute's *Zeitschrift für Sozialforschung*, "Freud's own insights into the historical character of the modifications of the impulses vitiate his equation of the reality principle with the norms of patricentric-acquisitive culture."[55] But, according to Marcuse, Fromm did not remain faithful to his beginnings and, even when he later continued to denounce capitalism, his critique remained superficial, limited to the question of the "values" to be lived within the very framework of an unfree society. Unlike Freud, Fromm did not want to see that these "higher values" are realized at the expense of individuals and their libidinal happiness.[56] In short, the revisionists, by eliminating Freud's most explosive concepts, would have yielded to a "desire for the positive." According to Marcuse, however, recognizing the "right to happiness" in the here and now, as Fromm preferred, implied defining it in terms compatible with this society, and thus making these values equally repressive forces. The metapsychology of Freud contains a greater critical potential than his therapeutics, which necessarily take into account the given reality and the need to cure patients without waiting for a change in civilization.

Revisionists oppose a "sociological" interpretation of the psyche to an individual-centered perspective. However, even Freud argues that the individual depends on a "general destiny," one that manifests itself mainly in early childhood. This is where "[t]he general repressiveness shapes the individual and universalizes even his most personal features."[57] According to Marcuse, revisionists overestimate individual differences: "The decisive relations are thus those which are the *least* interpersonal. In an alienated world, specimens of the genus confront each other: parent and child, male and female, then master and servant, boss and employee."[58] Marcuse argues that it is precisely the most "rigid," most "biologistic" Freud that contains the most critical truth about capitalist society: "In contrast, Freud's basic 'biologistic' concepts reach beyond the ideology and its reflexes: his refusal to treat a reified society as a 'developing network of interpersonal experiences and behavior' [as the "humanistic" neo-Freudians do] and an alienated individual as a 'total personality' corresponds to the reality and contains its true notion. If he refrains from regarding the inhuman existence as a passing negative aspect of forward-moving humanity, he is more humane than the good-natured, tolerant critics who brand his 'inhuman' coldness."[59] The "static" Freudian concept of society, according to Marcuse, is closer to reality than the "dynamic" concept of the revisionists, because every society is based on the repression of drives. Freud's minimal program is to limit unhappiness; to believe that more can be done in the present state of society implies an excessively angelic conception of society itself.

Revisionists want to develop the "potential" of their patients, but if society is as alienated as Fromm claims, how would it be possible to create responsible, productive, and fulfilled people? This is an idealist ethic, in contrast to Freud's vision, which, even when using irony, "refrains from calling repression by any other name than its own; the Neo-Freudians sometimes sublimate it into its opposite."[60] Fromm is indeed critical of commodity society and competition, but believes that it is still possible to realize "higher values" and to "work constructively" within it. He also overlooks the fact that erotic drives are always intertwined in some way with destructive drives. Freud, on the other hand, knows that "our civilization" has no room for a love that is both tender and sensual. But, according to the revisionists, a harmonious solution can be found. For them, the essential conflicts, such as social repression, are not even sociological; they are banal moral conflicts. They thus return to the devaluation of material needs and do not believe in a fundamental conflict between the pleasure principle and the reality principle: humanity's instinctual nature can find a socially recognized happiness. Their "humanism" thus falls short of Freud's terrible lucidity, for which the fundamental misfortune of repression can never be compensated for by its sublimation into "productive love" and other forms of pseudo-happiness.

Revisionists have spiritualized happiness and freedom, and so they can believe that happiness is possible even in a repressive society. On the other hand, it is Freud's recourse to biology that reveals the extent of repression and does not allow for the facile illusions of the "culturalists." Rather than "adding" a sociological dimension to Freud's theory, the sociological and historical content of these apparently biological categories must be extrapolated. The weakening of the individual has made it impossible to apply psychology to social phenomena. It is now necessary to "develop the political and sociological substance of the psychological notions": society is found within the individual, rather than the other way around.[61] An autonomous psychology is no longer possible.[62]

Fromm could not help but be surprised at the virulence of this polemic advanced by a former ideological companion. In the context of the conformist and anti-communist United States of the 1950s, he probably considered his own position to be already highly exposed, heretical, and subversive. Moreover, he opposed the reduction of psychoanalysis to a simple cure for individual neurosis, which was very common in the United States at the time, and reminded us that the sick individual is instead the consequence of a sick society and that the very founding principles of American society—such as competition—are pathological as such. It must have seemed strange to him that another Marxist should give him such a lesson in radicalism, reproaching him for having done exactly what he claimed to have always fought against: the adaptation of psychoanalysis to a repressive context, stripping it of any genuinely subversive character. How could a Marxist *criticize* him for emphasizing the role of adult relationships, and thus of society, in the psychic structure of individuals?

Fromm replied sharply in *Dissent*, the same journal that published Marcuse's attack.[63] His response begins by pointing out that Marcuse amalgamates the often-divergent positions of the various "revisionists" and that he unduly attributes to Fromm opinions that are properly those of Horney or Sullivan, who are much less interested in social criticism.[64] The critique then turns to Freud himself, to his "Darwinian" vision of human beings and his inability to historicize society. By reducing love to sexual desire, Freud can only conceive of an irreducible conflict at the basis of all civilization. Thus, no society can escape the repression of drives, even of love; only a few timid reforms in the field of sexual morality would be possible, as Freud himself says. How could this, Fromm asks, possibly pass for a radical critique of alienated society?

The "materialism" that Marcuse praises in Freud—in contrast with the supposed "spiritualism" of the revisionists—is, according to Fromm, nothing more than the "bourgeois" and pre-Marxian physiological materialism of the nineteenth century. On the contrary, Fromm argues, it is on the basis of Marx's materialism, as a dialectical relationship between nature and culture under the sign of "praxis," that it is possible to conceive of a human being who does not limit itself to the satisfaction of its impulsive needs. On the other hand, the demand for unlimited sexual satisfaction—which he attributes to Marcuse—is not radical: the Nazis of their time, and especially postwar consumer society, also proposed it. Aldous Huxley's *Brave New World* anticipated it, where conflict-free, happy people do not need to be coerced into obedience.[65] Fromm emphasizes that his conception of happiness and love is quite different from the dominant one, but that it is not impossible—only very difficult—to implement it in an alienated society. To do so, he adds, would even amount to a form of social critique and rebellion. The neglect of the "human factor," and more precisely the nihilistic attitude towards human beings, was one of the defects of Leninism and Stalinism. He concludes that "Marcuse's position is an example of human nihilism disguised as radicalism."[66]

In his reply to Fromm's response, Marcuse states that neither he nor Freud ever identified unlimited and immediate sexual satisfaction with happiness. But he also points out that all sublimation contains an element of unfreedom and repression. The *implications* of Freud's theory—beyond its effective permanence in the horizon of its time—are far more anti-capitalist than Fromm's nonsense about workers' participation in management. There is no nineteenth-century materialism in Freudian metapsychology, argues Marcuse; it even sometimes refers to Plato! "'Nihilism,' as the indictment of inhuman conditions, may be a truly humanistic attitude—part of the Great Refusal to play the game, to compromise with the bad 'positive.' In this sense, I accept Fromm's designation of my position as 'human nihilism.'"[67]

In his last response, Fromm again cites Freud to demonstrate, while criticizing him, that for Freud happiness does indeed lie in unrestricted sexuality—thus confirming that Fromm is not diverging from Marcuse's reading of Freud, but from the Freudian conception of sexuality itself. Neither Fromm nor Marcuse quote Adorno's aphorism in *Minima Moralia*: "Wrong life cannot be lived rightly"—although they might as well have.

Marcuse provided his own interpretation of Freud in *Eros and Civilization* (1955).[68] It is undeniably disturbing for those who think that a recovery of Freud's thought from a Marxist perspective—to which, as we know, Marcuse remained much closer than other authors of the Institute—can only consist in an explanation of individual neuroses by social repression, eliminating the "anthropological invariance" so present in the thought of the late Freud. However, it is exactly the metapsychological Freud that Marcuse highlights, and in particular the concept of the "death drive"[69] and the importance given by Freud to the prehistory of humanity in order to explain contemporary societies: the "primitive horde" and the "murder of the father" are said to be at the origin of persistent feelings of guilt that would explain even the "Thermidor," that is, the return to pre-revolutionary states of society.[70] For Marcuse, Freud's greatness resides precisely in his ruthless insistence on the existence of the death drive and on the fact that the unsublimated satisfaction of libidinal drives does indeed threaten the edifice of civilization in its present form. Freud does not suggest that human beings could live in harmony with this society; he only suggests that they should limit their drive satisfactions—without ever denying this to be a very painful renunciation—in order for the individual not to enter into a devastating conflict.

The question, therefore, is whether to accept repression and sublimation as the inevitable price to pay for preserving civilization. Freud's analysis, says Marcuse, is correct—provided, however, that it is not situated at the ontological level. It applies only to capitalist society (or other repressive societies). The abolition of labor—the radical reduction of working time and the transformation of work into libidinal activity—made possible in postwar capitalist society by the development of technologies for replacing living labor, paves the way for a historical transformation of the structure of the drives and their reconciliation with civilization. In this "concrete utopia," Narcissus and Orpheus succeed Oedipus.

No therapeutic intervention, no moral effort can succeed in reconciling the individual and society as long as alienated labor and surplus repression (to be discussed shortly) continue to exist. The neo-Freudians are mistaken in claiming that this agreement is possible. But Freud was also mistaken in claiming that the pleasure principle must remain forever subordinate to the reality principle, because nothing will stop the domination exercised by *Ananke* (Greek for necessity, need, lack, scarcity, etc.). Until now, Marcuse concedes, various societies have indeed developed within the framework of a scarcity of resources wrested from nature. Consequently, life has consisted of a struggle for survival. Under these conditions, the repression of drives and the coercion of labor have been, at least in part, a condition for human survival.

But the result of this long history of repression and alienation is to have created the precondition for its overcoming: thanks to technology, society is now ready to live with a minimum of alienation and repression. Anything beyond this inevitable minimum constitutes "surplus repression," with no other function than to maintain existing structures of domination for the benefit of a minority. It therefore has no real justification, which makes it possible to consider that a profound change in the drive structure of human beings is possible, even in the short-term. The death drive can be greatly reduced if society allows the constructive forces of Eros to occupy as much space as possible in individual and collective life. In a way, Marcuse reverses the Freudian assertion that the rather fixed drive structure sets narrow limits to any social transformation. According to him, the drives, both aggressive and libidinal, remain barely integrated into capitalist society and constitute a potential for rebellion, discontent, and malaise that will undermine any attempt to create a "smooth" or "pacified" society.

Eros and Civilization is now often seen as a book linked to the atmosphere of the sixties, when it was intensely discussed in many countries.[71] However, it cannot be reduced to a *vade mecum* of the "sexual revolution" or identified with the students who shouted "Marx-Mao-Marcuse" during demonstrations. Indeed, the book was born in a profoundly different context and has fueled debates up to the present, as shown by its frequent reissues. From the point of view of the critique of the commodity fetish, however, several criticisms can be made. We can note that Marcuse's effort to go beyond traditional Marxism, along with Adorno, is quite important in many ways, but does not prevent him from remaining within this framework on certain points. For example, he criticizes "alienated labor" (without defining it), but never arrives at the category of abstract labor, and thus neither at value, money, nor the fetish-character of the commodity. The critique of the "commodity" refers less to the product of labor in its dual nature (concrete and abstract) than to the objects of consumption, often considered in a way more akin to what Thorstein Veblen called "conspicuous consumption." This is a trait Marcuse shares with almost all authors critical of "the commodity" in the sixties.

Marcuse, like traditional Marxists in general, continued to demonstrate great confidence in "progress" and in the benefits of technology, provided that it is well utilized! He proceeds very far down this path, considering the automation of production as a *sine qua non* for the establishment of an erotic society,[72] thus implying a curious return to the "civilizing mission of capital."[73] According to him, automation threatens the very "domination" which would attempt to limit it! Marcuse also agrees with Fromm when he cites him: "Never before has man come so close to the fulfillment of his most cherished hopes as today. Our scientific discoveries and technical achievements enable us to visualize the day when the table will be set for all who want to eat."[74] But Marcuse adds that never have so many obstacles stood in the way. Liberation has never been so close, and only an anachronistic class domination, having lost all historical function, still opposes it. This is a far cry from a critique of fetishism!

Technological progress remains important for Marcuse as a precondition of liberation. It is the cunning of reason, a dialectical reversal: it is the reality principle that ultimately results in its transformation and the overcoming of its antagonism with the pleasure principle. This optimistic dialectic could be seen as another version of the traditional Marxist idea that the productive forces created by the bourgeoisie will eventually overturn the relations of production. But this technological progress is not for Marcuse a *goal* as such, and the number of television sets or tractors (an allusion to the Soviet Union) do not provide criteria for the good life.[75] In this regard, Marcuse cites the beautiful phrase of Baudelaire from *My Heart Laid Bare*: "True civilization does not lie in gas, nor in steam, nor in turntables. It lies in the reduction of the traces of original sin."[76] Certainly in the thought of Marcuse one can also find the premises of ecological conscientiousness. But the confidence in technology expressed in *Eros and Civilization* can only strike us today with its naivete—even if it is shared by almost all the thinking of its time, and particularly by the thought of the "left"!

This praise of technology and its importance in abolishing alienated labor shows remarkable parallels with the ideas the Situationist International had developed in the same period. Asger Jorn, Constant, and Pinot-Gallizio, but also Guy Debord himself, were convinced that technology had objectively rendered the capitalist mode of production obsolete and that it would allow a free association of individuals no longer based upon labor.[77] If in postwar society it had become possible to move towards a civilization of "leisure" and play, it is the direct consequence of the "victory over nature," which includes the possibility of abolishing work and the economy.

For the Situationist International, labor and the economy are only kept alive to safeguard class domination. It is now a matter of executing this sentence already enunciated by history. The recent opening of Debord's archives has made available his reading sheets and preparatory notes for the drafting of *The Society of the Spectacle*, wherein he emphasizes the great resemblance between the theories of Marcuse and his own theory of the spectacle. He nevertheless held reservations about technology and, from 1971 onward, began a fairly strong shift towards an increasingly pronounced criticism of its role.[78]

Marcuse attributes to technology an indispensable role in overcoming an original historical condition of poverty where the whole of human life revolved around its simple reproduction. Where available resources are scarce, *Ananke* dominates, and no emancipation is possible. Technologies, by creating abundance, are therefore, in the eyes of Marcuse, a kind of "necessary evil." This vision, according to which capitalism would have been a terrible but ultimately inevitable step in lifting humanity out of material poverty, is in truth contradicted by numerous historical and anthropological studies that generally appeared a little later.[79] Pre-capitalist societies did not always or everywhere live in discomfort; oftentimes, existence was less painful than in modern societies. The hypothesis of an original material distress, of a lack of resources forming the basic condition of humanity, is itself rather a bourgeois ideological construction. Marcuse, like many Marxists, accepts this presupposition of modern utilitarianism without question.

Another feature in Marcuse that may today seem outdated is the overestimation of sexuality in general, and of "polymorphic perverse sexuality" in particular as a vehicle of emancipation. The concept of repressive desublimation was intended to denounce the inadequacy of a simple increase in "tolerance" in postwar societies towards "normal" genital sexuality. It designates the recuperation of infantile and total eroticism as the real stakes of liberation. But today it is clear that even a certain progression of polymorphic perversion (which has undoubtedly taken place, even if still in commodified forms and rendered harmless *a priori*) has obviously not subverted society. It is not difficult to admit that sexuality *per se* is not revolutionary.[80] It is not incompatible with labor, nor is it only compatible with heavy physical work—the "new spirit of capitalism," as analyzed by Zygmunt Bauman, Luc Boltanski and Ève Chiapello, and Dany-Robert Dufour, libidinizes labor and human relations in its own way. The contemporary recuperation of erotic energy through the valorization of value and the becoming-total of the value-form modifies the way we regard some elements of previous social criticism. What presented itself as an instance of liberation reveals itself *a posteriori* as an involuntary contribution to the passage into the next stage of capitalist development. This is also the case for the critique of authoritarianism, oedipal structures, and prohibitions that is characteristic of the sixties, even if at the time this seemed to be the *most advanced form* of protest.

Today it can be said that these rebels often only applied the exhortation of Nietzsche: "if something is falling, one should also give it a push!" The identification of the heart of capitalism with structures of personal authority and an "oedipal" superego was at the very least one-sided (even if this identification persists in many minds up to today). We have subsequently seen that the capitalist system can function just as well with a lesser dose of authoritarianism (even if it cannot disappear altogether) and with more "liquid" structures (Bauman). The real authoritarianism, then, is that of the "automatic subject" (Marx): value and its fetishistic logic.

In his time, Marcuse was sometimes accused of promoting a "regressive utopia" that located the true human dimension, that which must be given the greatest possible value, in the less "mature" stages of psychological development. This objection was clearly conservative in tone, assuming the standpoint of an "adult condition" that was difficult to distinguish from mere social adaptation. Marcuse nevertheless distanced himself from discourses that seemed to him regressive and rejected Wilhelm Reich's "radical primitivism," in which "no essential distinction is made between repressive and non-repressive sublimation" and which aims only at sexual liberation.[81] For Marcuse, the "liberation" of the libido must be accompanied by its "transformation": the transformation of sexuality into Eros and an eroticization of the entire body, and also an eroticization of all social relationships, including labor, to the point where "Ananke itself becomes the primary field of libidinal development."[82]

The reverence towards Narcissus in *Eros and Civilization* is problematic.[83] Although Marcuse had in mind something very different from the consumerist narcissism of today, his interpretation of Orpheus is more convincing than that of Narcissus, and his praise of the latter proved prophetic beyond what the author might have wished. But at the same time—and this is part of the richness of his thinking—Marcuse already emphasized, as early as 1963, that a child born into a "permissive" family is less capable of opposing the world as it is.[84] He foresaw the development towards a "fatherless society,"[85] an expression that became the title of a book published in Germany in 1969, whose author, analyst Alexander Mitscherlich, was close to the Frankfurt School.[86]

Christopher Lasch: Narcissism as a Critical Category

In the United States, the concept of narcissism was introduced into the field of social critique with Christopher Lasch's *The Culture of Narcissism* (1979), an analysis Lasch extended in *The Minimal Self* (1984).[87] This unclassifiable author offers a devastating interpretation of North American society between the 1960s and the 1980s.[88] Today, he is often credited with anticipating trends that, almost forty years later, can be found everywhere. His rich and original critique endeavors to identify the signs, through rather detailed analyses, of a fundamental narcissism in society as a whole.[89] Particularly remarkable is the fact that Lasch does not limit his research to behaviors of "social predation," but finds narcissism in the desire for technical conquest as well as in its apparent opposite, the desire for a return to nature; he finds narcissism in virilism as well as feminism, in state structures as well as in the protest movements of the sixties. He owes this original reading to a rather broad conception of narcissism, understood as a denial of dependence on the mother and of the original separation from her. He is concerned to link his conception of narcissism to Freud's theory, particularly to his late works, by connecting the "sociological" dimension to the psychoanalysis of the individual.

Lasch himself first used the notion of narcissism in a rather descriptive manner to characterize visible social behavior. In the 1990 afterword to *The Culture of Narcissism*, Lasch clarifies his analysis: "the concept of narcissism had much broader implications than I had suspected. My earlier immersion in the clinical literature on 'secondary narcissism' . . . had convinced me that the concept of narcissism helped to describe a certain type of personality, one that had become more and more common in our time. Further reading suggested that it also described enduring features of the human condition."[90]

Lasch's own conception of narcissism is well summarized in the following paragraph:

> In its pathological form, narcissism originates as a defense against feelings of helpless dependency in early life, which it tries to counter with 'blind optimism' and grandiose illusions of personal self-sufficiency. Since modern society prolongs the experience of dependence into adult life, it encourages milder forms of narcissism in people who might otherwise come to terms with the inescapable limits on their personal freedom and power—limits inherent in the human condition—by developing competence as workers and parents. But at the same time that our society makes it more and more difficult to find satisfaction in love and work, it surrounds the individual with manufactured fantasies of total gratification. The new paternalism preaches not self-denial but self-fulfillment. It sides with narcissistic impulses and discourages their modification by the pleasure of becoming self-reliant, even in a limited domain, which under favorable conditions accompanies maturity. While it encourages grandiose dreams of omnipotence, moreover, the new paternalism undermines more modest fantasies, erodes the capacity to suspend disbelief, and thus makes less and less accessible the harmless substitute-gratifications, notably art and play, that help to mitigate the sense of powerlessness and the fear of de-

pendence that otherwise express themselves in narcissistic traits.[91]

Lasch often repeats that the narcissist is not necessarily a selfish person, but someone unable to define the boundaries between the self and the non-self.

Despite his avowed affinity with the Frankfurt School and its best-known representative in the United States, Lasch was highly critical of Marcuse. It is necessary to follow his rather subtle arguments when he essentially endorses Marcuse's critique of the neo-Freudians but in turn rejects Marcuse and Norman Brown's particular revisions of Freud. Lasch proposes his own version of the return to the late Freud and reproaches Marcuse for having remained, in spite of himself, within the bounds of the culture of narcissism.

According to Lasch, narcissism is as much at work in *mainstream* culture as in alleged protests against it: "Strategies of narcissistic survival now present themselves as emancipation from the repressive conditions of the past, thus giving rise to a 'cultural revolution' that reproduces the worst features of the collapsing civilization it claims to criticize."[92] This "cultural radicalism" only criticizes values and models that have now been overcome by the very development of capitalism. It thus presents itself as a questioning of authoritarian structures in the name of the development of the individual, and therefore an attack on the "father" and the superego, the latter conceived as the main agent of a repressive society. To be free, says the culture of personal liberation, the individual must free itself from the superego. However, Lasch warns against this illusion: there are superegos much worse than the classic "father" and his social extensions. The decline of the family only generates an archaic and ferocious superego within the "liberated" individual.

For Lasch,

> [t]he changing conditions of family life lead not so much to a 'decline of the superego' as to an alteration of its contents. The parents' failure to serve as models of disciplined self-restraint or to restrain the child does not mean that the child grows up without a superego. On the contrary, it encourages the development of a harsh and punitive superego based largely on archaic images of the parents, fused with grandiose self-images. Under these

conditions, the superego consists of parental introjects instead of identifications. It holds up to the ego an exalted standard of fame and success and condemns it with savage ferocity when it falls short of that standard. Hence the oscillations of self-esteem so often associated with pathological narcissism. The fury with which the superego punishes the ego's failures suggests that it derives most of its energy from aggressive drives in the id, unmixed with libido. The conventional oversimplification which equates superego and id with 'self-restraint' and 'self-indulgence,' treating them as if they were radically opposed, ignores the irrational features of the superego and the alliance between aggression and a punishing conscience. The decline of parental authority and of external sanctions in general, while in many ways it weakens the superego, paradoxically reinforces the aggressive, dictatorial elements in the superego and thus makes it more difficult than ever for instinctual desires to find acceptable outlets.

The alliance between the superego and Thanatos "directs against the ego a torrent of fierce, unrelenting criticism."[93]

These observations seem to ring even more true today than in Lasch's time. To cite a particularly widespread phenomenon: in the depression experienced by those who "put on some weight" or fail in adapting to specific standards of beauty, a ferocious superego asserts itself and is always ready to overwhelm the ego with reproaches and to blame it for its failures in life. This superego is all the more insidious and difficult to escape because it no longer speaks in the name of external demands (duty, country, religion, honor, etc.), but in the name of the desires of the individual itself, working against itself if it fails to achieve success in life, which, it is assured, depends only on itself. The contemporary individual feels eternally guilty for not meeting expectations that, in the context of declining capitalism, are completely unrealistic, and for whose satisfaction all the means are lacking.[94] Thus, the citizens of contemporary society continually oscillate between feelings of omnipotence and impotence. From this derives the well-known ambition to control or "manage" everything in individual and collective life (it is "the extension of the domain of management" to all spheres of life, as described by Italian sociologist Michela Marzano).[95]

The liberation movements that took center stage during the sixties and seventies therefore aimed at fighting against the superego, whose source was allegedly to be found in the resolution of the Oedipus complex: the (male) child accepts his defeat and ends up identifying himself with the father, who denies him access to the mother. This becomes the model for all successive prohibitions and power structures. The struggle against the castrating father was therefore seen as the beginning of the struggle against all forms of repression. In this way, the revitalized Freudian Marxism of that period proposed to unite personal liberation and social revolution.

But Lasch rejects this perspective as a trap, as another form of adhering to the narcissism that lies at the heart of contemporary capitalism. Yet, to carry out his critique of "cultural radicalism," Lasch refers to the late Freud.[96] "The superego represents internalized fear of punishment, in which aggressive impulses are redirected against the ego. The superego—the primitive, punitive part of the superego, anyway—represents not so much internalized social constraints as the fear of retaliation, called up by powerful impulses to destroy the very source of life."[97] The Oedipus complex is "another variation on the underlying themes of separation, dependence, inferiority, and reunion," after the failure of oral fantasies to face reality. In *Inhibitions, Symptoms and Anxiety* (1926), Freud himself referred to a *"Minoan-Mycenaean layer"* underneath the Oedipal conflict, stating that "'anxiety due to separation from the protecting mother' is the original source of mental conflict,"[98] including the Oedipal conflict. "It now appears that it is the child's growing awareness of the disparity between his wish for sexual reunion with the mother and the impossibility of carrying it out that precipitates the Oedipus complex." In other words, the imagination of the child exceeds its actual physical capacities. "[T]he precocity of the child's mental and emotional development, the precocity of his sexual fantasies in comparison to his physical capacities, holds the key not just to the Oedipus complex but to much of his later development as well."[99] It is not only paternal prohibitions but also the lack of physical maturity that prevents the realization of the incestuous desires of the child (of both sexes). "Penis envy embodies the 'tragedy of lost illusions,'" in the words of Janine Chasseguet-Smirgel, a French psychoanalyst to whom Lasch often refers. "She goes onto argue [notes Lasch] that because we can never completely reconcile ourselves to the abandonment of those illusions, we continue to elaborate fantasies that deny any knowledge of sexual differences."[100] This is not, of course, an individual question, but rather one of a human condition: "Premature birth and prolonged dependence are the dominant facts of human psychology."[101]

According to Lasch, "[i]f the designation of contemporary culture as a culture of narcissism has any merit, it is because that culture tends to favor regressive solutions instead of 'evolutionary' solutions, as ChasseguetSmirgel calls them, to the problem of separation. Three lines of social and cultural development stand out as particularly important in the encouragement of a narcissistic orientation to experience: the emergence of the egalitarian family, so called; the child's increasing exposure to other socializing agencies besides the family; and the general effect of modern mass culture in breaking down distinctions between illusions and reality."[102] Central to Lasch's critique is the fact that contemporary society prevents "evolutionary solutions." But of what might these consist? "The inescapable facts of separation and death are bearable only because the reassuring world of man-made objects and human culture restores the sense of primary connection on a new basis. When that world begins to lose its reality, the fear of separation becomes almost overwhelming and the need for illusions, accordingly, more intense than ever."[103] The best response to this need for reassurance is, according to Lasch, the "transitional object" referred to by English psychoanalyst and pediatrician Donald Winnicott, author of *Playing and Reality* (1971).[104] It is not only a substitute for the breast, but also allows for the conquering of an external world that is at the same time recognized as autonomous. It thus makes it possible for the child to emerge from the state of fusion. In the end, the child outgrows the need for transitional objects because transitional phenomena have spread everywhere and have occupied the entire intermediary ground between the inside and the outside. For Winnicott, Lasch recalls, play and its development in art are therefore not, as for many psychoanalysts, substitute gratifications, but constitute essential mediations between emotional separation and union with loved ones.

It is the intermediate realm of man-made objects, then, that threatens to disappear in societies based on mass production and mass consumption. We live surrounded by man-made objects, to be sure, but they no longer serve very effectively to mediate between the inner world and the outer world. . . . The world of commodities has become a kind of 'second nature,' as a number of Marxist thinkers have pointed out, no more amenable to human direction and control than nature herself. It no longer has the character of a man-made environment at all. It simply confronts us, at once exciting, seductive, and terrifying. Instead of providing a 'potential space between the individual and the environment'—Winnicott's description of the world of transitional objects—it overwhelms the individual. Lacking any 'transitional' character, the commodity world stands as something completely separate from the self; yet it simultaneously takes on the appearance of a mirror of the self, a dazzling array of images in which we can see anything we wish to see. Instead of bridging the gap between the self and its surroundings, it obliterates the difference between them.[105]

Lasch clearly distinguishes his own reading of social reality and his interpretation of psychoanalysis from that of Marcuse. He distinguishes three "parties" in the American culture of the seventies: the "superego" party (conservatives), the "ego" party (humanists and cultural liberals, but also the old left) and the "ego ideal" party (the party of the "cultural revolution," which is not only against capitalism, but also against industrialism). He places Marcuse in this last field, which he also calls the "party of Narcissus."

According to Lasch, in a few dense pages in the last chapter of *The Minimal Self*, entitled "The Ideological Assault on the Ego," Marcuse, like Norman Brown, had good reason to attack the previous radicalism of Reich, Fromm, Horney, and other neo-Freudians, who insisted on cultural causalities and wanted to liberate Freud from the mechanical science and bourgeois and patriarchal culture of the nineteenth century.[106] "Feminism, Marxism, and psychoanalysis thus appeared to converge in an exposé of the authoritarian family and of the 'patricentric' personality who experiences suffering as guilt instead of injustice" and identifies with the aggressor.[107] Lasch summarizes the reproaches Marcuse and Brown addressed to the neo-Freudians, and essentially endorses them.[108] But he expresses reservations about the centrality of the Oedipus complex in Marcuse, who even considers its origin in the "primitive horde" to be a historical fact. According to Lasch, Freud, in his late sociological writings, especially in *Group Psychology and the Analysis of the Ego* and *Moses and Monotheism*, bases himself "on a model of mental conflict already discarded in the more strictly psychological writings of his last phase."[109] In the late writings focused on the psychology of the individual, says Lasch, Freud returns the essence of mental conflict to an earlier stage of individual development, where it is not the father who prevents the realization of incestuous desire, but the child's own physiology. This stage is marked, above all, by the anxiety of the initial separation: first the exit from the intrauterine condition, followed by the end of its prolongation during the first months of life. The result of the Oedipus complex, claims Lasch, who considers himself in full agreement with the late Freud, is not only submission to the reality principle: as a matter of fact, the agent of repression is not only "reality." "The entire conceptual scheme that opposes pleasure and reality, equating the former with the unconscious and the latter with conscious adherence to parental morality, has to give way to a different model of the mind."[110] In commenting on Marcuse's 1963 essay, "The Obsolescence of the Freudian Concept of Man," Lasch approves of the central thesis, according to which we are moving towards a "fatherless society." Here, it is society itself that directly models the ego, and "[t]hese changes led to a 'tremendous release of destructive energy,' a 'rampant' aggressiveness 'freed from the instinctual bonds with the father as authority and conscience.'"[111] However, Lasch continues, what "these developments invalidate, of course, is not the 'Freudian concept of man' but a social theory 'extrapolated,' in Marcuse's own words, from Freud's extrapolations of clinical data into prehistory. They invalidate the idea, already weakened by Freud's later work and by much of the work subsequently produced by Kleinians, object-relations theorists, and ego psychologists, that repression originates in the subjection of the pleasure principle to the patriarchal compulsion to labour. Yet Marcuse continues, even in his later writings, to condemn the 'performance principle' as the primal source of human unhappiness and alienation."[112] For Marcuse, labor will always be an alienation;

the liberation of Eros demands the technological abolition of labor. Marcuse, continues Lasch, disavows "any intention of advocating a 'romantic regression behind technology,' he insists on the liberating potential of industrial technology. . . . Automation alone makes it possible for Orpheus and Narcissus to come out of hiding. The triumph of polymorphous perversity depends on its antithesis: instrumental rationality carried to the point of total regimentation. Presumably an exercise in dialectical thinking. . . . The achievement of 'libidinal work relations,' it appears, requires the organization of society into a vast industrial army."[113]

In Lasch's eyes, Marcuse has much more in common with Fromm and Reich than he thinks:

> In spite of his attempt to confront the profound pessimism of Freud's later work, Marcuse's interpretation of psychoanalytic theory, like that of the neo-Freudians, rests almost entirely on Freud's early work, in which mental suffering originates in the pleasure principle's submission to an oppressive, externally imposed reality. In spite of his condemnation of the neo-Freudians' 'moralistic philosophy of progress,' Marcuse shares their faith— part of the intellectual legacy of the nineteenth-century socialist movement and of the Enlightenment in general—that the progress of reason and technology, once these are freed from capitalist constraints, will eventually make life pleasant and painless.[114]

Lasch also offers a rather subtle analysis of Brown's work, which he considers superior in many respects to Marcuse's reading of Freud. For Lasch, Brown "is a more trenchant critic of neoFreudian revisionism than Marcuse. It is not only the 'revisionist emphasis on the influence of 'social conditions' that is misguided, as Marcuse contends. Revisionist theories of culture rest on the more fundamental misconception that repression originates in parental control over infantile sexuality."[115] If revisionist theory were true, repression could be lessened through educational or social reform—as neo-Freudians wish, but also Marcuse, only in a more radical way. According to Lasch, Brown better recognizes the incompatibility between infantile drives and any form of culture and, like Freud, refuses any easy consolation. He discards the notion that sexual pleasure is the only object of repression, and its corollary that neurosis originates in a conflict between pleasure and the patriarchal work ethic, between Eros and civil morality. He explains that these ideas derive from naïve theories about historical progress that Freud himself abandoned in his late psychological work.

While Lasch's analysis of Brown's work cannot be traced here in detail, its conclusion must nevertheless be recovered. For Lasch, play and art are important modes of establishing a non-narcissistic relationship to the world: it is not a question of denying the separation, but of first recognizing it and then offering compensation. Art and play are therefore not merely, as for Marcuse and Brown, substitute gratifications.

> Notwithstanding their contempt for ego psychology, Brown, Marcuse, and their followers fall back on the very same strategy . . . of exempting certain favored activities from psychoanalytic scrutiny. . . . for the Freudian left [they are] art and play. . . . Whereas Freud insisted on the underlying kinship between art and neurosis, Brown, Marcuse, and Dinnerstein try to salvage art and playful creativity from the psychoanalytic critique of human pretensions, just as Hartmann tries to salvage perception, language, and memory. Art resembles the most deeply regressive psychosis in its attempt to restore a sense of oneness with the primal mother. What distinguishes art from psychosis or neurosis is that it also acknowledges the reality of separation. Art rejects the easy way of illusions.[116]

Even if the final result of the work of art may be serene, it always elaborates a conflict between union and separation. The role of art and play is thus to allow human beings to bear the renunciations that culture—any culture—imposes upon them: psychoanalysis "refuses to dissolve the tension between instinct and culture, which it regards as the source of the best as well as the worst in human life. It holds that sociability not only thwarts but at the same time fulfills instinctual needs; that culture not only ensures the survival of the human species but also provides the genuine pleasures associated with collective exploration and mastery of the natural world; that exploration, discovery, and invention themselves draw on playful impulses; and that culture represents for man precisely the life 'appropriate to his species.'"[117]

Lasch therefore claims to have struck a decisive blow against what he also calls the "party of the ego ideal"—the left of 1968—on an essential argument: the role of the superego. Still claiming to be following Freud's late writings, Lasch affirms that the superego is not the representative of the external world, but an advocate of the internal world. It is not only the result of the internalization of repression from the outside (from society through the father).

> On the contrary, the superego consists of the individual's own aggressive impulses, directed initially against his parents or parental surrogates, projected onto them, reinternalized as aggressive and domineering images of authority, and finally redirected in this form against the ego. Images of destructive and punitive parental authority originate not in the parents' actual prohibitions but in the unconscious rage of infancy, which arouses unbearable anxiety and therefore has to be redirected against the self. . . . we might say that castration anxiety itself is merely a later form of separation anxiety, that the archaic and vindictive superego derives from the fear of maternal retaliation, and that, if anything, the Oedipal experience tempers the punitive superego of infancy by adding to it a more impersonal principle of authority, one that is more 'independent of its emotional origins,' as Freud puts it, more inclined to appeal to universal ethical norms, and somewhat less likely, therefore, to associate itself with unconscious fantasies of persecution.[118]

The Oedipal superego is more closely related to the desire for reparation, to gratitude towards the mother, thus forming the primary nucleus of moral consciousness.

But what are the *historical causes* of this rise of narcissism? A widespread return to pre-Oedipal psychic forms constitutes a real anthropological mutation and must have very important causes. The question remains poorly elucidated by Lasch, as by the other authors examined here.[119] On this point, his explanations remain somewhat superficial: he mentions in particular the decline of small business (especially the family business, the site *par excellence* for the formation of the bourgeois superego) in favor of large corporations, the disintegration of the traditional family and the bureaucratization of existence (which reduces the citizen to a situation of total dependence, like a baby fed and taken care of by large institutions), and the overabundance of the commodity. Like almost all the observers of his time (in this field he is much less original than elsewhere), Lasch considers the replacement of competition by the management of monopolies (state or large corporations) as the definitive result of the deployment of capitalism. A few years later, the triumph of neoliberalism demonstrated the opposite—and above all made it possible to see that it was neoliberal culture, and not the latest avatars of Fordism-Keynesianism, that elevated narcissism to the rank of a universal *forma mentis*. In this identification of the profound logic of capitalism with the suppression of competition (and the residual spaces of freedom linked to it) and with an omnipresent bureaucracy, Lasch merely repeats, without realizing it, the assertions of Marcuse and the entire Frankfurt School.[120] One reason for this is that his work was written at the time of the transition from the Fordist-modern era to the postmodern period, and he sometimes designates phenomena that belong to the Fordist-modern past as "narcissistic" (for example, the welfare state with its maternal characteristics). It is therefore hardly surprising that the remedies he advocates are mainly a return to a kind of patriarchal life as it would have been known in the United States during the nineteenth century.

To understand the nature of the link between narcissism and capitalist modernity, even Adorno and Marcuse are of little help. Marcuse too explains the psychic changes and the "technological abolition of the individual" by the twilight of individual enterprise, the reign of "monopolies," and the "decline of the social role of the family." In his view, there used to be, especially in the resolution of the Oedipus complex, genuine personal experience, which "left painful scars" and allowed the constitution of a "sphere of private non-conformity. Now, however, under the rule of economic, political, and cultural monopolies, the formation of the mature superego seems to skip the stage of individualization: the generic atom becomes directly a social atom."[121] Thus the quasi-abolition of competition—which he takes for granted—standardizes individuality.

A Short History of Narcissism

Obviously, narcissism has always existed. Examples of "narcissistic rage" are not lacking in any historical period. Alexander the

Great, opposed by his best friend Cleitos, killed him in a fit of rage, only to bitterly repent for his actions. Around 1300, Italian poet Cecco Angiolieri, angry with his father for denying him money to satisfy his vices, wrote this famous sonnet:

If I were fire, I'd burn the world away
If I were wind, I'd toss it in a storm
If I were water, I'd drown it
If I were God, I'd send it to the depths

If I were Pope, then I'd be happy,
for I would trouble all the Christians
If I were Emperor, know what I'd do?
I'd chop off heads all around

If I were death, I'd visit my father
If I were life, I would get the hell out of his house
I would do the same with my mother

If I were Cecco, which I am and was,
I'd take all the young and pretty ladies,
and leave the old and homely ones to someone else.

But why did narcissism become, in the course of the twentieth century, the dominant pathology that dethroned the "classical" neuroses treated by Freud?

The connection between narcissistic perversion and capitalist logic is quite obvious: exacerbation of competition, frigidity, egoism (both at work and also in the family context), lack of empathy, etc. All this is true in terms of social psychology and observable behavior. However, from our point of view, narcissistic perversion—or the quasi-equivalent "narcissistic personality disorder"—is only the "phenomenon"; the "essence" is secondary narcissism as an economy of the libido. We can also distinguish between, on the one hand, people clearly affected by narcissistic perversion—who do not necessarily suffer from it because they are unaware of it—and, on the other, narcissism in the general sense, as a component, more or less pronounced, inherent to almost all contemporary psyches—just as it is often said that we are all more or less neurotic. It is less a question of a clear demarcation between narcissists and non-narcissists than of a diffusion of narcissistic attitudes to varying degrees. Over the course of the twentieth century, there has been a real "rise in the rate of narcissism" in society, rather than increase in the number of completely narcissistic people.

The "victory" of narcissism has been so great in recent decades that it has abolished itself. In 2012, for example, the media announced that the category of "narcissistic personality disorder" would disappear from the fifth edition of the *Diagnostic and Statistical Manual of Mental Disorders*, the American Psychiatric Association's manual, used worldwide to classify mental disorders—a book as well-known as it is criticized for its positivist and purely descriptive approach. Its symptoms were supposedly no longer considered pathological, or were now thought to belong to other disorders. Although narcissism was "saved" in the final version of the manual released in 2013, the lesson is clear: very often, narcissism is no longer seen as a disease because it is everywhere. It is a variation on the English proverb: when so many people violate the ban on stepping on the grass, they simply remove the sign.

The search for the historical causes of the rise of narcissism must also take into account another important element: returning to very early childhood, the pre-Oedipal phase, is also a return to a stage of life outside of any social logic. In the Oedipal conflict, the father already appears as the representative of a social and "patriarchal" order that enforces the laws established by the culture to which the child belongs. He is the representative of "culture" and the laws that disrupt the purely "natural" life led by the child and its mother in their symbiosis; he thus forces the child to abandon this naturalness. Psychoanalytical interpretations that shift the essential center of conflict to the pre-Oedipal phase risk falling into an even more "biologistic" perspective than the one of which Freud is often accused. The earlier the phase, the more children are supposed to resemble each other, regardless of the socio-historical context, insofar as they are said to be "driven" only by physiological needs. All children breastfeed, suck their thumbs, desire affection, become anxious when the mother steps away, etc. Should the above mentioned culturalist school be followed, which relies on comparative anthropology to examine the different methods of weaning and forms of early education, in order to draw conclusions about the behaviors of a given culture?

The social construction of a newborn child actually takes place in other ways. On the one hand, adults are responsible for transmitting ways of being in the world to the child from the very beginning. A particularly striking example is the difficulty that children today often experience in *meeting the gaze* of their mother, which should awaken them to life and respond to their primary (healthy) narcissism: a parent hidden behind sunglasses and busy on their mobile phone while pushing the baby carriage drives the child into an unhealthy solitude, especially if this inattention of the adult is repeated in other activities. It may seem trivial, but the accumulation of these attitudes results in an environment that is markedly different from those that children in other eras would have experienced. Similarly, early exposure to the world of technological devices certainly plays an important role. In addition, changes due to social developments, such as the possible absence of a father, early socialization (in daycare), or successive rearrangements of the child's environment also contribute to changing the condition of early childhood.

But above all, the difficulties that arise at the moment of the emergence of primary narcissism must not be imagined to operate as a kind of definitive and irrevocable stunting for the remainder of one's life. It is the social factors that can decide whether a child's initial refusal to establish real objectal relationships will later give rise to a permanent structure or not—by arousing narcissistic behavior, encouraging and valuing it, or, on the contrary, penalizing it, as was generally the case in pre- and proto-modern cultures. If the formation of secondary narcissism begins at the moment when the child emerges from primary narcissism, the former is only really formed if reinforced at each stage of psychological development.

The spirit of competition and the affirmation of the isolated self at the expense of its social bonds characterize the whole of capitalist modernity, not only the phase when narcissism became visible (mainly after the Second World War), but also and above all during the phase of "liquid modernity" that gradually took hold after 1968. In contrast, the main pathology in Freud's period was obsessive neurosis, corresponding to the dominant features of "classical" capitalism. Work and saving formed the basis of the dominant social character at a time when capital needed all available labor-power and cash reserves. This society channeled libidinal energy into labor and repressed sexuality, especially in its unorthodox forms. Excessive inhibition and repression produced personalities impoverished by the repression of their desires. The teacher who punishes their pupils and the petty military officer who mistreats their recruits were paradigmatic figures of this social world, as was the hysterical or "neurasthenic" woman cut off from her desires. In the twenties, Wilhelm Reich described the "character types" and Erich Fromm, as we have seen, spoke of the "anal character" of the typical bourgeois: an individual who remains at a stage where everything revolves around "give and take," and whose life is devoted to the accumulation of objects and wealth. The violence with which this individual distances his other desires transforms him into a rigid and hateful being (especially in obsessive cleanliness, leading to the cult of "purity").

The successive phases of modernity have gradually replaced the repression of desire with the permanent solicitation of desire for commercial purposes. The obsessive saving of the "anal character" has given way—not completely of course—to oral greed as socially validated behavior. The generalized regression to oral modes of behavior—which goes back to the very first, most "archaic" phases of life—is part of an infantilization that constitutes one of the most striking features of postmodern capitalism and which will be discussed in the next chapter. In many ways, the narcissistic organization of the personality is the opposite of the neurotic organization. Narcissism is as much a part of postmodern, liquid, flexible, and "individualized" capitalism—which finds its fullest expression in the "network"—as obsessive neurosis was for Fordist, authoritarian, repressive, and pyramidal capitalism, which found its characteristic expression in the assembly line.

One of the historical factors that have contributed most to the rise of narcissism has been the development of technology, and especially its application to products and procedures of everyday life from the 1950s onwards, with the rise of "consumer society."[122] With technology embedded in everyday life, subjects constantly experience an enormous power that is not the result of an individual compromise with reality, but has all the features of magic: it is enough to push a button. Individual adherence to the feeling of omnipotence provided by technology takes two forms: the personal exercise of this power—by hitting the accelerator or having a machine wash the dishes—or the identification of with large-scale technical achievements—such as enthusiasm for missions to space or advances in medicine. What is always at stake is the struggle against feelings of impotence that reactivate the helplessness of the infant.

One example is domestic heating: in a traditional peasant context, people used to heat their domiciles—at least in France—by first chopping wood at the front door. Although a tiring and time-consuming endeavor, one only depended on oneself or those in the immediate vicinity. Today, all you have to do is turn a knob, which effectively turns everyone into an all-powerful magician who only has to announce: "I want." At the same time, everyone is placed in a state of increased dependency: all it takes is for a tyrant on the other side of the world to decide to reduce fossil fuel supplies for political or economic reasons, and we find ourselves without heating, without understanding why and unable to return to chopping wood.[123] This is the result of the "increasing integration of the world," which also means, for example, that it is possible to lose one's job because the Tokyo stock exchange collapsed as the result of a local election. The condition of the narcissistic human being is thus a dialectic of omnipotence and impotence. "Complexity" and "generalized interdependence" mean that people are no longer dependent on themselves or their own strength, not even for the most mundane of tasks like opening a door (pushing a button) or talking with a neighbor (sending a text message). The ability to reproduce biologically, once the inalienable property of the "proletariat," is also being taken away from humanity, especially as a result of "medically assisted procreation." The result is a deep sense of degradation, even if it remains generally unconscious. In exchange for the comfort gained, we accept very strong infantile dependencies, even a certain helplessness, and thus find ourselves in the "distressed state" of the newborn unable to survive a day without the help of a third party. It is the denial of dependency that creates historically unprecedented forms of dependency; it is the fantasy of omnipotence that creates impotence.

The Fetishist-Narcissist Paradigm

The importance of narcissism can be assessed in a new way on the basis of the critique of value and commodity fetishism, that is, by defining a *fetishist-narcissist paradigm*. It seems that no one thus far has attempted to explore the link between narcissism and the logic of value. Yet this paradigm promises to explain many of the seemingly disparate phenomena of the contemporary world.

Secondary narcissism can be considered as a real *absence of the world*. The affected subject has never accepted, beyond apparent behavior and at a deeper level, the separation between its ego and the world. It has not integrated the world into its self; the world exists for it as a space of projection and as a momentary concretization of its fantasies. It cannot conceive of relationships of equality with other people, nor understand the autonomy of objects. This is why the narcissist tends to manipulate or exploit others—especially in order to be admired—and why he does not truly love anyone and instead moves from one relationship to the next. From this point of view, "dating sites," a sort of vast "supermarket of amorous relationships," both index and serve as the springboard for an unprecedented narcissism. Ultimately, in the eyes of the narcissist—or at least their unconscious—all people are of equal merit and interchangeable. Indeed, they are not perceived as autonomous beings, each with their own history, who should be respected in order to establish mutually enriching relationships, but viewed as extras forced to play a role in the narcissist's inner scenario. This is why, as has already been mentioned, the inner world of the narcissist is so impoverished: one "invests" nothing in these relationships and therefore derives nothing in return. The narcissist has a similar relationship with objects: they are not interested in them because they are different from them. Nor does the narcissist want to know them, but only use them, to manipulate and dominate them. If objects prove to be irreducible to the subject and have a life of their own, the narcissist may enter into a fit of rage and break the refractory object, such as a machine that does not work or a drawer that refuses to open. This is exactly how the narcissist acts, or would like to act, towards humans who evade their power and disappoint their expectations, whether it be a romantic partner or a subordinate at work (it is well known, for example, that the managerial level is one of the best places to find "narcissistic perverts" and empirical surveys have even shown that among company managers, narcissists are greatly overrepresented. It seems that being a narcissistic pervert does wonders for one's career).

The first chapter demonstrated that Descartes' philosophy contains a preliminary formulation of the narcissism and solipsism constitutive of the modern subject-form. This discourse can be extended to capitalist society in general, as a society based on value and abstract labour, the commodity, and money. Rather than seeking to establish a relationship of cause and effect, base and superstructure, or reality and reflection, it is more appropriate to speak of a *parallelism* or *isomorphism* between the narcissistic structure of the subject of value and the structure of value itself—which is a "total social form" and not merely an "economic" factor. If the value-form is the "basic form" or the "elementary form" of the whole of capitalist society, using Marx's formulation, but also a "total social fact," according to the formulation of Marcel Mauss, this also means that value, as a form of social synthesis, has two sides: an "objective" side and a "subjective" side—even if these terms, it must be admitted, are problematic. One side cannot be given priority over the other, neither chronologically nor causally.

The value of the commodity also entails a kind of "annihilation of the world" (we are not referring to its effects, but to its basic logic). Value recognizes only quantities, not qualities. The multiplicity of the world disappears in the face of the ever-equal value of commodities produced by the abstract side of labor. This side, it should be recalled, implies the erasure of all particularity proper to concrete labor, reduced to a simple expenditure of human energy measured in time and stripped of specific differences. The only difference between two labors, from the point of view of abstraction, is the amount of value—especially the surplus-value—they generate. It is irrelevant whether surplus-value is produced by making bombs or toys—this indifference to the material "bearer" of value is a structural law that completely overrides the intentions of the actors involved. Thus, commodities, in which the abstract side of labor is "crystallized," are distinguished solely by the amount of undifferentiated value they represent. They must have some use-value and satisfy some need or desire, but these use-values are interchangeable. The logic of value consists in a gigantic *reductio ad unum*, a liquidation of all the particularities that form the true fabric of human and natural existence. The logic of value produces a structural *indifference* towards the contents of production and the world in general. Value, produced by abstract labor, passes from one object to another. From money it becomes a commodity, then money again, so on and so forth; from capital it becomes a wage, then capital again, so on and so forth. Thus, an "essence," an invisible "substance," moves from one object to another, without ever identifying itself with any of its objects.

When Marx describes fetishism as a *real* phenomenon, and not as a mere mystification of consciousness, he is aiming at this fact: the concrete loses its central role in life and is reduced to being only a supportive moment in the self-movement of abstraction—although the latter is ultimately extracted from the concrete! This is a real ontological inversion. It is a movement from the same to the same, a tautological movement where capital expands in order to be reinvested, to expand again, *ad infinitum*. The real and material world, nature, people, and their needs and desires appear only as forms of recalcitrance, often as obstacles that must be overcome or pushed aside. The deliberate aggression towards the world, people, and nature that characterizes capitalism is not the result of any leader's bias towards evil—although this can sometimes be a supplement—but is itself the consequence of fundamental indifference. From the standpoint of value, the world and its qualities simply do not exist.

This summary description of the logic of value makes it possible to grasp its similarity to the logic of narcissism. The (secondary) narcissist reproduces this logic in his relationship to the world. The only reality is his self, an ego that has (almost) no qualities of its own because it has not been enriched through object relations, relations to the other. At the same time, this self tries to extend itself to the whole world, to envelop and reduce it to a simple representation of itself, a representation whose figures are inessential, ephemeral, and interchangeable. Starting from its own organic body, the external world has no more consistency for the narcissist than use-value has for value. In both cases, there can be no peaceful relationship, but only domination and exploitation to feed a voracious appetite. If it is so voracious, it is because it is by nature insatiable. We return again to the myth of Erysichthon: value must increase by progressing indefinitely, since it has nothing concrete as its goal. A thirst can be quenched, a pyramid completed, the whole world conquered, but the process by which value and capital increase can never reach an end, balance, or stable situation of satisfaction.

Similarly, the narcissist can never be truly satisfied. His body, and as a consequence his genital satisfaction, remain alien to him. He lives in a world of projections and fantasies where, like Tantalus, he fails to really "touch" others. He may experience this as a form of superiority born of detachment, as a series of situations where he takes more than he gives. However, the sensation of "emptiness," which is one of the main manifestations of narcissism, and one of the few moments when the narcissist can suffer from his condition, proves to be the ultimate failure of this strategy. This is followed by a repetition compulsion, since he still hopes to one day achieve the imagined satisfaction.

If it is recalled that all commodity values are equal, that they are merely different quantities of the same phantasmagorical substance, abstract labor, then the role of the unlimited and tautological in contemporary society can be better understood. The fact that everywhere, there is the movement from the same to the same, without encountering otherness, such that everything is equal to everything, as shown by the liquidation of the boundaries between generations and sexes, genetic manipulation and assisted procreation, the possibility of choosing one's own body, or even a world without bodies and without limits, without boundaries between the self and the non-self, such as video games—it seems impossible to study all these phenomena without taking into account the logic of value and that of narcissism.

This reductionism is one of the most characteristic features of advanced capitalist society: everywhere, the heterogeneity of the world is reduced to a single substance. In turn, objects, which in principle are irreducible to one another, become in the end only larger or smaller quantities of this substance without quality. Barcodes are one example: any commodity can be identified with a single succession of bars with varying widths. QR codes extend this process to any "object," material or immaterial. They are part of the process of "digitalizing the world," the real significance of which we are only just beginning to understand. Within binary code, there are only two possible situations: 1 and 0, closed and open circuit. Their combination is sufficient to identify every single *ens* in the world, not only as a category, but also as an individual object: RFID chips (radio-frequency identification) can follow the life of every yogurt cup until they are consumed. The encounter between the digitalization of the world and genetics promises a kind of apotheosis, which might signal an apocalypse. DNA itself can be read as a binary code: it consists—or, more precisely, it can be interpreted—as the combination of two chromosomes, X and Y, which can supposedly explain the multiplicity of life on earth. Clearly, there is a link between the digitalization of the world in recent decades and the enormous growth of genetic research and its practical applications. The "deciphering," or more precisely, the decoding of the genomes of living species, including humans, has advanced—without knowing how far nor the implications—thanks to computers that "read" the genomes as if they were software, doing so using specific software. On the other hand, the development of information technology has, from a certain point onwards, acquired great advantages from the study of genetics, itself interpreted as a marvelous "computer," or software, possessing a complexity not yet reached in human constructions. Bioinformatics has yielded its most worrying fruit with genetically modified organisms (GMOs). But rather than speak about their well-known dangers, let us here draw attention to the epistemological and ontological basis of these apocalyptic-like technological advances: the denial of the multiplicity of the world, its reduction to an indistinct mass whose only function is to be at the disposal of the subject and to provide it with a feeling of omnipotence.

A question, or rather an objection, may arise with regard to the formulation of the paradigm of the fetishist-narcissist constitution. This question concerns the historical nature of narcissism. Capitalist society has been based on value, money, and abstract labor since its inception. From the fourteenth century onwards, money gradually became the primary social mediation.[124] A second important threshold was crossed in the seventeenth century with the scientific revolutions, and a third in the eighteenth century with the industrial revolution. We have focused on Descartes because his philosophy corresponds to the historical moment when the commodity, and especially money, really began to shape everyday social relations. It appears then, according to the argument developed thus far, that capitalist society (or commodity society, or the society of value—these terms can be considered synonymous) has always been narcissistic—and not by accident, but in its very essence. How then can the prevalence of narcissism, which comes into view only after the Second World War, be explained as a social pathology? Why is it that for such a long period of time—centuries, if we consider the Cartesian starting point, or at least a century and a half, if referring to the fully developed capitalism of the ruling bourgeoisie—it was obsessive neurosis that dominated? That the anal character, the diminished self in the face of the collective, the institutional superego, the priest and the teacher's corporal punishment, the barracks-factory and the morality of austerity and self-sacrifice imposed itself? These are hardly narcissistic features! Why did Freud not think it necessary to give central importance to narcissism? Why did we have to wait until 1970 to see such a strong interest in this phenomenon, for both researchers and the general public?

The answer is that it is necessary to distinguish between the conceptual "core" of a historical phenomenon and its concrete unfolding in empirical reality. The distinction between an "exoteric Marx" and an "esoteric Marx" resides in this fact: Marx had recognized, behind the colorful façade of capitalist reality, the work of "abstract" factors, such as value. At the deepest level, he demonstrated that it is the accumulation of abstract labor in the form of value and then money that explains visible phenomena and directs their development. However, it can be recognized today, in retrospect, that this analysis of the "esoteric" Marx concerned the still semi-hidden core of this social formation. It was largely concealed by a social reality that retained many features of pre-capitalist societies. These two tendencies could even sometimes develop in opposite directions. The visible phenomena can, for example, conceal the conceptual essence for a long time, or even appear as its opposite. Thus, from the point of view of the "pure" logic of value, the seller of labor-power is a seller like any other and has the right to do whatever it takes to obtain the best price for their commodity. They contribute to the accumulation of capital as a living bearer of variable capital. They are therefore of commensurable "dignity" to the capitalist, the living bearer of fixed capital. Yet the actual conditions of capital's reproduction, still greatly imbued with feudal elements, meant that, in Marx's time, workers remained largely subjects with minor rights, their associations and strikes repressed, and their aspirations to realize themselves as commodity subjects deemed illegitimate in comparison with the same aspiration expressed by other social strata. It was inevitable that even Marx was not always able to distinguish between the "essence" of capitalism as such and the forms of compromise that existed in his time between pure logic and the survival of other forms of social synthesis—especially when he attributed to class struggle the function of overcoming the commodity system as such. In the century following his death, we witnessed the gradual "integration" of the proletariat and the triumph of the "pure logic" of value. To condense it into a single image: it was understood that a worker who does not stand up, hat removed when the boss enters the room, but who instead is on first-name basis with him, can just as easily create surplus-value. On a more structural level, it has become clear in the last decades that surplus-value created by a "multitude" of self-employed workers, without bosses or individual exploitation, is just as valuable on the market as surplus-value produced in India under Dickensian conditions. The workers' movement abandoned its initial "radicalism" as soon as the representatives of capital exhibited a willingness to compromise by renouncing certain forms of domination that were often irrational from the point of view of capital itself, but rather the fruit of an outdated mentality.

The history of capitalism is thus the history of the process by which it gradually came to "coincide with its concept," to put it in Hegelian terms. This "concept"—which cannot be observed empirically, but only discerned through analysis—eventually became increasingly visible and freed itself from the debris inherited from previous social formations. At the same time, this affirmation of the "pure" abstract form of value does not constitute a definitive triumph, but indicates the beginning of its ultimate crisis. Indeed, these pure forms, which imply the subordination of all concrete content to the accumulation of an empty and abstract form, are incompatible with the pursuit of "life on earth"—they could only govern society, if at all, when they still possessed some residual "substance" derived from pre-capitalist forms. In other words, their total victory is also their defeat.

The "automatic subject," self-valorizing value as subject, is already implied by the very existence of abstract labor, value, and money as forms of social synthesis. It has existed *in nuce* for over half a millennium. By its very nature, capitalism is not a regime of domination exercised by people—"the capitalists" or "the bourgeoisie"—but an anonymous and impersonal regime of domination, exerted by "functionaries" of valorization, the "managers and petty-officers of capital," as Marx calls them—"personifications of economic categories, embodiments of particular class relations and class interests."[125] It is, in Marx's words, the "fetish-character of the commodity." But for centuries, this anonymous fetishistic structure remained almost entirely invisible in relation to the surface of flesh-and-blood actions of individuals. Their role has been steadily diminishing over the course of the twentieth century, which has seen the establishment of the "automatic subject" (the capitalist relation as such)—even if many people still do not want to understand it and continue to attribute all the ills of the world to the "one percent," as they once did in France with the "two hundred families." The consequence of this change—or, more precisely, of this "becoming visible"—for "direct democracy" and other emancipatory perspectives will be examined in the epilogue.

Classical neurosis was the result of the relationship with an authority figure where fear and affection, libidinal and aggressive drives, are combined—producing a personalized superego. Narcissism, on the other hand, is the psychic form that corresponds to the automatic subject. Just as the automatic subject needed a very long incubation period to appear in its "pure" form, while existing in germ form from the very beginning, narcissism took a long time to become socially *in actu* what it already was *in potentia*. Money, in its impersonal equalizing power, has always been a vehicle for the narcissistic spirit. As is well known, Marx's approach is by no means based on an examination of the psychology of economic actors. However, in the final chapter of the *1844 Manuscripts*, entitled "The Power of Money," which he wrote at the age of twenty-six during his stay in Paris, Marx analyzes money—notably through an interpretation of passages from Goethe's *Faust* and Shakespeare's *Timon of Athens*—as the narcissistic medium *par excellence* (without, of course, using the word). Money provides absolute power and all qualities to the individual, transforming impotence into omnipotence and erasing the specific qualities of both objects and people.[126]

Return to Nature, Conquer Nature, or Overcome Capitalist Regression?

It has already been mentioned how, for a very long time, the right has spoken of "nature," and above all "human nature," whereas the left has spoken of "culture." For the right, this nature sets very narrow limits on the possibility of transforming life; for the left, almost everything is the fruit of society and education and can therefore be changed. This is the eternal debate between Hobbes and Rousseau: is the human being an incorrigible beast who simply needs to be restrained in order to limit the damage, therefore legitimizing the state and other repressive institutions? Or is the human being "good," or at least "neutral" by nature, and it is society that corrupts, especially with the appearance of private property? As is well known, each of the two hypotheses has historically led to violence and even totalitarianism: the Hobbesian approach justifies all infringements of individual freedom in order to struggle against an evil human nature present in each of us, while the Rousseauean approach can lead to the attempt to force the "really existing" individual into conformity with his supposedly true nature, obscured by society, by claiming to create a "New Man" and violently eliminating all residues of the corrupted society. The first position—that of the immutability of the foundations of human existence—implies renouncing the hope for change and elevating the modern bourgeois subject to the rank of human being *in-itself*, which is contradicted by numerous anthropological studies, especially those that have dealt with the theme of "the gift." The second position, that of the plasticity of human nature, is too often contradicted by experience and thus often ends up giving arguments to its opponents.

Both positions persist today. Is the leftist position necessarily emancipatory? Is it not somehow compatible with techno-scientific projects of remaking the world, with contempt for all limits, which is seen at work in both excessive consumption and ecological crisis? Does not the idea of the infinite plasticity of the human being continue to haunt the contemporary "left-wing" imagination, particularly in its enthusiasm for medically assisted procreation techniques? Technophilia, whatever its ideological justification, necessarily reinforces narcissism.

Tertium datur? Is there another approach that goes beyond a simple "neither nor" and banal assertion that "human nature" is probably somewhat alterable, but not excessively so? It could consist in examining the solutions that various human cultures have given to the problems that are so widespread, even in the most diverse cultural and social contexts, that they can be considered as part of a kind of "human condition" (a term that is, in any case, preferable to "human nature"). This line of inquiry reveals some rather interesting perspectives: it is no longer a question of deciding whether human beings are "by nature" "greedy, tyrant, lustful, slovenly,"[127] selfish and stingy, whether they seek only power and wealth and seek to dominate their neighbors and be served by others.[128] In order to maintain a perspective of emancipation after the wreckage of this aspiration throughout the twentieth century, it is perhaps not necessary to insist on the assumption that all the unpleasant aspects of mankind are the result of a bad social organization that can eventually be removed, like a layer of mold from a jar of jam. Admitting that even in the midst of revolutions, people have not often become prodigies of virtue does not necessarily lead one to assert, with resignation or enthusiasm, that Hobbes was right and then slipping into depression or making peace with the world under the banner of "realism." Nor is it necessary to conceive of human history as a "fall from grace" following an original balance that must be restored, nor to rejoice at the "end of history" reached with the universal diffusion of market democracy, imagined as a final renunciation of all the dangerous and potentially totalitarian illusions of curbing man's "natural selfishness."

We can thus agree, without being "reactionary," that certain characteristics of our biological nature—"first nature"—as well as the limitations that any culture places on aggressive and libidinal drives, can be found in any place and time, in any culture and society. For example, kinship structures may vary—in some cultures, male authority is embodied in the brother of the mother, not the biological father (ethnologists call this "avunculism"). However, the anguish deriving from the separation from the primary mother figure, as well as some form of "castration"—the prohibition of polymorphic desire—on the part of the entourage is part of a universal human condition, until proven otherwise. This applies *a fortiori* to factors such as the premature birth of the human infant in comparison with other animals. The consequences seem as inevitable as they are universal, such as the persistence of the primary prohibition figure in the form of a "superego" where individual experience and social structure are entangled.

This theme could be tackled by examining the notable differences between psychic lives in different cultures. In other words, is the Oedipus complex universal? Do the Japanese have an unconscious? Jacques Lacan doubted as much. Do Samoans experience neurosis as a result of sexual repression? In the thirties, anthropologist Margaret Mead denied as much. Ethnopsychiatry and ethnopsychoanalysis as developed by Géza Róheim, Georges Devereux, and others have challenged this and proposed useful approaches for our argument. They examined how different cultures around the world treat psychic pathologies differently and provided examples of dealing with them, such as turning the psychotic into a shaman or exorcizing collective fears through appropriate rituals. This research has also produced investigations into the formation of the "self" in non-Western cultures[129] that need to be considered for a broader examination of the "subject"—especially if it is to be demonstrated as a historical construct.[130]

French anthropologist Pierre Clastres, who analyzed how certain "primitive" societies prevent the formation of separated power, made one of the first attempts in this direction.[131] According to him, the desire to become "chief" can exist in all societies, but some societies, fearing the establishment of lasting power structures, have sought and sometimes succeeded in preventing as much. Among the indigenous of the Americas, for example, Amazonian tribes opposed the Andean societies, which produced vast empires and highly hierarchical societies. One of the most common strategies for channeling the ambition of certain individuals consisted in bequeathing them "prestige" without any real power, which would be impossible to accumulate and always revocable. In some Native American cultures, those with the greatest wealth acquired the right to spend it on grand celebrations and feasts for the community and thus to earn the gratitude of others![132]

This approach merits further elaboration. How do different cultures react to phenomena unconnected to individual pathology in its relation to the "normality" of the group, but which, while having the appearance of normality, are considered undesirable? If, to take up Lasch's thesis, the initial separation anxiety is part of the history of each individual in any socio-historical context, and cannot be related to an external repression (as is the case of the enthronement of the superego through the threat of castration, according to the Freudian-Marxists), and if no general cultural or educational reform will ever be able to ensure a childhood free of conflict and anxiety, it does not follow that this anxiety should receive the same responses in every society. Humanity has developed very different ways of coping, and not all solutions are equal. Confronting trauma, acknowledging separation, and accepting substitute solutions—"transitional objects," from toys and crafts to art, but also friendship and love—is not the same as denying separation and clinging for a lifetime to fantasies that maintain the initial illusions of omnipotence (including the fantasy of uniting with one's parent of the opposite sex and having a child with them, denying the reality of castration and gender differences, etc.). The path of the individual in this respect depends not only on individual circumstances. The environment can compel an individual in one direction or another. But this environment cannot be reduced to the family atmosphere—as "classical" psychoanalysis would have it—nor only to social class, as Fromm would have said in his early years. There is also a notable, even determining influence of what has often referred to here as the "principle of social synthesis" or the "social *a priori*."

We have already outlined the danger of favoring "regressive solutions over developmental solutions" with regard to the problem of separation, as discussed by Lasch with reference to Janine Chasseguet-Smirgel. This idea deserves to be pursued. Although Lasch remains distant from any discourse formulated in terms of the critique of political economy, even when he examines the role of the "commodity"—which he identifies with its "concrete" form as the industrially produced object of consumption—he nevertheless understood the psychological effects of commodity consumption: "The consumer's complete dependence on these intricate, supremely sophisticated life-support systems, and more generally on externally provided goods and services, recreates some of the infantile feelings of helplessness. If nineteenth century bourgeois culture reinforced anal patterns of behavior-hoarding of money and supplies, control of bodily functions, control of affect—the twentieth-century culture of mass consumption recreates oral patterns rooted in an even earlier stage of emotional development, when the infant was completely dependent on the breast. The consumer experiences his surroundings as a kind of extension of the breast, alternately gratifying and frustrating." Neither reality nor the self appears as solid and durable. "Partly because the propaganda surrounding commodities advertises them so seductively as wish-fulfillments, but also because commodity production by its very nature replaces the world of durable objects with disposable products designed for immediate obsolescence, the consumer confronts the world as a reflection of his wishes and fears."[133]

The production and consumption of standardized commodities, removed from individual control, thus constitutes the very opposite of those "transitional objects"—the products of "meaningful" work, derived from play—which for Lasch, as we have seen, represent the only possible way to establish a "friendly" relationship with the world and to reduce the weight of the "human condition."[134] However imprecise his conception of capitalism may be, and however questionable his positive references may be (work, community, family, and even religion), Lasch makes a very strong argument here: capitalism has inaugurated a real anthropological regression. It has destroyed the modest but effective means with which humanity had long tried to master the contradictions of life. Capitalism has broken them for the sole purpose of selling commodities.

For Lasch, the conflict between drives and civilization is therefore not reducible to historical circumstances, but is rooted in the very structure of the drives as it already manifests itself in the newborn child. What changes historically, and can constitute an object of critique, are the regressive or developmental ways that different civilizations respond to the initial anxiety. Lasch condemns commodity society—without naming it as such—because it imposes particularly regressive responses to this problem. This is where his critique of consumer society finally meets Marcuse's, albeit freed from certain illusions. In any case, it still seems particularly appropriate for our times, characterized as they are by the capture of desire by the commodity.

From this perspective, the establishment of a world of standardized and rapidly obsolete commodities, with which the subject cannot establish lasting and personal relationships, can be described as regression on a grand scale. There is no longer an environment in which the subject can recognize itself as the fruit of its encounter with the world (in the words of Baudelaire: "The shape of a city, as we all know, changes more quickly than the mortal heart"). As has been said, technologies and commodities cultivate a magical and all-powerful relationship with the world and contribute to holding the individual back at an early stage of its development.

A similar discourse applies to fusional experiences that are not, in essence, either narcissistic or non-narcissistic. The search for fusional experiences, as a return to the primary unity, also exists in many non-narcissistic contexts: dance and music, alcohol or other drugs, mysticism or the worship of an ideal, festivals and crowds, not to mention love, are obviously all universal experiences. What characterizes narcissistic society is the importance and specific features assumed by the search for a momentary fusion. For example, classical music consists of alternating moments of separation (tension) and of harmony and joyful union. This is why Lasch claims that art, as a transitional object, can sooth the separation anxiety that follows us throughout our lives: separation is not denied or hidden, but first acknowledged and then, at certain moments, overcome. The experience of classical music is thus quite different from that of a rock concert, rave, or love parade accompanied by techno music, which are more akin to a relationship with hard drugs.

The education of a child's taste for certain flavors is another example of the "regressive" or "developmental" solutions provided by different cultures, a beginning point in the individual process of humanization. Young children spontaneously enjoy sweet tastes, while rejecting acidity and bitterness even more so. However, after a while, they accept salty tastes without difficulty. If adults do not force them to taste bitter foods, they will never take the initiative to do so themselves; but it is quite possible to leave them in this initial condition, which is currently and most frequently the case. A whole multinational industry, from fast food to sweetened drinks and cookies, deploys enormous resources for keeping "consumers" in this state of sensory deprivation. Beyond the strictly economic aspect, this is part of a general infantilization linked to narcissism, which will be discussed in the next chapter. Here, as elsewhere, a "developmental" solution must take note of the initial inadequacy of human beings and compel them towards overcoming this condition, even if it means facing some resistance. If we try to quietly sneak past this intersection between the "the narrow path of virtue and broad path of vice," we risk losing access to entire sections of the richness of human experience developed over many generations and, in this case, lose access to the plenitude of culinary experience.[135]

As can be seen, it is not a question of proposing a return to nature, as Rousseau argued, or of pronouncing unconditional adoration for childhood, so fashionable in recent years. Human beings are not born perfect and then perverted by society. The restrictions that society imposes upon the individual during their development are not always mere emanations of an inescapable "reality principle" against which only "utopians," "immature people," "fanatics," or "abstract ideologues" could rebel. Many of these restrictions serve to perpetuate the fetishistic societies that created them. It would make no sense to oppose them with an abstract "freedom," especially when it comes to childhood. The problem is not so much that there are restrictions as such, but that these restrictions unnecessarily prevent individuals from accessing the fullness of life that social and cultural development has made possible. Yet the solutions vary greatly, even though all cultures that exist or have existed seem in one way or another more repressive than "necessary," for example with regard to the status of women. But this is not to say that these solutions are lost in a night where all cats are grey, nor that there is an identifiable "progress" that has led to a gradual expansion of freedom that culminates today at the summit of history—nor, conversely, at the end of a continuous regression from some past golden age.

It would be interesting to establish a classification of human cultures and societies according to the solutions they provide to the limits of the human condition, such as separation anxiety, incestuous desires, and destructive impulses. Capitalist society would perhaps appear as the most "regressive" society, the one that has done most to prevent the maturation of individuals; the one that has abandoned many of the achievements of previous societies. This would provide a basis for the assertion that capitalism constitutes an "anthropological rupture," a "generalized regression," a "de-civilization," a "barbarization," or a "reverse anthropogenesis." Among the basic elements of the "human condition" with which every culture has to contend is first and foremost what can be called "aggressiveness," the "destructive drive," or the "death drive." Aggression has been one of the main issues in the debate between the left and the right on possible freedoms and necessary constraints. Here, the boundaries tend to be particularly sharp. For the right, the tendency to aggression is part of the deepest and most "animal" nature of man and justifies, on its own, the existence of institutions whose purpose is to channel and limit what can never be fully suppressed. For the left, aggression is only the consequence of circumstances that, at the individual and collective level, produce tension and frustration—intermediate positions can of course exist as well. According to Hobbes, Carl Schmitt, or Samuel Huntington, war is an anthropological invariant, whereas the left explains war as resulting from the greed and rapacity of the ruling classes. The approach proposed in this work, however, is not to determine whether societies necessarily "generate" aggression and destruction, but how they "manage" them. It has been demonstrated that the "absence of the world" characteristic of value corresponds to the empty world of the narcissist; similarly, it will be shown that the expansion of the "death drive" in the contemporary world is also a consequence of the subject-form, and above all, its ultimate implosion.

Social atomism, that is, the radical separation between members of society resulting from abstract labor as a principle of social synthesis, gives rise to fantasies of total fusion characteristic of the narcissist. This isolation is obviously a product of history, not a biological constant. What embodies contemporary forms of individual and collective decomposition is therefore not, as is often thought, a lack of subjectivity, that is, insufficient access to the status of subject, but rather an *excess* of the subject-form. The fetish-narcissistic constitution is contradictory in itself and therefore dynamic; it tends towards a catastrophic outcome by seeking to annihilate what has been projected outwards: it is indeed animated by a "death drive." Modern rationality always has its hidden and "irrational" side, just as Sade is the dark side of Kant.

There is a link here between two parallel processes: on the one hand, the dissolution and constitution of the subject in and through narcissism, which, since the "birth" of the subject in the seventeenth century, has formed its core; on the other hand, the diminishment of value production resulting from the replacement of living labor by technologies. These two trajectories have been in their most acute phase for about half a century. There is an identity at the deepest level between the modern subject and value: that of *the basic forms* that precede all concrete content. These true *a priori* involve the same emptiness, the same indifference to the world, the same self-referentiality whose identity ultimately leads to the annihilation of both the world and the self. This is the last consequence of the subject and value. Pre-capitalist ways of life were far from perfect, but at least they did not bear these characteristics.

CHAPTER 3
CONTEMPORARY THOUGHT IN
THE FACE OF FETISHISM

At the risk of being schematic, two phases in the "psychic history" of capitalism over the last 250 years can be distinguished: a first "Oedipal" phase and a second "Narcissistic" phase. The "Oedipal" phase, characterized by authoritarian structures and a highly visible and "masculine" superego, is a direct continuation of certain pre-modern structures. The "Narcissistic" phase partially began in the 1920s, although its precursors can be found in bohemian artistic culture, particularly in France, during the second half of the nineteenth century, of which Baudelaire is emblematic, followed by the Romantics. This development decelerated with the rise of totalitarianism and began to impose itself more widely after the Second World War in Western countries, making a qualitative leap after 1968. As has been mentioned, this victory of narcissism is nothing other than the becoming-visible of the hidden essence, the core, of commodity society, which goes back at least to the period of Descartes.

A Loss of Limits?

Obviously, the narcissistic "geological layer" has not simply replaced or expelled the Oedipal layer, especially since each individual psyche, as well as the collective psyche—as Freud never tired of repeating, using the image of Rome and its composite constructions—are patchworks of elements dating back to different eras that overlap and superimpose, amalgamate, and oppose each other in the most varied combinations. It would be quite erroneous to imagine that the authoritarian phase is simply behind us—either regrettably, in the eyes of the reactionary, or happily, for the optimistic progressive. However, the opposite error is much more common, which consists in continuing to identify the capitalist system with Oedipal structures, as if nothing essential distinguishes the present situation from that of the nineteenth century. With so-called "postmodern" thinking, narcissistic forms are even often mistaken as moments of liberation. Indeed, if capitalism is identified with only one of its phases—the rigid, pyramidal, overtly authoritarian phase—there is the risk of not understanding what Zygmunt Bauman has described as its "liquid" phase, as opposed to the preceding "solid" phase. Postmodern life consists in making individual happiness the goal of society. The individual is no longer asked to sacrifice himself for the interests of the collective, and it is the satisfaction of desires, not the fulfillment of duty, that is proposed as the general rule of life. This results in more flexible and less hierarchical relations between social classes, between the elderly and young, men and women, whites and non-whites, as well as social mobility and the possibility of "choosing" one's destiny independently of origins (social, geographical, sexual, etc.) instead of adhering to a predetermined script received at birth. Further indexes of this shift appear in the realm of sexual freedom, extended now to "sexual minorities," as well as an education system that respects the personalities of children, in the family and at school. Finally, there is the possibility for women to make the same choices as men.

Critical thinkers will immediately retort that this is "only" an "appearance," that this is at best only very partially true. What is needed is to continue to struggle for real equality and a democracy that is truly embedded within everyday life, since such advances are only partially realized, at best. They are permanently threatened, as reactionary forces are always on the move to reverse such achievements and return to the society of yesteryear. Certainly, there is no shortage of examples to confirm this perspective. The "liquid" society is indeed a *tendency*, a very strong one, but it does not occupy the totality of the social field. It is true that even today's reactionaries are necessarily postmodern and "liquid" and that even neo-fascists no longer march in lockstep. But all this is not enough to explain why the Manichean vision of a struggle between progress and reaction, darkness and enlightenment, often ends up unintentionally endorsing the most contemporary and insidious forms of domination in capitalist society.

A study of the subject-form corresponding to "liquid" reality through the categories of psychoanalysis has been conducted since the end of the 1990s by authors—psychoanalysts by profession or otherwise—who refer to the thought of Jacques Lacan. The critique that these authors make of "Western madness" is one of the major attempts to understand the most recent developments of the subject-form, especially in its everyday dimension.[1] Their examination of the forms of subjectivity that have taken hold under neoliberalism—they speak of (neo)liberalism rather than capitalism, as we will soon grasp more precisely—is based on the observation of an *abolition of all limits*. One of the first books of this trend, published in 1997 by Jean-Pierre Lebrun, is titled *Un monde sans limites*.[2] Additionally, psychoanalyst Charles Melman recalls in *L'Homme sans gravité*, his book of interviews with Lebrun, that for two centuries Hilbert, Gödel, Marx, and Freud were devoted to identifying *limits*.[3] But "the century to come will be the century of their removal: nothing will be impossible," and the initiators of this reversal were "Foucault, Althusser, Barthes, Deleuze, who proclaimed the right not to happiness, but to jouissance."[4] Philosopher Dany-Robert Dufour announced that one of the ten commandments of the psychic economy in the era of triumphant liberalism proclaims: "Thou shalt liberate thy impulses and seek unlimited jouissance! (This leads to the destruction of an economy of desire and its replacement by an economy of jouissance)."[5]

In a series of books published back-to-back after 2000, Dufour examined, with undeniable verve, the origins, history, and present of the psychic economy of the unlimited market. He agrees with Melman and Lebrun that the passage from the economy of desire to the economy of *jouissance* is an echo "in the psychic economy of the changes that have occurred in the commodity economy with the spread of liberalism."[6] These authors also note that the unconscious has changed a great deal since the time of Freud and that its current forms—which they consider to be very negative—are a consequence of changes in other spheres, notably the transition to a liberal economy.[7] Dufour traces the many stages in the development of the liberal spirit, reserving a place of "honor" for Bernard Mandeville and his *Fable of the Bees* (1714). According to him, liberalism consists in the abolition of everything that imposes limits, from childhood onwards, upon the spontaneous impulses and passions of the human being; it presents itself as a liberation of the individual and seems, from this point of view, to have completely triumphed in recent decades. In reality, this liberation, according to Dufour, has another aim: to transform autonomous subjects into docile consumers, into a "ego-herd" who are easily governed and ready to swallow whatever industry offers them.[8] The "autonomy" of the previous subject was the result of an internalization of the need to relate to a great "Other," a necessity that goes back, in the final analysis, to *neoteny*:[9] "Man is an animal that comes into the world unfinished, unfinalized and thus deprived of objects which, in other animals, are prescribed by genetic code. Nature certainly flows within man and pushes him very strongly towards . . . that which he knows not what."[10] This is why humanity essentially requires a great Subject, even if its expression changes historically: totem, physis, god, king, people, race, nation, proletariat, etc. If an idol is no longer useful, it is destroyed and another is created, even for those who consider themselves atheists.[11] In the old patriarchal and religious order, this Other who allows access to the status of subject was an external figure; later, Kant and Freud transferred the figure of the "father," and of authority in general—long synonymous with subjugation—to the interior of the individual, thus creating a "strong subject." According to Kant, it is the figure of the master who "makes it possible to subject man to the laws of humanity (which man does not carry within himself, but upon which he must elaborate),"[12] provided that the master eventually allows the subject to proceed without him.[13]

Kant's transcendental and Freudian psychoanalysis would therefore emerge as the great adversaries of liberalism. In truth, psychoanalysis concurs with liberalism in the assertion that the human drive is by nature egoistic and only seeks its own satisfaction; but Freud also knew that "it is necessary to suppress this liberated drive for pleasure, and this was to be carried out from the very beginning of the formation of the individual, otherwise it would be too late afterwards"—a conviction that would have come from his Kantian background.[14] Dufour recalls that, according to Freud, Kant's categorical imperative was the direct heir of the Oedipal complex, thus adding to Kantian morality the unconscious mechanism that brings the subject to consciousness. Indeed, in order to function, the paternal fiction—of which there are many variations in history—must remain unconscious and unrecognized as a fiction.[15] Otherwise, no social cohesion would be possible.

Through education and self-education, the human being becomes master of itself. It learns to control its passions and to accept limitations—the first of which is always the renunciation of the mother and the acceptance of differences between sex and ages, as well as the resulting prohibition on incest. The whole of human culture is based on this acceptance. Yet market liberalism has shattered these secular or millennia-old constructs with the sole aim of selling more commodities: *desire*—which is often satisfied with a substitute (whether a neurosis or sublimation) or with a general representation or metaphor—is replaced by *direct pleasure [jouissance]*. Thus today, a universal and unlimited right to *jouissance* is proclaimed, which manifests itself in a frantic and unrestrained consumption of commodities and in a complete loss of autonomy with regard to one's own impulses. Dufour observes that "the extreme exploitation of the drives, especially for commercial gain, destroys the subject that is also at once its source," noting that among the most visible consequences of liberalism is the massive diffusion of pornography.[16] This constitutes the ideal condition for a new form of tyranny. The abolition of the figure of the master and of the very idea of education, combined with the rejection of all rules in the name of freedom, has been ardently defended by Michel Foucault, Roland Barthes, Gilles Deleuze, and Pierre Bourdieu: "The blunder of postmodern philosophies . . . was to believe that the little subject could have managed perfectly well on its own, if only institutions and the great despotic Signifiers had not set out to alienate it."[17] The real purpose of school should be, according to Dufour, to enable young people to control their passions (in the etymological sense of the term). In antiquity, music, dance, poetry, and grammar taught self-control and harmony in order to transform passion (in which the subject remains "passive") and outcry into expression, transforming excess into measure.[18]

Dufour is in complete agreement with the thesis defended in this book that modernity's departure from religion is only an appearance, since it has proceeded with the emergence of a new divinity: the Market.[19] Yet the Market, for Dufour, can never really replace religion. It only functions in the present and "does not provide in fiction what is lacking in human reality." It leaves the "little subjects" to cope with their "need for an origin." The Market "no longer completes in nature what the latter was unable to," whereas classical neurosis "implies this structure of alienation from the Other as the figure of the origin."[20] To truly abandon religion, it is necessary to abandon the "total liberalism" that believes in a hidden spirit that ensures the spontaneous harmonization of private interests and vices; this can be achieved by reintroducing regulation into all human economies.[21] In a few informative pages, Dufour reminds us that Adam Smith was also a theologian who wanted to establish the free market and the "invisible hand" as a new form of providence. For Smith, who adopted much of his argument from Mandeville (without the more provocative aspects), it was possible to escape from all morality.[22] Both Kant and Smith set out to apply Newton's lesson to social life, and "selfish interest" played the same role in Smith's work as "attraction" did in Newton's scientific theology.[23] However, for Smith, it was necessary to *deregulate* as much as possible in order to fulfill divine purpose, while for Kant it was necessary to *regulate*. The whole of modernity consisted of a balance between these two tendencies, and today, moral, political, and economic deregulation has now spread to all spheres of life. It is as such not merely a question of economic "deregulation": Dufour sees Foucault as a prophet of deregulation (even in his praise of madness), which would explain why he is so favored by the right.[24] Similarly, Deleuze's "schizo" subject is the ideal subject of the market, as is the hacker or the corporate predator.[25] By destroying the "despotic signifiers" described by Deleuze, it is ultimately the market that has imposed itself as master. According to Dufour, Deleuze even goes beyond liberalism: for the author of *Anti-Oedipus*, all identity is paranoid, and so one must constantly invent new ones. This, Dufour observes, corresponds perfectly to the new spirit of capitalism, which does not favor self-owning subjects.[26] Deleuze wanted to go faster than capitalism itself by introducing the language of economics into the analysis of symbolic processes.[27] Consequently, his praise of "nomadism" and the "machine" has been fully recuperated by the most contemporary marketing strategies.[28]

Despite the good intentions of these authors, there is, according to Dufour, a risk of reinforcing capitalist barbarism because of a "postmodern collapse of the two founding symbolic references through which the oedipal knot is resolved, identified by Freud as being at the heart of the civilizational process."[29] This can be seen, Dufour continues, in the increase of incest and child rape, which expresses the denial of generational difference. Before, there were forbidden desires— the desire for the mother, classically—that had to be renounced. A certain type of psychoanalysis (of the Deleuzian type, says Dufour) encouraged people to envisage the realization of these desires and escape from the Oedipal knot—for example, by *physically* changing one's sex.[30] However, this has not yet created the possibility of having children. A *market of children* has therefore been created, once again placing capitalism one step ahead.

For Charles Melman too, the unconscious of the "liberal man" is different from the Freudian unconscious. "Psychic liberalism" tempts with the possibility of leading multiple lives, of experiencing a variety of different pleasures, of exploring all situations, even in terms of sexual identity. This "sometimes obviously entails effects of derealization. It is not polygamy but poly-subjectivity," in which the subject attempts to experience, simultaneously or consecutively, "several life trajectories totally different from a subjective point of view."[31] The new psychic economy does not render us into adults by emancipating us from the father, but rather makes us infants, entirely dependent on satisfaction. In other words, the new psychic economy is the ideology of the market. It "is anonymous without anyone in control, which is what makes it so unsettling."[32] Melman's approach presents itself as a radical critique of commodification: "The process depends on no one, in other words, on no ideology. It depends solely on the people whose accelerated, magnificent, globalized economic expansion needs to see timidity, modesty, moral barriers, and prohibitions broken down in order to sustain itself. This is to create consumer populations, eager for perfect enjoyment, without limits and addictive. We are now in a state of addiction to objects."[33]

Like Dufour, Melman notes a general de-symbolization: it is no longer a question, as before, of an "approach organized by representation, but of going to the object itself."[34] What is expected are object satisfactions, not representations.[35] What links the new psychic economy and the economy as a whole is that "it is in a way a new relationship to the object, insofar as the object's worth is not determined by what it represents, or by that of which it is representative, but rather by what it is."[36] Advertising that makes fantasies more explicit prevents people from fantasizing, and literature that renounces metaphor in favor of a supposedly direct language prevents people from imagining. Even political power descends into barbarism when it is no longer symbolic and "seeks to defend and protect nothing other than its existence as power."[37]

Evoking Authority to Escape the Market?

These analyses seem to capture certain aspects of contemporary subjectivity that few others want to recognize, especially those features that do not fit into the commonly accepted model of progress and reaction. They express a resolute opposition to *French theory* and to the pantheon in which the eternal Foucault, Deleuze, Althusser, Barthes, etc. are now enshrined, often passing for the *ne plus ultra* of intellectual opposition. It is clear that Dufour, Melman, and Lebrun are not enticing an audience eager to see certain attitudes—such as a fascination with unorthodox forms of sexuality and parenting— recognized as the new frontiers of an emancipated civilization in the making.

However, certain limitations to their discourse quickly become apparent. Firstly, as with almost all contemporary authors, their critique of "capitalism" is limited to that of neoliberalism alone, even when they call it "hyper-capitalism" or "postmodern capitalism." Implicitly or explicitly, the "excesses" of an "unhealthy" capitalism beginning after 1970 are opposed to the more "solid" capitalism of the past. Thus, Dufour deplores the transition from "entrepreneurial capitalism" to shareholder capitalism, and thus the financialization of the economy.[38] In this he believes he sees the "tyranny without tyrants" described by Hannah Arendt, as if it had never existed before.[39] In his criticism of large international financial institutions, such as the IMF, or in his illusions about democracy, citizens, or the "participatory" economy[40]—whether in the factory or *via* the internet[41]—or in his comments about a "better distribution of labor,"[42] Dufour proves himself to be very unoriginal.

Nostalgia for the supposedly "healthy" capitalism of the Keynesian-Fordist era is today quite widespread, especially in France. It is accompanied by a neo-Lacanian nostalgia for the "strong subject" and "solid realities," such as work, the "republican" school, and the family. The new psychic economy thus appears as a kind of psychic counterpart to financialization.[43] On the other hand, Dufour establishes no link with the fundamental structures of capitalism (value and abstract labor). The *decline* of the subject is thus lamented, rather than criticized. Kant is presented as the one who opposed the "dignity" to the "price" of something and thus gave the individual the strength to resist the permanent seduction of consumption. His role as a champion of the abstract and purely formal spirit that characterizes commodity society is overlooked. The internalization of social norms, in which Dufour sees Kant's great merit, has a drawback that Dufour completely neglects: these norms are not neutral and do not represent "culture" as such, against which all else is barbarism. On the contrary, these specific norms defended by Kant are themselves, as we have seen, possible vehicles of barbarism, especially in their promotion of contentless "laws" that should be obeyed without question.

Many of the social and psychological phenomena described by Dufour, Melman, Lebrun, and others existed long before the neoliberal era, even if it has exacerbated them. The civilizational divide did not emerge from the recent past, somewhere between solid capitalism and its sad degeneration—which would make classical capitalism, and all of its basic categories, fall on the side of "civilization." It took place a few centuries earlier. Contemporary "hyper-capitalism," based on finance and the excessive commodification of all aspects of life, has only developed to the extreme what was already contained in its earlier stages. Capitalist logic has always been incompatible with the human dimension!

This nostalgia for the lost subject has at least two problematic consequences: on the one hand, a positive appreciation of historical forms of the lost subject, such as religion and patriarchy. Despite assertions to the contrary, these authors are tempted to extol the virtues of authority, earlier stages of capitalism, and Oedipal structures. Lebrun is thus obliged to ask Melman, in their book of interviews: "There is this critique addressed to psychoanalysts, and especially to Lacan's work, where it is said that, under the pretext of appealing to the laws of language or the symbolic order, there is the question of advocating for a return to patriarchy. How do you respond to this criticism?"[44] Melman refuses any nostalgia for the old patriarchal and religious order: "The only way to be human is to take into account the determinism imposed on us by the laws of language. Not to celebrate them, not to venerate them, not to engage in skepticism or resignation," but to see what can be done with them once they are recognized.[45] Despite his claim not to want to turn back the clock, Melman considers religion as the lesser evil, wondering whether it will be possible "for many people to continue to respect this debt which allows for the possibility of subjectivization, the consequences of this relationship with the Other, without believing in a God inhabiting the heavens."[46] An "empty heaven" is even regarded as the cause of the weakness of individuals in the face of the Sirens of consumption—of the "object," as Melman calls it. Lebrun himself reminds us in his preface to the 2011 reprint of *Monde sans limites* that a better distinction than the one he made fifteen years earlier needs to be made between the "decline of the paternal function" and the "decline of the patriarchal function."[47] Dufour asks himself the same question: "How can we get rid of patriarchal ideology without at the same time destroying the paternal function?"[48] He responds by suggesting that the Kantian-Freudian subject be reevaluated. He argues that resistance of the neurotic—depression included—and the refusal to renounce its symptoms is the best resistance against liberalism. Neuroses commit the subject to seeking satisfactions different from drive satisfactions, and thus to embark upon the path of "civilization." The subject's unsatisfied desires, forbidden by the "name of the father," are thus to be transformed by sublimation, a conclusion similar to Lasch.

Even if they claim to oppose authoritarianism, the concern about the loss of authority leads these authors to very one-sided views on contemporary freedom.[49] They thus take the appearance of freedom at face value. Today, says Melman, "everyone can publicly indulge all their passions and, what is more, demand that they be socially recognized, accepted, even legalized, including sex changes."[50] "No one can be denied the legitimacy of their satisfaction, neither the transsexual nor the elderly woman who wants a child."[51] Melman thus forgets that this applies—at most—only to the family and sexual sphere. Nor does he take into account the social nature of, for example, the demand to live without permanent fear for one's material survival, or to possess legal documents when one was born outside one's country of residence. The criticism made against the fact that any desire can today be publicly claimed as satisfied does not distinguish between justified claims—because they belong to the order of what society itself has made and can therefore undo—and questionable claims—because they touch on a sphere that can be called "natural." This critique is blind to the fact that in some respects there are more limits than ever, more walls, more electronic barriers, more prohibitions, more "security measures," more states of emergency.

On the other hand, a second consequence of nostalgia for a lost subject, which would have disappeared only very recently, produces a curious incoherence: while insisting, often rightly, on the "anthropological revolution in progress,"[52] Dufour and Melman explain this far-reaching event by quite contingent factors.[53] If our form of the unconscious dates back to the emergence of neoteny, or at least to Roman antiquity, as Melman thinks; if it is therefore several thousand years old, it seems curious that a rupture of such importance could be the consequence of recent financialization or of the upheavals of the education systems in recent decades. Lebrun, for his part, attributes the new psychic economy to the "conjuncture of the development of techno-sciences, the evolution of democracy, and the rise of economic liberalism," which, according to him, began with the fall of the Berlin Wall.[54]

If the word "economy" appears frequently among the neo-Lacanians—mainly in the expression "psychic economy," or "new psychic economy"—it is, as with Freud himself, largely metaphorical. In their perspective, the economy in the narrow sense dissolves into a "symbolic economy" with very vague contours and which is instead rooted in an ontology of language. The driving force of change would ultimately always reside in family structures (which obviously remain central to the psychoanalytic worldview). They argue that limiting is the function of the father, and what they see as a "contemporary return to matriarchy"[55]—for example in the single-parent household—is in their view an invitation to remain in the "unlimitedness" of the original maternal regime.[56] The loss of limits is thus, in a way, due to the preponderant role of mothers in contemporary society and in the claim of gender equality.

However, unbridled consumption also plays a role in this loss of limits: "There is no longer a driver at the wheel," says Melman, "and is it so reassuring that in its place, in the seat, is the object? It is the object that has now arrived, after having taken the place of the figure of God, conceived first with an animal and then a human face: it is the object that is invested with authority in our present third phase."[57] This object promises unlimited *jouissance*, a "surplus of pleasure," with "drugs being the most remarkable case," adds Melman. One might think that we are talking here about the "automatic subject," but this "object" is in reality simply the commodities of consumption coveted by subjects. Their role as bearers of value produced by abstract labor remains completely beyond these considerations. Dufour also aligns himself with the critics of the "proletarianization of the consumer," who he says include Guy Debord, Jean Baudrillard, Christopher Lasch, George Ritzer, and Bernard Stiegler. It is therefore hardly surprising that he exhibits nostalgia for "real work" (artisanal, worker-controlled, meaningful) and "real money," not based on speculation.

Conceiving the existence of various "human economies"[58] allows Dufour to recognize that their changes contribute to a redefinition of the unconscious.[59] Consequently, he accuses psychoanalysts of believing too much in the "extraterritoriality" of the unconscious and forgetting that it is subject to historical variations. One wonders, however, whether the recent changes in the psychic economy indicate a dangerous departure from the "essence" of man described by Freud and—according to these authors—Lacan, or whether they demonstrate, on the contrary, that the concepts of classical psychoanalysis referred only to a brief phase in the psychic history of man. For the Lacanians, there is an eternal law, that of language. But, Melman admits, this law develops and does not necessarily take the form of the Oedipus complex. The "classical" unconscious, in which the father forbids desire and in so doing re-introduces it, would thus be only *one* of the possible forms of prohibition, this "fall" that "the proper functioning of the chain of language includes" and which is therefore the consignment of every "speaking being."[60] In other words, different forms of the unconscious have existed in the past or in other cultures, and others will exist in the future.

The discourse of Dufour, also shared with a large part of psychoanalysis, is based on a central presupposition: the imperfections of human beings are not only the result of a bad social order, but above all of the *naturally unlimited* character of human drives and passions, especially in the domains of the libido and aggression. This assumption is shared by Thomas Hobbes, truly the father of bourgeois ideology, right down to his assertion that desires are by nature infinite.[61] The need to educate the "little subjects"—real individuals, in Dufour's terminology—is obviously one of the consequences. Additionally, Dufour attributes an important place to "pleonexia," that is, greed, insatiability, the desire to always seek more, and especially more than others.[62] But is this condition "natural," such that culture must serve as a necessary barrier against man's greed? This is a very big question, one running through the pages of this book. Without postulating an "original innocence" of the human being, we can nevertheless suggest that the extraordinary power of the drives—which seems self-evident—could itself be a specifically modern condition. The observation of certain "primitive" societies suggests rather that the pursuit of material wealth and sexual satisfaction is much less compulsive than in more "developed" societies. In his *Politics*, Aristotle said of man that "when destitute of virtue, he is an animal most unholy and most savage, and most viciously disposed towards sensuality and gluttony."[63] Indeed, the Western conception of man is largely based on this assumption—but it could also be interpreted as a distinctive feature of the West itself, which would explain its enormous aggressiveness and desire for conquest.

Recourse to the psychological and ethical category of "greed" also presents another limitation. When Dufour writes, for example, that "the indefinite increase of wealth [is] the only true aim of capitalism,"[64] he does not distinguish between abstract and concrete wealth.[65] As we have said, in capitalist society, concrete wealth is strictly secondary to the amount of abstract time it represents. The bulimia of the capitalist subject does not therefore derive from its insatiable natural passions. Montaigne mentions an ancient figure, Pheraulas, a protégé of the Persian king Cyrus, who "has passed through both kinds of fortune and found that increase of possessions was not increase in appetite for drinking, eating, sleeping, and embracing his wife,"[66] and therefore judged that "on the loftiest throne in the world we are still sitting only on our own rump."[67] All concrete desire is thus constrained by our body's limited capacity to assimilate what gives it pleasure. In traditional and naïve representations, kings and heroes consume an enormous amount or possess harems at their disposal. But the possibility of surpassing others in these areas remains very limited. The sorrow of kings who no longer know what to do with their power, or even how to enjoy it, is also the subject of legends, such as Cleopatra dissolving pearls in vinegar or Caligula caressing the necks of his lovers while telling them that they will soon be decapitated.[68]

In his logical and historical genealogy of money, Marx demonstrated that hoarding, which was the prevalent form of wealth accumulation in pre-capitalist society, was a first, though very imperfect, manifestation of the nature of money. It already contains unlimitedness *in nuce*:

> The desire after hoarding is in its very nature unsatiable. In its qualitative aspect, or formally considered, money has no bounds to its efficacy, i.e., it is the universal representative of material wealth, because it is directly convertible into any other commodity. But, at the same time, every actual sum of money is limited in amount, and, therefore, as a means of purchasing, has only a limited efficacy. This antagonism between the qualitative limits of money and its qualitative boundlessness, continually acts as a spur to the hoarder in his Sisyphus-like labour of accumulating. It is with him as it is with a conqueror who sees in every new country annexed, only a new boundary.[69]

It is precisely the *detachment* of money from all natural needs that makes it unlimited:

> All other commodities are accumulated either as use values, and in this case the manner of their accumulation is determined by the specific features of their use value. Storing of corn, for example, requires special equipment; collecting sheep makes a person a shepherd; accumulation of slaves and land necessitates relations of domination and servitude, and so on. Unlike the simple act of piling up, the formation of stocks of particular types of wealth requires special methods and develops special traits in the individual. . . . Gold and silver constitute money not as the result of any activity of the person who accumulates them, but as crystals of the process of circulation which takes place without his assistance. He need do nothing but put them aside, piling one lot upon another, a completely senseless activity, which if applied to any other commodity would result in its devaluation. . . . His imaginary boundless thirst for enjoyment causes [the hoarder] to renounce all enjoyment. Because he desires to satisfy all social requirements, he scarcely satisfies the most urgent physical wants. While clinging to wealth in its metallic corporeality the hoarder reduces it to a mere chimera.[70]

Only when it becomes "money as money," ready to be reinvested in an expanded cycle of production through the creation of surplus-value obtained through unpaid surplus labor, does money begin to "coincide with its concept" and unfold its full potential. As has been said, unlimitedness only becomes truly unlimited when the multiplication of value through the multiplication of abstract labor becomes the principle of social synthesis. The abstract, the pure unit, knows no limits to its growth. This is therefore the complete opposite of a natural "pleonexia." Just as narcissism is the psychic form corresponding to fetishistic society of the commodity, the "world without limits" is indeed a major feature of our time, although it also produces, by implication, the multiplication of borders and walls. As in the case of narcissism, it is neither an eternal element of human life nor a purely contemporary reaction to recent economic and political changes. It is the core of the commodity regime that has finally eliminated all remnants of the old regimes—and especially the limits they set or respected.

On Idealism and Materialism

Their inability to understand the *causes* of the phenomena they describe remains a point of weakness of the neo-Lacanians. Either they attribute the greatest anthropological revolution in millennia to a specific phase of capitalism that has lasted barely thirty or forty years, or they attribute responsibility to certain intellectuals (without questioning the reasons for their audience), or they attribute, in looking for more distant causes, changes in the sphere of production to changes in the symbolic sphere (notably philosophical). Thus, Dufour devotes often remarkable pages to Pascal and Descartes, to the *Port-Royal Logic*, to Mandeville and Adam Smith, to Kant and Sade. These are largely the authors examined in this book, and the conclusions drawn are sometimes similar. However, Dufour's idea of the birth of capitalism from the spirit of metaphysics, that is, as a secularization of religion, is quite different from ours. Descartes, for example, appeared above as a *witness* to a change that took place in the sphere of everyday exchanges, and in particular in labor and in the circulation of money. However removed our approach may be from "historical materialism," it still remains a form of materialism for which the essential lies in the unconscious or semi-conscious acts performed countless times every day. Dufour's explanation remains ultimately "idealist" in the banal sense of the term—a fault he shares with Serge Latouche, whose analyses of the birth of economics are interesting in many respects, as well as with Louis Dumont and his analyses of the genesis and development of economic ideology, and with Cornelius Castoriadis and his study of the imaginary institution of society.[71] For these authors, modernity, utilitarianism, and economism are essentially a matter of imagination and ideology, not of *real* history, part of that real history of capitalism, which began with the introduction of firearms at the end of the Middle Ages and continued *via* the competition between the owners of capital, soon to be established as a general social principle. This demonstrates that the "new imaginary" they solicit, while surely necessary, is not sufficient. We have returned to the story of the philosopher who thinks it enough to free oneself from the *idea* of gravity in order to avoid drowning . . .

This difficulty in describing the causes of phenomena is clearly a consequence of the almost total absence of any reference to the critique of political economy and its categories.[72] Despite Dufour's intention to "speak the whole," to denounce the "fragmentation of knowledge,"[73] and despite his references to the concept of "transduction,"[74] he shares with postmodern thought, as do the other authors mentioned who so eloquently criticize it, an abhorrence of any "one-sided" explanation, especially when it comes to what they call "the economy." In fact, these authors fail to distinguish between "economics" and the critique of political economy. When Dufour speaks of the danger of reducing the various human economies to the capitalist economy alone, he seems to identify a possible abusive reductionism at the level of theory with the *real* reduction actualized by capitalist society—a difference which we have already addressed on several occasions. He writes that "the use of economic analysis in this linguistic, aesthetic, and symbolic field amounted to repeating the error made by economics when it addresses the question of the exchange of goods between men. It postulates rational subjects defending their interests, and it never questions the production of these subjects, that is, the symbolic economy that refers to an economy of people irreducible to the economy of goods."[75] To attribute to all subjects, as a matter of principle, the pursuit of rational and conscious self-interest is certainly an error that Marxism shares with utilitarian and liberal frameworks; but it must be recognized that "really existing economism" does in fact attempt to impose such behavior on all subjects and is not a figment of the imagination.

Despite repeated references to Marx, Dufour underestimates the latter's contribution to defining the "common ground" of the various problems Dufour describes so effectively.[76] Instead, Dufour indulges in the banal and false opposition between a young humanist Marx, critic of alienation, and an old economist Marx, concerned solely with economic exploitation.[77] According to him, the critique of value asserts that "the productive force of labor is no longer labor, but the new forms of cognition and automation permitted by computers," citing Marx's "Fragment on Machines" from the *Grundrisse*.[78] Here, Dufour erroneously attributes to the critique of value the position of Toni Negri's post-operaismo and the proponents of "cognitive capitalism" gathered around the French journal *Multitudes*—who are in fact the antithesis of value critique.[79] The critique of value does not propose a "schema of emancipation [that] favors the techno-sciences (which have become the main producers of wealth)."[80] Contrary to the blissful optimism of cognitive post-operaismo, for whom the smooth slide towards a post-value society has already begun, the critique of value considers that the greatly increased role of the "general intellect" in the production of commodities *diminishes* their value and thus reinforces the crisis of this mode of production.[81]

While Dufour writes that "the proposition of value critique is strong and we can only subscribe to it,"[82] he shares a widespread misunderstanding when he asserts that value critique believes that "capitalism will collapse all on its own,"[83] or worse still, that it is necessary to wait for the full development of capitalism to reach the remotest parts of the world before even being able to think its abolition—and finally, that this expresses a form of excessive "optimism"!

This ambiguity must be clarified. If capitalism has already survived several crises, this does not mean it survives "by feeding on its own weaknesses"[84] or that it "finds in crises the means to regenerate itself by conquering new markets."[85] There is an enormous difference between the cyclical crises belonging to the growth phase of capitalism and the absolute limits it has reached in recent decades, which are due to the decrease in the mass of value produced by living labor as a whole.

In the face of the postmodern denial of the natural bases of human existence and attempts to consider them as mere "constructs," Dufour's discourse is salutary; on the other hand, its similarities with classical reactionary discourse can certainly cause irritation. We recall the words of French philosopher Maine de Biran, delivered as early as 1816 in the Chamber of Deputies, in defense of the principles of the Restoration: "If we wish to restore to the people the moral habits analogous to their position by making them know and love their duties instead of maintaining them with chimerical rights; if the tender feelings of the family, neighborly relations, simple and moderate tastes are the primary pleasures of man in all conditions and the only compensations for the sorrows which so often overwhelm the lower classes, let us be careful not to withdraw such satisfactions."[86]

Dufour's discourse therefore risks drifting towards a defense of the most banal "realism," but also of every constraint that should be integrated. The alternative to narcissism cannot consist in the simple acceptance of given realities and the erasure of oneself in the face of what is, in a unilateral adherence to the reality principle at the expense of the pleasure principle.[87] If we consider any attempt to radically change the conditions of life in society to be a matter of narcissism and fantasies of omnipotence, we arrive at the liberal equation that utopia = totalitarianism. Not every search for the absolute can be labelled "narcissistic," where all the great ambitions and grandiose projects of the past and present appear as fantasies of omnipotence, such that only everyday grind and "realistic" reformism might escape narcissism. Freud's invitation to be content with the "ordinary unhappiness" of family and work cannot be the last word—even if it says more about bourgeois society than all other recipes for happiness, even if they are psychoanalytically adapted. We thus always come back to the same question: what should be done today with the superego, the fruit of the Oedipus complex? Is its decline positive, does it mean a greater form of individual freedom, the end of patriarchy, or even the end of work? Or has it given rise to a new form of fetishism, even more difficult to understand, to name and fight, because it is so deeply embedded within individuals and so seemingly in accord with their desire for "*jouissance*"?

New Forms, Old Woes?

The New Spirit of Capitalism (1999) by sociologists Luc Boltanski and Eve Chiapello has quickly become a seminal book and, for once, it is deserved. Their basic thesis is clear and well argued: the "classical" spirit of capitalism, based on the patriarchal and bourgeois small enterprise, is the one described by Max Weber at the beginning of the twentieth century. The second spirit of capitalism reached its peak between 1930 and 1960, with large organizations at its core. The third spirit began after 1968 and continues today. What characterizes these different "spirits" are not only social, economic, or technological factors, but also systems of *justification*. Justification not only consists of ideology, but also, and above all, in the daily motivations of actors and in the parameters that measure the relative "status" of the actors. This aspect is particularly important because, as the authors admit from the outset, "[i]n many respects, capitalism is an absurd system" and therefore has to resort to many justifications in order to draw actors into a game where their chances of success are low.[88] Weber developed the idea that "people need powerful moral reasons for rallying to capitalism" because it is so contrary to tradition.[89] Wages alone do not cultivate a real commitment to work, nor is mere compulsion enough. Above all, modern capitalism requires active engagement and mainly needs to mobilize the energy of senior staff—executives and managers—by presenting itself to them not only as a livelihood, but also as an opportunity for freedom and self-realization.

Boltanski and Chiapello distinguish six "cities" (or "logics") in contemporary society that correlate with different historical periods and which form the totality of the "justifications" that can provide motivations for social actors: *inspirational* (the saint, the artist); *domestic* (hierarchal position in a chain of personal dependencies); *reputational* (the opinion of others); *civic* (in which the "great man" is the representative of the collective); *commercial* (supplying desired commodities); and *industrial* (efficiency, professional skill). The first spirit of capitalism consisted above all in a compromise between the domestic city and the commercial city; the second spirit between the industrial city and the civic city. The "third spirit" is characterized by the "city of projects," where status is based on the activity of "mediators," and the general equivalent is "activity," which overcomes the oppositions between work and non-work, stable and unstable employment, wage-laborers and non-wage-laborers.[90] Each city places specific constraints on accumulation and imposes real limits, which are not simply intended to conceal the reality of economic forces.

What is truly interesting and innovative in Boltanski and Chiapello's approach, despite the theoretical weakness of their conception of capitalism,[91] is the attention paid to the recuperation of the critiques addressed to each "spirit" of capitalism, which were subsequently used to forge the subsequent spirit, transforming the response to old weaknesses into new strengths: "The notion of the spirit of capitalism equally allows us to combine in one and the same dynamic the development of capitalism and the critiques that have been made of it. In fact, in our construction we are going to assign critique the role of a motor in changes in the spirit of capitalism."[92] Capitalism must therefore have recourse to extra-economic motivations, which may even have been, at the beginning, anti-economic motivations: "To maintain its powers of attraction, capitalism therefore has to draw upon resources external to it, beliefs which, at a given moment in time, possess considerable powers of persuasion, striking ideologies, even when they are hostile to it, inscribed in the cultural context in which it is developing. The spirit sustaining the accumulation process at a given point in history is thus imbued with cultural products that are contemporaneous with it and which, for the most part, have been generated to quite different ends than justifying capitalism." If capitalism proved to be so robust it is "because it has discovered routes to its survival in critiques of it. . . . It is probably this surprising capacity for survival by absorbing part of the critique that has helped to disarm anti-capitalist forces. The paradoxical consequence is that in periods when capitalism seems triumphant—as is the case today—it displays a fragility that emerges precisely when real competitors have disappeared."[93]

Critique can have three main effects: it can delegitimize previous spirits, it can help capitalism to incorporate some of the values of its opponents, and it can push capitalism into rendering itself more difficult to decipher. The consequences for critique are distressing: "Short of steering clear of the capitalist regime entirely, the only possible fate of radical critique . . . is to be used as a source of ideas and legitimacy for escaping the unduly normative and, for some actors, costly framework inherited from a prior state of capitalism."[94] Thus critique and capitalism are always renewing themselves, and often the changes achieved by critique create new problems that give rise to another type of critique.

Boltanski and Chiapello also introduce a distinction between "social critique" and "artistic critique" that has had some success. Since its beginnings, indignation against capitalism has been nourished by four main sources: disenchantment and inauthenticity; oppression by the market and the wage condition; poverty and inequality; opportunism and selfishness. The artistic critique draws mainly from the first two, while social critique from the latter two. These two types of critique were not always in agreement, the social critique often accusing the artists of immoralism and egoism, and the artists accusing social critique of conformism and narrow-mindedness. The relations between the French Communist Party (PCF) and the artistic avant-gardes were an illustration of this reality. Each critique can present itself as the most radical, and each possesses a modernist and anti-modernist side.

After 1968, faced with the impossibility of stemming protest among workers with wage increases and concessions to the unions, management opted for another strategy: accommodating the demands for personal autonomy that had spread especially among the middle and upper strata of the workforce.[95] "[N]eo-management aims to respond to demands for authenticity and freedom, which have historically been articulated in interrelated fashion by what we have called the 'artistic critique'; and that it sets to one side the issues of egoism and inequalities traditionally combined in the 'social critique'. Challenging the hitherto dominant forms of hierarchal control and affording greater freedom are thus presented . . . as a response to demands for autonomy from more highly qualified wage-workers [who] trained in a more permissive familial and educational environment [and] find it difficult to tolerate the discipline of the firm."[96]

It was a success not only because the number of strike days decreased eightfold between 1972 and 1992, but also because the concessions made to the type of demands (authenticity, freedom) that traditionally emanated from artistic milieus and that, after 1968, became a mass phenomenon, gave a new lease on life to the modalities of accumulation and the justifications that accompanied them.[97] "[T]he qualities that are guarantees of success in this new spirit – autonomy, spontaneity, rhizomorphous capacity, multitasking, . . . conviviality, openness to others and novelty, availability, creativity, visionary intuition, sensitivity to differences, listening to lived experience and receptiveness to a whole range of experiences, being attracted to informality and the search for interpersonal contacts—these are taken directly from the repertoire of May 1968," but now serve an opposite purpose.[98] The critique of hierarchy and surveillance is thus detached from the critique of commodity alienation. The critique of inauthenticity is also recuperated by conviviality, opposed to the bureaucratic formalism that tries to eradicate everything irrational.

Nevertheless, many avowed critics of capitalism did not understand, or did not want to understand, this change. For them, it was only a matter of concessions made reluctantly by an essentially nineteenth-century form of domination which always had a tendency to "quell" social and societal "conquests."[99] Boltanski and Chiapello's portrait is effective: "A majority of intellectuals made as if it was nothing, and continued . . . to regard as transgressive moral and aesthetic positions that were now incorporated into commodity goods, and offered without restriction to the public at large. [They] found an outlet in the critique of the media and mediatization as the derealization and falsification of a world where they remained the exclusive guardians of authenticity."[100] Artistic critique was therefore undermined by blurring the opposition between intellectuals and artists (the representatives of idealism) and economic elites (the representatives of realism). The contemporary artist has become a small-business owner, while the manager presents himself in turn as a "creative," moving from project to project. After authors like Bourdieu, Derrida, and Deleuze denied the very concept of a subject facing the existential alternative between authenticity and inauthenticity, it was no longer possible to denounce the "spectacle" from an external standpoint.[101] The various critiques of the concept of authenticity debased the "artistic" rejection of consumer goods, comfort, and daily mediocrity, and have rid many intellectuals of the contempt for money. A certain sociology of art, by affirming that the artist is a worker like any other, contributed to the loss of art's "aura."[102]

Boltanski and Chiapello also underline the gradual shift in the meaning of the magic word "liberation": "it can be shown that the cycles of recuperation created in the framework of capitalism play on the confusion between these two different meanings [of 'liberation'] . . . Liberation can be understood as *deliverance* from a condition of *oppression* suffered by a people, or as *emancipation* from any form of *determination* liable to restrict the self-definition and self-fulfillment of *individuals*."[103] The first term evokes the alienation specific to a group, for example workers, whereas the second is more characteristic of the artistic critique and registers the specific alienations which derive from any form of necessity, integration, or identification with a nation, trade, sex, etc. (which gives rise, for example, to struggles against "stereotypes"). In this redefinition of liberation, the legacy of the artistic avant-gardes and their search for a non-bourgeois life played an important role: "demands for autonomy and self-fulfillment assume the form given them by Parisian artists in the second half of the nineteenth century, who made *uncertainty* a lifestyle and a value: being able to possess *several lives* and, correlatively, a *multiplicity of identities*, which also presupposes the possibility of freeing oneself from any *endowment* and rejecting any *original debt*, whatever its character."[104] Artistic and literary activities had remained on the fringe of capitalism because of the indistinction between professional and personal activity, a division that, for others, proved fundamental for the sale of labor-power or for qualifications.

Today, on the contrary, features characteristic of the life of an artist in the nineteenth century, like the "lack of any distinction between time at work and time outside work, between personal friendships and professional relationships, between work and the person who performs it," have become widespread. They also generate anxieties specific to the "connexionist world."[105] Indeed, in the connexionist world, which Boltanski and Chiapello also call the "projective city," to which they devote many pages of analysis, the inability to establish lasting family, friend, or work relationships is experienced as a personal failure and leads to a devaluation of oneself that makes it difficult to form new bonds. "[E]very entity . . . exists to a greater or lesser extent depending upon the number and value of the connections that pass via it."[106] The connexionist world thus creates new forms of suffering and will therefore give rise to new forms of critique. Just as the emergence of the second spirit of capitalism partially took into account the critique of the first spirit (more security for wage-earners also means more freedom), after 1968 it was argued that this freedom had become a new form of oppression (bureaucracy, rules). Similarly, the third spirit then incorporated this critique. Is it possible today to demonstrate "that the promises have once again not been kept, and that new forms of oppression have emerged?"[107] The increase in constraints, work rhythms, and responsibilities is an unfreedom, as is the reciprocal self-discipline of workers in teams, the "control via the market and computerized control in real time but from a distance."[108] In the connexionist world, Boltanski and Chiapello tell us, critique must propose a new type of justice. The "projective city" does not "enable us to engage in activity intended to restrict the extension of commodification. Yet is it arguably there that the only critical designs capitalism cannot recuperate are to be found, because it is as it were, in essence, bound up with the commodity."[109] For the authors, if capitalism "does not restore some grounds for hope to those whose engagement is required for the functioning of the system as a whole,"[110] it could be heading towards a fatal crisis. It is therefore always a lack of consent that allegedly hurls capitalism into crisis!

New Discourse on the Miseries of Our Time

If we have referred in detail to *The New Spirit of Capitalism*, it is because the book—although far removed from the critique of value, as much in its theoretical bases as its political consequences (which remain within a "reformist-democratic" perspective)—has the advantage of attempting a global analysis of the current situation. The same cannot be said of the majority of recent descriptions, even critical ones, of the social transformations currently underway. The modifications of the subject-form, and in particular the transformation of former instances of liberation into market subjectivities, have been observed often enough. But what is generally lacking is the identification of a deeper reality, one that is more difficult to appreciate: the fetish-character of the commodity as the consequence of abstract labor. The interest of these approaches lies therefore in the accuracy of the description of the phenomena and not in their provided interpretation.

The transformation of what was subversive into an auxiliary of the new tyranny never ceases to amaze. For example, in the repressive American school of the 1950s depicted in Peter Weir's *Dead Poets Society* (1989), the nonconformist teacher tries to impart upon his students the subversive aphorism *Carpe Diem* ("seize the day") in opposition to a sacrifice to supposedly "higher" values. Today, this could be a Nike slogan—perhaps it already is. Similarly, the poem "Les Oiseaux de passage" (1876) by Jean Richepin, set to music by George Brassens, could probably be sung in unison today in any airport by yuppie neo-nomads, beneficiaries of globalization, and those that scoff at bourgeois mediocrity. Every day offers new examples of this kind of shift. Just observe the way advertising uses the words "revolution," "rebel," "escape," "subversion," or "real life."

Recent forms of colonization of the imagination have been described in detail in Naomi Klein's international bestseller *No Logo* (2000).[111] Additionally, the specific role played by counterculture and the "cool" and "youthful" spirit of the sixties is the subject of a book by Thomas Frank.[112] However, one of the authors who has best criticized the commercial exploitation of the imagination is French author Annie Le Brun. As she writes:

> Such is the nihilism that underlies technical reason, playing precisely on the missing link between cause and effect, to prevent us from representing what we are doing. The result is a real breakdown of the imagination, at the origin of the phenomenon of *generalized de-metaphorization*, through which, with the help of narcissism, most people today are pleased to find themselves; unrelentingly reinforced as avoidance of the other, this de-metaphorization precipitates a collapse of representation to such an extent that the current period endeavors to disguise it through its aesthetic of the Same, spreading itself in the art of recycling when it is not a matter of pleonasm.[113]

In a remarkable phrase, Le Brun writes that "there is no doubt that the devastation of the natural forest goes hand in hand with that of the mental forest."[114] The "de-metaphorization" evoked by Le Brun obviously refers to the importance of the metaphor not only in all poetry, but in particular with the Surrealists—among whom she claims membership. For the Surrealists, the creation, or the discovery, of unheard-of metaphors was to lead to a reversal of the relationship between things, including elements of reality. The metaphor is always to be reinvented or transformed by those who resort to it—not only in written poetry, but also in everyday life. It thus represents a true form of freedom. This distinguishes it from the "symbol," whose decline is of such concern to Dufour and other neo-Lacanians. "De-symbolization" is today as apparent as de-metaphorization. Yet the symbol necessarily retains an authoritative character: symbols are always already there and speak on behalf of a higher power. They do not lend themselves to individual inventiveness but demand respect. They are the emanation of a Grand Subject inaccessible to the "small subject." The dismantling of Grand

Subjects (if it actually took place) can indeed lead to barbarism if it occurs within the turmoil of a capitalism in crisis, replacing the bad with the worse. But if the only alternative consisted in a return to the adoration of symbols, then all attempts at liberation, like those undertaken by the Surrealists, would have been in vain.

The impoverishment of the imagination is partly due to what could be described as the *disappearance of childhood*. If it is true that childhood has never constituted an Eden of innocence, as some like to imagine, it is no less true that never in history has childhood been so widely the terrain of shameless economic exploitation. The reduction of child labor in the "developed" countries cannot hide the fact that today children must earn their right to life by massively *serving* in the running of the economy. This fact is obvious. It must be recognized that the damage inflicted upon their psyches is no less severe than that inflicted upon their bodies, when subjected to heavy physical work. The standardization of the imagination by video games, to cite only one particularly flagrant example, impoverishes the developing human being as much as carrying bricks all day deforms its body. The excess of images is already an attack on the blossoming of human potential: a chasm opens up between content transmitted by words, with the possible support of some images through stories and books, and hyper-realistic images that prevent the formation of a personal imagination. This difference is much more important than whether the content is "violent" or not. A healthy childhood in a world where Baby TV exists (launched in 2003 by the Fox corporation) is easier said than done . . . Besides, the kind of addiction created by electronic images seems to be quite similar to the effects of hard drugs, and saving your child from the effects of permanent exposure to electronic devices can be as difficult as keeping them away from drugs and gangs when you live in a favela. To speak of a "stolen childhood" today not only refers to the abuses and deprivation that so often occupy sensational media attention.[115]

At the same time, while the status of childhood has changed radically, we have to admit of the *infantilization of adults*. For a long time, childhood represented the *other* of capitalist society, its opposite: play rather than work, spending rather than saving, immediacy rather than expectation, enjoyment rather than renunciation, joyful disorder rather than patient construction, desire rather than asceticism, emotion rather than cold rationality, spontaneous chatter rather than structured language, seduction rather than effort, enthusiastic scribbling rather than constructed perspective, etc. Children were brutally educated in the values of society and "remaining a child" was incompatible with participation in community life. "Humanity had to inflict terrible injuries on itself before the self—the identical, purpose-directed, masculine character of human beings—was created, and something of this process is repeated in every childhood," wrote Horkheimer and Adorno in their work on the genealogy of the Western man.[116] In the course of the twentieth century, a lot has changed: critique of the capitalist way of life has often taken the form of an exaltation of childhood, especially in the artistic world. Today, it is the values of childhood (or presented as such) that drive capitalism, particularly its high-tech sectors. The perfect capitalist subject often behaves like a child—in consumption, but also sometimes with regard to management (thus, in financial markets, the time horizon is extremely short-sighted and erratic behavior is rampant). In the past, capitalism could be accused of bullying the child in each of us; today, we should rather accuse it of infantilizing us. Rather than speak of a "disappearance of childhood" as described by media theorist Neil Postman,[117] we can say that "[n]owhere is there any entry into adulthood," as Guy Debord already noted in 1961.[118] Additionally, American political scientist Benjamin Barber has published the highly acclaimed book *Consumed: How Markers Corrupt Children, Infantilize Adults, and Swallow Citizens Whole*.[119] But infantilization is not only a process specific to the world of consumption; there is also an infantilization of production that results from the loss of skilled craftsmanship.[120] Many activities are transformed into games and work is presented as "fun." But at the same time, the logic of work and "performance" is extended to the whole of life and fun is transformed into work, both of which are governed by the laws of competition and efficiency. This abolition of the boundary between work and leisure leads to a society without rest.[121] The permanent acceleration and, paradoxically, the resulting "lack of time" have been described by Lothar Baier and Hartmut Rosa,[122] and long before them by Paul Virilio.

Almost all human faculties have been outsourced and entrusted to machines that even a child can operate at the touch of a button. In many ways, individuals in pre-industrial societies seem more "adult" while modern individuals seem to be "regressing." The more "advanced" a society becomes, the more infantile it appears to many observers, especially in the United States. This is evident, to cite an example already mentioned, by the rise of preference for sweetness in taste and junk food at the expense of bitter and/or finer foods, such as certain traditional wines (replaced by peach or vanilla flavored wines) and certain artisanal cheeses (sometimes banned for "hygienic" reasons). This is also evident in the diminished importance, in almost all productive processes, of the physical strength, skill, and experience on which crafts and agriculture were based, while an eight-year-old child can become a "computer genius." Also worth noting is the preference given to images over speech and the almost non-existent role of individual memory in relation to external memory aids, as well as the greatly increased role of children within the family, especially where they influence purchasing decisions. Previously, life was a long apprenticeship, even after reaching adulthood, where any abilities were acquired through a demanding process for which one could not take shortcuts, one that required above all practice and time. Technological advances, while relying on complex yet hidden procedures that the user need not understand, allows for the simplification of each stage and for these shortcuts. The slow formation of a personality through the valorization of "character," "common sense," "experience," "long-term reflection," or "patience" is no longer required. Growing up does not bring much benefit anymore. It is no longer a matter of gradually entering the fascinating and previously unattainable world of adults. Becoming an adult no longer means gaining autonomy and a better understanding of the mysteries of the world, nor does it mean acquiring additional rights that somehow compensate for the loss of childhood privileges. Children, and *a fortiori* adolescents, now have little incentive to grow up.

This joint absence of childhood and adulthood has undermined a central aspect of human existence: *experience*. Experience can be understood as the ability to learn from what one has lived through with an eye towards the future, and as the integration of life's events into a *meaningful whole* that goes beyond any particular event. It is closely related to *narrative*, which has also disappeared from the horizon of modern life.[123] Over the course of the twentieth century, experience (*Erfahrung* in German: what one has gone through, from which one learns a useful lesson) has been increasingly replaced by the event (*Erlebnis* in German: what has occurred, what has merely happened without knowing how), akin to emotion. The *Bildungsroman*, a specific product of bourgeois culture, was based on the *construction of experience*. Whether the hero succeeded, like Wilhelm Meister, or failed, like Julien Sorel, he always achieved the essential: meaning was given to his life and the particular elements, including those that were painful, were conceived as part of a whole that freed them from their insignificance or negative character. In the end, it comes full circle. The increasing impossibility of writing a *Bildungsroman*—which today sounds meaningless and dull if it does not end with the realization of the *impossibility* of such a harmonious conclusion—is an eloquent indication of the loss of meaning in capitalist society and the fragmentation of experience.

Narcissism and experience are two antithetical forms of existence. The narcissist, by relating everything to oneself and being incapable of establishing objectal relations, cannot truly have experiences: these require losing oneself in the surrounding world in order to find oneself again, enriched by what was found.[124] Consequently, the rise of narcissism went hand in hand with the replacement of experience by *Erlebnis*— discontinuous occurrences. In contrast to experience, which always includes the ability of the individual to elaborate upon the experience undergone and which ideally leads to a form of wisdom, *Erlebnis* can be sold as a commodity and used to sell other commodities. This is evident today: on the one hand, the sale of emotions has become the driving force of advertising, which associates unrelated feelings with the most banal products. One does not buy a pair of shoes for its qualities, but for the emotions it supposedly represents. The sophisticated boutiques of the most fashionable brands invite people to spend time there as an *Erlebnis*, to experience the emotion; the purchase of any product is instead a secondary consequence (a "shopping experience" in the "shopping temples").[125] The organization of "events" and "adventures," be it an artistic performance or a trip to Tibet, has also become a "cutting edge" economic sector. In addition, the *experience economy* is based on the ability to turn anything into an *experience*, an emotionally moving event.[126]

This arbitrary association between a commodity and emotional value is predominantly based on the external *form* of the commodity: it is the *aestheticization of the world* and the *triumph of design*. Design was invented by William Morris, the Bauhaus, and the Russian Constructivists between the end of the nineteenth century and the 1920s with a democratic purpose: to allow for the large-scale production of high-quality objects, especially artistic ones, thus favoring their distribution to all segments of the population. But its nature changed completely after the Second World War and ended up swallowing all sectors of culture: visual arts and everyday objects, film and photography, architecture and urban planning now exist almost exclusively as branches of a unified design. This is particularly visible in architecture, which often only aims at "creating emotions" for visitors. The extreme utilitarianism of the commodity has been accompanied for some decades now by an extreme aestheticism.[127]

Without going into detail, it is also clear that the virtualization of the world and life in "social networks" have enormously increased narcissistic tendencies, which are not limited to the culture of the "selfie" and the permanent customizing of one's "profile" in order to obtain as many "likes" as possible. Rarely has there been a more accurate and perfect realization of market democracy and equality than in Andy Warhol's prophecy: "In the future, everyone will be world-famous for fifteen minutes." The internet represents both the dream of capital—that of a potentially infinite expansion, without physical constraints—and the narcissistic dream of subjects—that of a life without limits. This derealization curiously goes hand in hand with a "reality overload," a "tyranny of reality," where we only pass from the same to the same, incessantly copying already existing realities *ad nauseam*.[128] But this paradox is only an appearance: the limitation of "reality," in the flattest sense of the term, the lack of imagination and the denigration of "utopianism" in the name of "realism"—this kind of capitulation to social reality, as if it were "natural," is accompanied by a replacement of directly perceived things by industrially manufactured images that often do not respect any form of "reality" or its limits.

We are only just beginning to measure the consequences of the anthropological revolution initiated by digitalization, not only at the social level but also at the neural level.[129] The very status of the subject and the individual seems to be affected: commentators speak—sometimes with enthusiasm, other times with concern—of the possible overcoming of the "individual" (the "indivisible") to the benefit of a "multividuum," where the individual human being would only exist as an element of a collective intelligence, comparable to bees, making it possible to talk of "distributed" or "swarm intelligence."[130] This intelligence would reside in the *cloud*, where all the data and memory needed by the individual would be stored; never mind if the entirety of knowledge becomes the property of a single corporation or if a solar storm wipes out all existing magnetic data.[131] Let us add to this the widespread aspiration towards the infinite manipulation of the human body, which is no longer accepted as a "limit" but as "material"—whereas genetic manipulation and fantasies about "transhumanism" confirm the marriage between technologies and human biology; not to mention that the narcissistic desire for omnipotence produces, *via* new technologies, heights of delirium unimaginable even just thirty years ago.

A Transformation Older Than Digital Technology

Other transformations of the subject began before the digital revolution. French sociologist Alain Ehrenberg was one of the first to analyze the permanent recreation of the subject through drug use, media exposure, and life-coaching. In *The Uncertain Individual* (1995), he emphasizes that the contemporary subject must struggle, often without succeeding, with tasks different from those of the past, but which remain quite severe: "We have entered a society of self-responsibility: everyone is compelled to find a project and act on their own behalf in order not to be excluded from social life, regardless of the weakness of the cultural, economic, and social resources at their disposal. . . . [There are] two sources for our confusion: the restoration of the feeling of the self, which drugs or psychotropic medication provide, and the reconstruction of the image of the self that television has been offering for years."[132] Life is no longer a collective destiny, Ehrenberg observes, but a personal story. It must be added that individuals depend as much as before on processes that they can neither perceive nor influence, but for which they are nevertheless completely responsible. Today, we are less compelled towards "automatic behaviors or attitudes" than to "be responsible for ourselves."[133] "The qualities of availability, openness to others, negotiation, and communication are required for everyone, whereas they were completely unknown to most people thirty or thirty-five years ago. Inhibition is becoming a handicap for social and relational integration, and self-confidence an increasing asset."[134] It is no longer just professional skills, but the individual's entire personality that must be sold, and a lot of energy must be devoted to making it suitable for available buyers.[135] Ehrenberg also notes that the injunction to constantly enjoy at all costs often crushes the individual: "There has been an exchange of moral guilt for guilt towards others and the self, along with no longer feeling capable of enjoyment and of making others enjoy themselves."[136]

Ehrenberg defines the seemingly chosen "uncertainty" of the contemporary individual as resulting from the need to construct a place for itself. Like Boltanski and Chiapello, he locates its origins in the artistic bohemia of yesteryear: "We are dealing here with the generalization of a mode of existence of individuality long limited to elites or artists, to a kind of experience discernible at the beginning of the nineteenth century in literature and polite society, through the dandy and the artist who were the first to construct their identity around an 'obligation of uncertainty.' This mode of existence is today that of everyone, but to different degrees and unequally in the upscale neighborhoods and in the slums."[137]

Faced with such overwhelming and difficult obligations, the individual is easily seduced by the support offered by the market and technologies: "The evolution of the relationship to television and psychotropic drugs is characteristic of the massive development of identity technologies and self-esteem industries. They are built on the integration of subjectivity in the technological, whether it comes from the fields of pharmacology or electronics. . . . The individual is *today* autonomous only insofar as it relies on the assistance of various mechanisms of external support."[138] Ehrenberg also emphasizes how individuals resort to drugs in order to continue working and assert themselves in competition. Drugs arrived in France as a form of *psychic-building* alongside "the spirit of enterprise, competition, adventure, and extreme sports."[139] They "are beginning to be perceived as the doping of individual action and are now the chemical assistants of an individual held to be the entrepreneur of its own life."[140] According to Ehrenberg, there is thus a link between the neoliberal rhetoric of the "responsibility of the individual" and the massive use of drugs. Psychotropic drugs "tend more to be a means of increasing one's performance and psychic comfort than an escape from reality, a form of passivity, or an aspect of hedonism." In short, it is simply a matter of *doping*.[141] Today, working on oneself is no longer a matter of introspection and discipline, but of chemical substances and self-help gurus.

The proliferation of socially accepted drugs, such as Prozac, entails three major risks, according to Ehrenberg. First, personal change is now less about understanding oneself than about being understood by a specialist. Secondly, depression is now considered an illness. Finally, "increasing difficulties in coping with frustrations, due to the lack of means for differentiating between pathological suffering and ordinary unhappiness, contributes, in a vicious cycle, to a decreasing capacity to cope with problems without chemical assistance. These difficulties can only increase in a society of self-responsibility, where academic, professional, or social failure is increasingly imputed to the individual itself and leads to mass frustrations that were unknown in previous societies of destiny."[142] The medicalization of psychological suffering—which leads to sadness considered as an illness—profoundly changes the relationship of the subject to itself: "We will follow Édouard Zarifian when he writes that 'we have progressively moved from the treatment of psychological disorders . . . to the systematic medicalization of simple existential psychological suffering.'"[143] It is thus no longer a question of solving a temporary problem, but of offering palliatives without which existence itself is impossible: "We know less and less how to heal, but will have to learn more and more how to give assistance."[144]

The individual is permanently required to be "responsible" for their own life, yet without having the means to do so. This, according to Anglo-Polish sociologist Zygmunt Bauman, is the basis of the opposition between "solid society" and "liquid society." The "scenarios" that used to guide us (discussed at the beginning of this chapter) have lost much of their importance in the context of an "advanced" society, and the struggle against what remains of them (especially in the area of "gender") has become a favorite activity of so-called "progressives." This is not to be nostalgic for such scenarios, but their disappearance, without giving people the opportunity to determine the course of their own lives, has made them extremely vulnerable. Contemporary individuals are disoriented by the incessant obligation to make decisions about almost every aspect of their lives, but without really being able to decide anything. They can no longer be excused for being born in the countryside, for being a woman, working class, being from an immigrant family, or for their specific physique: if they do not have the life they want, it is their fault and their fault alone. It is because they did not work hard enough, did not follow their diet properly, did not purchase the right laptop model, did not "manage their relationships" well enough . . .

CHAPTER 4
THE CRISIS OF THE SUBJECT-FORM

Like value, the subject-form—which at once both creates value and is created by it—has been in crisis for several decades. According to the usual understanding of the term, the subject is self-preservation, an affirmation of the self. In the words of Spinoza: "No virtue can be conceived as prior to this—namely, the endeavour to preserve oneself."[1] This assertion is the basis of modern thought.[2] However, as we have seen, the subject-form is far from being based solely on rationality and on a rational pursuit of its "interests": it also has a "dark side." This dichotomy of the subject-form refers both to the "splitting" between the sphere of value and the sphere of non-value and to the fact that actions which seem to obey the reality principle are often only detours for realizing more sinister designs which origi-nate in early childhood, especially in the case of the narcissist.[3]

The Death Drive of Capitalism

This "dark side" finds its most extreme form in endless destruction and self-destruction. Aggression is not in itself inexplicable or irra-tional behavior: it can be aimed at appropriating property or bodies, either to enslave them or to obtain libidinal satisfaction from them. What is much more difficult to explain is "autotelic violence," as German sociologist Jan Reemtsma calls it in *Trust and Violence*.[4] This is violence whose aim is its own satisfaction and which not only does not increase the well-being of the aggressor, but often costs them dearly, committed at the cost of damaging oneself and, in some bor-derline cases, of self-destruction. Acts incompatible with the simplistic assumption of an omnipresent "survival instinct" have always existed. Today, however, suffering, destruction, and death—of others as well as of oneself—are no longer a *means* of achieving a goal belonging to the order of life's interests, but have become *ends in themselves.*

Since the late nineties, there has been a proliferation of premeditated massacres in schools, universities, workplaces, and other public spaces, mainly but not only in the United States; attacks labeled as "jihadist" without fitting into the traditional categories of politics and religion; unmotivated attacks, even murders—often as a result of a "sidelong glance"—in public places; ferocious attacks on immigrants, marginalized people, or homosexuals. We can also cite the 2015 case of Germanwings flight 9525, whose co-pilot intentionally flew the aircraft into a mountain. We know of the sadistic violence deployed by criminal organizations linked to drug trafficking, especially in Brazil and Mexico, whose perpetrators know with near certainty that they will die young. We are also aware of the "senseless killing" in families deemed to be "ordinary," often in suburban areas; the acts of dangerous vandalism, such as throwing rocks off highway overpasses; and the torture and murders committed by upper class youth with the sole aim of experiencing an "exciting thrill."[5] Even the revolts in the poor suburbs of major French, English, and North American cities have increasingly lost their political character and are sometimes reduced to mere outbursts of rage. Despite their obvious differences, and the unfathomable element of any individual act, a certain "family resemblance" emerges from these actions that goes beyond classification and statistics.[6] Their increase, but especially their specific features, call for particular attention. We will attempt to explain them here, at least in part, by the general crisis of the subject-form, which corresponds to the crisis of the value-form and leads to a real "death drive," where destruction and self-destruction coexist. The suicidal tendencies of globalized capitalism have their counterpart in the suicidal tendencies of many individuals, whether latent or declared. In other words, the irrationality of capitalism corresponds to the irrationality of its subjects. This phenomenon expresses all too well the decline of the subject-form and the becoming-visible of its hidden essence, which has existed since its origins.

These forms of violence cannot be explained by the "interests" of the perpetrators and thus belie the utilitarianism dear to both liberals and traditional Marxists alike. Nor would it make sense to evade the issue by citing the numerous manifestations of violence observed throughout history, in order to conclude that we are not worse off today than in the past and that such acts are nothing new under the sun. This diffusion of the death drive on such a large scale and in such varied forms, in all strata of the population and across the whole surface of the globe, is, at least in times of "peace," historically unprecedented. The question, however, is not whether violence has increased, but rather, what are the *characteristic forms* of contemporary violence.

It was Freud who first asserted the existence of a "death drive" that goes beyond simple aggression. It is also one of his most difficult and controversial notions to grasp. We will limit ourselves to recalling that Freud introduced the term, breaking with many of his previous concepts, in *Beyond the Pleasure Principle*, where he attempted to elaborate a reflection on the experience of the First World War. In particular, he confronted phenomena that seemed incompatible with the fundamental psychoanalytic principle that every human being seeks only their own pleasure. In his essay, Freud moves quickly from the historical situation to a level that he himself describes as "very speculative" by emphasizing the death drive, in the final analysis, as a cosmic tendency towards decomposition and to the return towards the calm of inorganic matter.[7] The death drive, however, is opposed by Eros, the force that seeks to compose and unite dispersed elements into more elaborate constructions, whether family, culture, or society.

Despite the highly speculative character of this "death drive," which contrasts with Freud's usual desire to remain strictly within the bounds of the scientific attitude, and despite the strong resistance this concept encountered from the outset among many of his followers, Freud retained it until his death. He gave it a central role in the last synthesis of his theory, *An Outline of Psychoanalysis* (1938). The libidinal drives and the drives of self-preservation, whose opposition had previously occupied an important place in his theoretical edifice, were reunited under the name "life drives," antagonistic to the "death drives." In *Civilization and Its Discontents* (1930) and *Why War?* (1933), Freud used this concept to explain the destructive impulses of contemporary culture.

Among the many opaque aspects of the concept of the "death drive" is its relationship to aggression. On the one hand, Freud identifies the death drive with the "Nirvana principle" or "principle of constancy," that is, with the supposed tendency of any organism to reduce tensions to the lowest level, or to maintain them at a constant level—which is not the same thing, as Laplanche and Pontalis emphasize, although that is not the essential point here.[8] It would thus consist in the search for a state without tensions or desires, a state of absolute rest. Apart from a return to the single-cell organism or inorganic matter, such a state can be found in the prenatal situation, with the death drive considered as the desire for its return—or the return to postnatal primary narcissism. The death drive is therefore linked to narcissism, although Freud does not place much emphasis on this connection.[9] On the other hand, the life drive pushes the death drive outwards to avoid the self-destruction of the living organism. It is then transformed into aggression and is much easier to observe. The requirements of life in society—which Freud calls "culture"—finally oblige the individual to renounce the integral practice of this outward discharge onto the external world and to direct part of its aggression towards itself. But human beings, Freud assures us, accept this restriction of their aggression with reluctance, which ends up constituting the basis of war and other violence.

The role of the death drive within Freud's late theoretical work—the "second topography"—poses many problems, especially with regard to its relationship with the "pleasure principle" and the psychic instances of the ego, id, and superego. Most psychoanalytic authors therefore abandoned the concept, either implicitly or explicitly. As we have seen, Marcuse is a notable exception: rather than rejecting a concept that seemed incompatible with any "progressive" interpretation of psychoanalysis, he accepted and confronted it. According to him, this drive does indeed exist, but it has historical causes and its impact on social life can be drastically reduced.

The strength of the Freudian concept of the death drive is that it not only refers to aggression as it has been so frequently analyzed, for example in ethology—to which Erich Fromm refers extensively in his late book *The Anatomy of Human Destructiveness* —where it explains the advantages it brings to the agent of aggression.[10] Freud also attempts to explain aggression towards the self, which is much more difficult to understand. The weakness of his explanation, in our opinion, derives from its anthropological, ontological, even cosmic character. Any form of violence appears there only as a particular case of a very general phenomenon. However, like Marcuse, who took the "death drive" seriously and built upon it a critique of capitalism, it must be admitted that some destructive drives have been present in human beings since the very beginning and do not derive only from a corrupted but otherwise pristine human nature. Capitalism did not invent these drives, but it broke down the barriers that restrained them and favored their expression, often in order to exploit them.

A different direction will be pursued here: rather than questioning the death drive as an ontological principle, we will try and use the concept to understand the present state of the subject-form in the period of the decomposition of capitalism. Let us leave the single-celled amoebas in peace and ask ourselves how this concept, even with its somewhat metaphorical significance, can help us understand the unleashing of destructive forces in the modern and contemporary era.

Running Amok and Jihad

A particularly striking manifestation of a pure "death drive" in contemporary society is *running amok*. It originally referred to an outburst of murderous madness existing in Malaysian culture, where it formed a "ritualized deviant behavior," as ethnopsychiatry puts it. It referred to an individual who, usually after being affronted, would rush out into the street and, in a trance-like state, start killing people at random with a knife, before being overpowered and eventually killed. For several decades, this term—made familiar by the title of a novel by Stefan Zweig published in 1922—has been used in Germany to describe acts that in English are generally referred to as "school shootings," "mass killings," "lone-wolf attacks," etc.

In its most characteristic form, *running amok* refers to the act of an individual who enters a school, university, cinema, or other public place and shoots people at point-blank range, usually ending with suicide. Although there have been killings of this kind since the beginning of the twentieth century, it was not until the 1990s that the phenomenon became so widespread. The so-called Columbine massacre, named after the American high school in Colorado and resulting in the death of fifteen people on April 20th, 1999, is the best known and constitutes a kind of "paradigmatic" example of *running amok*. It is also the most studied. The deadliest mass killing was at Virginia Tech University in the United States in 2007, where thirty-two people were killed. The vast majority of these killings have occurred in the United States, Germany, and Finland, but at least thirty other countries have experienced *running amok* in schools in recent decades.

A sort of "ideal type" portrait can be drawn of the school mass murderer: a young man, even a teenager, who grew up in a "quiet" family, even if his parents are often divorced. He is not known to be violent and has no criminal record. Not very sociable, he spends a lot of time on the internet and playing video games. Excluded from social life and struggling with school or work, he has a painful relationship to his own life and future. He is gradually overtaken by resentment and depression and, unable to envisage any positive outcome to his life, conceives the project of leaving this world with a bang, in a spectacular display, taking with him as many people as possible. This day of glory is carefully prepared, sometimes through his journal or on the internet, sometimes by providing vague hints to his classmates. The modern scenario of *running amok*, unlike the ethnological case to which it owes its name, is not spontaneous and does not arise from a sudden burst of anger. It is the result of calculation, of slow ripening.

Usually, the "lone-wolf" acts alone—the two Columbine massacre perpetrators were an exception—after obtaining weapons.[11] When the planned day finally arrives, he "posts" a message on the internet or leaves a kind of testimony. At the scene of the killing, often dressed in black and without saying a word, he begins shooting in cold blood those he finds in his path. He continues until he is killed by police or turns the gun on himself, sometimes after a shootout. Some commit suicide after their arrest. Almost every killing is a kind of "extended suicide."

These traits form a kind of "common basis" with many variations. For example, some of them kill relatives, especially their mothers, before leaving the house. They are not known to be directly politically motivated in the sense of participating in organized activities—the future perpetrator of *running amok* lives at home and does not regularly socialize, nor does anything enthuse him. However, some of them are openly racist and display sympathies with the extreme right. The two teenagers who committed the Columbine massacre consciously chose April 20th, the anniversary of Hitler's birth, and one of them had expressed racist, antisemitic, homophobic, and sexist beliefs in his journal.[12]

The location of *running amok* is usually somewhere the killer has experienced a series of what they considered to be unbearable humiliations: above all high school, sometimes universities, more rarely the workplace, but also in places such as the German employment office.[13] Massive resentment, the feeling of having suffered an injustice and of not having received what one deserves invariably form the psychological background of the one who *runs amok*. The cases of "classic" *running amok*—a few dozen killings which, in total, have resulted in a few hundred deaths—have aroused considerable emotion, especially in Germany, where there is now a rich literature on the subject (the peculiarity of the French scenario will be mentioned shortly). *Running amok*, although very rare, tends to seize the collective imagination because of its highly significant character.

Beginning in 2010, numerous events occurred that had several elements in common with the "classic" *running amok*, but differed in important ways. In 2012, in a cinema in Aurora, Colorado, a young man dressed as "Batman" killed twelve people at the premiere of a film about the superhero, but did not commit suicide afterwards. The act of the Germanwings co-pilot who crashed his plane into the French Alps in 2015 bears many similarities to *running amok*, although it seems that the perpetrator hesitated until the last moment between a "normal" and "extended" suicide—he had been suffering from depression for a long time and feared losing his job precisely because of his illness and other related disorders.

More recently, the lines between an "unmotivated" *running amok* and ideologically motivated acts have begun to blur, opening a new chapter in the history of mass murder. Suicide bombings by Islamists in the early eighties already had some features in common with *running amok*—including the recording of a video testament before the act. A few rare commentators have not failed to make this connection clear. As early as 2001, shortly after the September 11th attacks, Robert Kurz wrote that the immolations could not be explained only by the particularities of an "archaic" religion or culture, but also demonstrated decidedly modern elements. He also recalled that the perpetrators of the Columbine massacre had also imagined hijacking a plane and crashing it into New York.[14]

The mass murder perpetrated in July 2011 by Norwegian Anders Breivik displayed certain characteristics of *running amok*, but possessed features that were altogether distinct. For example, the perpetrator did not commit suicide and turned his trial into a political forum, justifying his actions with racist ideological considerations. The Charleston massacre in June 2015, which left nine people dead in a Black Methodist church, was perpetrated by a white "supremacist" who also left a "manifesto" and hoped to incite further acts—he too did not commit suicide.

But it was mainly the attacks attributed to the Islamic State (ISIS) that mixed the genres. The attacks on *Charlie Hebdo* and the Bataclan theater in January and November 2015 in Paris, as well as the one in Brussels in March 2016, were still classic political attacks carried out by prepared commandos who had been operating in the Salafist movement for years. The case of the San Bernardino, California shooting is more complicated: on December 2nd, 2015, a couple of Pakistani origin who had just had a child opened fire in a medical center, killing fourteen people before fleeing and being shot by police. In Orlando, Florida on June 12th, 2016, a man of Afghan origin, twice married and a father known for his violent temper, murdered forty-nine people in a gay nightclub before being shot by police. The Islamist motivation was most evident in Mohamed Merah's March 2012 attacks on a Jewish school. The very troubled personality of the killer is undoubtedly a determining factor in the act. The framework is further challenged in the case of the employee of North African origin who beheaded his boss in Isère in June 2015 and then displayed an Islamic State flag; it is also challenged in the case of the Nice massacre on July 14th, 2016. We can also mention other, less striking actions where individuals with a Muslim immigrant background, but who were not distinguished by any particular religious observance and had backgrounds of erratic behavior punctuated by minor offenses, decided to make a dramatic exit from a personal situation they perceived as utterly hopeless. This generally occurred after what the media call a "flash radicalization," often carried out on the internet. These individuals acted alone but chose, at the last moment, to claim themselves as members of the Islamic State, thus giving "meaning" to their actions by linking them to an imaginary community. Shouting "Allah Akbar" at the moment of the act, even if nothing in his life had predisposed him towards Islamic martyrdom, also ensures the killer a certain media resonance, by referring to the idea of an international nihilism. This obviously does not prevent others from faithfully pursuing this path for years before making the ultimate sacrifice.

It is not possible here to examine a subject like jihadism at length, even if we limit ourselves to its European dimension. The phenomenon has too many different facets and is constantly changing. Let us just say that recalling the psychopathological dimension of acts described as "jihadist" in no way means denying or underestimating the dimension that could be called "political." The biographical trajectories that lead killers to commit their acts are not the result of "personal" problems but are the direct reflection of social factors. Even if some of those *running amok* or jihadists were undergoing psychological or psychiatric treatment, often for depression, this does not mean that we can account for these phenomena by looking at individual psychologies. It would be just as erroneous to take their ideological motivations literally. Islamist terrorism would never have found such a high number of adherents in Western countries if it had not been able to draw on a reserve of people ready to commit homicide-suicide out of a desperation caused by ongoing social collapse. The increasing diversity of the profiles of killers testifies to how much this form of self-destructive hatred has spread throughout very different groups of the population. Men and women, "native" Europeans or immigrants, rich or poor, misfits or university graduates—anyone can be captured by hatred and the desire to sacrifice themselves in a final blaze of glory.[15]

Another indication of the kinship, even parallelism, between *running amok* and jihadism is their geographical distribution. France had long been spared the school shooting, but this "French exception" came to an end in March 2017, when a student, explicitly inspired by the Columbine massacre, injured several people in his Grasse high school.[16] This quite "typical" case of *running amok* in school fortunately did not achieve the tragic fate of its original. Until then, France had only known two cases close to *running amok*: the killing in Tours in October 2001, when a former railway worker killed four bystanders in the street, and the vaguely politically motivated massacre of the Nanterre city council by Richard Durn in March 2002. The latter wrote a testimonial letter quite characteristic of *running amok*: "I will become a serial killer, a murderous madman. Why? Because I am frustrated but I don't want to die alone, because I've had a shitty life, I want to feel powerful and free just once." France, on the other hand, holds the sad record for jihadist acts in Europe. Germany, on the other hand, has the highest number in Europe of *running amok* in schools or on the street—such as the shooting in a Munich McDonald's in July 2016—as well as fatal assaults without motive or caused by trivial altercations in public spaces. It is as if these two forms of killing, jihadist acts and "classic" *running amok*, beyond their apparent motivations or lack thereof, occupy roughly the same "niche" in collective psychology.[17] Furthermore, if the psychological profiles of the perpetrators differ, what they have in common is a nameless and boundless despair and hatred that aims at self-destruction as much as destruction. The targets (infidels or homosexuals, classmates or politicians, teachers or simple bystanders) seem interchangeable. Moreover, different modalities of violence are amalgamated within everyday life, including traditional and archaic forms, essentially focused on the defense of "masculine honor," even expressed through technology, such as livestreaming the crime on social networks.

Explaining the killings by the "hatred of the other" is a rather limited approach. Racism and homophobia are not new. What needs to be explained is the "action itself." We are probably not so much faced with an increase in murderous impulses as with the *levée des garde-fous* (a very beautiful French expression, unknown in other languages) that prevented the realization of those impulses.[18] It is not necessarily the hatred that is new, but the large number of people who are willing to die to satisfy it without any other benefit. The social transformation of the last decades has deprived many individuals of the antibodies necessary to contain the "sad passions" which, if they are not always products of capitalist society alone, have certainly flourished there like poisonous flowers on a rotting corpse.

Mutatis mutandis, one might be tempted to draw a parallel with another very rare pathology, observed since the 1980s but which is also striking because of its highly symbolic character: multiple chemical sensitivity disorder. Anyone suffering from this serious condition is forced to live in a sterile environment because they cannot survive contact (in the most severe cases) with certain common chemical substances. These substances are generally from industrial production (pesticides, exhaust fumes, dyes, solvents, and other industrial compounds). However, as in the case of allergies and their tremendous rise in recent decades, the problem is not only the presence of harmful substances in the environment, however important, but also a dramatic decrease in antibodies, natural defenses, and the immune system in general. This decrease seems to be one of the most dramatic consequences of capitalist and industrial society for the human psyche and body, and could well constitute in the next

few years one of the main battlegrounds of the war between eco-
nomic-technological rationality and living reason.

Understanding *Running Amok*

As just mentioned, Germany is the European country most affected by school shootings. The considerable emotional distress caused
by these acts has as much to do with the fact that the victims were
children or young people as with the lack of motivation that makes
them difficult to understand and rationalize. Among the many authors who have studied the subject, with very different results, Götz
Eisenberg has best analyzed the causal link between *running amok* and
capitalist society. Trained in the Frankfurt School tradition and close
to the critique of value, he worked for decades as a prison psychologist, where he met many violent offenders. He has written four books
since 2000, which mainly derive from articles and essays written in
many cases immediately after new cases of *running amok*. Eisenberg
not only examines *running amok* in schools, but also other forms of
violent and criminal behavior, especially those that appear "gratu-
itous" and "explosive." He also relates them to many behaviors considered "normal," such as the resurgence of xenophobia in Germany or the addiction to cell phones. He does not think of *running amok*
as a mysterious and incomprehensible irruption of a foreign element
in "our" lives, but as the extreme point of a "cold" society governed
by the principle of economic rationality and which subjects young
children to its demands at an early age. According to him, it is surprising that there are not *more instances* of *running amok*, since, as he
writes, "who could say that they have never felt the temptation to
destroy everything and end it all?" The large number of more or less
serious threats of *running amok* after each massacre demonstrates, if
it were even necessary, that for every actual instance of *running amok*,
there are a hundred more merely contemplated.

According to Michel Foucault, the "disciplinary society" that
emerged with the Enlightenment designates a society governed by
a form of power based on an increasing internalization of social
constraints. This form of power was the response to a particular

problem: "How to make men work willingly and to allow the products of their labor be appropriated from them without protest?"[19] It was through the formation of the superego, which created an active identification of subjects with the state and the economy, that this problem found resolution. Traditional education was often brutal, and what human beings had to repress in pain and fear was projected onto others in order to rid themselves of it, to objectify and hate it. These forms of education aimed at subjecting the rhythms and needs of children to a rigid organization, generally through physical punishment and humiliation. The child reacted by developing a "shell," preventing them from feeling their own body and emotions as well as those of others. This produced, says Eisenberg, the insensitivity necessary to face competition in bourgeois society and to kill without hesitation in modern warfare.

Authoritarian education—"poisonous pedagogy," in the words of child psychologist Alice Miller—was gradually replaced, especially after 1968, by other forms of education that also subjected children to the demands of capitalist society, although less by direct violence than by *indifference*. From an early age, children are often made to believe that work, consumer objects, and especially electronic "communication" devices are more important to their parents than are the children themselves. Behind the alleged tolerance of today's educational system, children are often left to fend for themselves and to their electronic devices.[20] The relationship of indifference towards meaningless and easily disposable things is also transmitted to the relationship between people: anyone can be replaced by anyone at the first sign of difficulty. Children feel lost in a world where no one responds to their cries for help.

Education today no longer serves to limit primary narcissism, nor does it teach how to bear frustrations. As such, sitting in front of screens, children develop limitless fantasies. Even parents who take education seriously and want to structure their children's superego find themselves struggling with the often more powerful influences that technology exerts on them, even within the confines of their bedrooms. The risk for children is to miss their "psychic birth," to no longer find limits that oppose their feeling of infantile omnipotence—limits that are embedded in living and loved ones and teach them to bear frustrations and criticism. This explains why children or adolescents sometimes prefer to resort to pain—through piercings or scarification, for example—experienced as a tangible "reality" that allows them to "feel" the presence of a limit, of something or someone, rather than becoming lost in an abysmal void. In a life dominated by audio-visual technologies, we no longer "touch" anything:[21]

> Nobody and nothing overtly oppresses them [children], but they have been robbed of the essential: they thus grow up as psychically frigid human beings not knowing who to blame for their nameless unhappiness or where they can direct their accumulated rage. Hatred and widespread narcissistic malaise are not today, in general, the consequence of failed object relations, nor of wounds inflicted by severe parents, but of a human and educational nirvana that is also found, and perhaps especially, among the middle classes. Nothing and nobody give the drives of children and young people a duration and a form, and their self-esteem cannot be increased by warming up to the market and monetary subjectivity of their environment. Neglected education and loneliness in front of screens can result in a hatred without subject and without object, totally 'pure,' generating a blind and free-floating violence, a 'purposeless' criminality that remains an enigma for its victims, the police, the justice system, and criminal psychologists. Their search for understandable motives leads to nothing concrete, but the absence of concrete motives is perhaps the real motive. . . . Hate and *running amok* are born from the cold, from the lack of relationship to the object, from the mounting indifference and emptiness.[22]

The problem is not that education has become too "free" and that it is necessary to return to an education that exercises a fair "reduction of *jouissance*," as the Lacanians would say. Contemporary education—which is obviously a widespread *tendency* that, fortunately, is far from being the case in all families—is as unfree as the old education system and cares just as little for the welfare of children, beyond the facade of proclaiming otherwise. It simply prepares children to live within the "new spirit" of capitalism, whose pronounced values, as has been said, are often the opposite of the old ones, without making individuals any freer or more fulfilled. In both forms of upbringing, people often retain a lifelong buried memory of childhood traumas that can reactivate and lead to violent or suicidal acts and, in the most extreme cases, mass murder.

The authoritarian personality—the psychic type that prevailed until the sixties and which is obviously far from having disappeared—feels, above all, a sense of "rage" and directs it towards a scapegoat. It projects onto external objects the impulses it must fight within itself. The narcissistic and borderline subject—indeed, narcissism is a borderline symptom in the sense that it is situated between neurosis and psychosis—that dominates today is inclined towards a hatred without object. This subject is devoured by the fear that their psychic structure might dissolve completely and the aggression serves as a mechanism to preserve the ego. Originally, the borderline is a person unable to integrate the good and bad images of the maternal figure—originally separate, according to Melanie Klein—and who continues to divide objects into "completely good" or "completely bad." Avoiding the destruction of the good objects by the bad ones is for them a question of psychic survival. Through archaic mechanisms such as splitting, denial, or "projective identification," the borderline subject strives to protect itself from even more radical fragmentation and from the fear of being devoured by a symbiotic mother. The rage is thus a protection against this fear. It finally detaches itself from its original motivation and becomes directed against the entire world.

Eisenberg underlines that "realistic compromises" between the drives and social requirements, which are essentially formed in childhood, have largely disappeared. From now on, society is immediately present within socialization and prevents the formation of individuality. During its ascendant phase, capitalism functioned on account of the persistence of pre-capitalist social forms, notably the family. A pure abstraction, such as money, cannot generate any libidinal investment and therefore cannot be the basis of any social bonds. The capacity of symbolization and sublimation, as well as a tolerance for frustration, are no longer cultivated in such a society. "The ego that is formed in this way is fragile, weak, and, throughout life, threatened by tendencies to regression, fragmentation, and dissolution. In situations of humiliation and separation that reactivate the core of early childhood traumas, the subject who feels threatened resorts to archaic mechanisms of defense in a struggle to displace the inner horror onto the outside world."[23]

The "ego" of the past was certainly a receptacle of subdued and internalized repressions. However, its dissolution was not the consequence of a social process of emancipation; on the contrary, it abolished what still allowed for some acceptable form of interpersonal relations. In the age of flexible capitalism, the old "characters" have become dysfunctional: the system now demands that people adapt to everything—subjects without subjectivity, "externally-driven" and no longer "internally-directed." The borderline subject with its unstable personality is thus constituted as a social model. More and more people are coerced into developing a fragmented identity in order to stay afloat in a world where everything is constantly changing and which demands "flexibility" on all fronts. This goes far beyond the management of a workforce:

> The neoliberal deregulation of the social state, the economy, and society goes hand in hand with a psychic and moral deregulation, which affects the superego as much as the ego and its modes of defense. It is as if human beings are being depleted by a vacuum of regressive de-structuring, whose consequences entail archaic mechanisms such as splitting and projection dominating the primary functions of the ego and the more mature defense mechanisms. Since at the same time the transformation of 'external constraints into internalized self-constraints' (Norbert Elias) no longer occurs with sufficient reliability, the tendency to transpose intrapsychic tensions and conflicts into the external world increases in the same proportion as the acting out.[24]

The more flexible a person becomes, the less they have internalized values—both cannot be maintained simultaneously. Those who do not know how to adapt, who continue to function according to old models, often lose their jobs and, above all, their bearings: "More and more people have the impression that the film of external reality is moving faster than the words describing it."[25] They easily harbor great resentment without knowing where to direct it; migrants are often the favorite targets. It is what nourishes populisms of every stripe.

Chronic depression is one possible reaction to this state of affairs—it is aggression against oneself. In depression and aggression, the same mechanism is at work. Statistics tell us that there has been a sharp increase in the number of cases of depression over the last few decades within "advanced" countries. There are two very different explanations for this phenomenon, both of which are quite disturbing: either the statistics correspond to reality, and society is literally becoming more pathological, or it is the pharmaceutical companies, and psychiatry in general, that have succeeded in excessively broadening the criteria for defining depression in order to sell more pills. According to the fifth edition of the DSM psychiatric manual, a person who remains in mourning for more than two weeks after the death of a loved one, showing feelings of emptiness, sadness, or fatigue combined with stress, should be considered depressed and can be treated with medication! In the third edition of the manual, published in 1980, one year of mourning was still considered normal; in the fourth 1994 edition, this period had already been shortened to two months.[26] Already twenty years ago, this is what Alain Ehrenberg had called the transformation of existential problems into psychiatric problems, to be treated medically.[27]

The borderline subject can, unlike the psychotic, maintain an appearance of normality until any insignificant event topples their fragile psychic balance. The humiliations that accumulate in individuals, especially in periods of crisis, can reactivate experiences from early childhood and tendencies towards splitting: "purely bad" objects then appear, representing evil itself. The loss of employment is often accompanied by a loss of identity and interpersonal structures which until that point allowed the precarious functioning of people with weak egos. Their latent psychopathology then explodes. As much as the society based on labor must be critiqued, says Eisenberg, it must be recognized that the disappearance of work also releases destructive energies which before were bound by labor but which now roam freely in the social space. Aggression no longer finds anyone to target and stumbles everywhere against anonymous structures—which can lead to attacking anyone, but also to the pursuit of explanations in conspiracy theories and other paranoid visions. It is like taking a stick and trying to whack the fog enveloping society that prevents one from seeing clearly.

Although women are "catching up" in the field of *running amok* and autotelic violence, these acts remain a largely masculine phenomenon. Apart from the historical reasons for the link between violence and masculinity, contemporary male violence is also a consequence of attempts to combat the fear of the devouring symbiosis with the archaic maternal figure—a fear reinforced by the disappearance of father figures in the family and society—and to safeguard a form of "self." Whoever has to prematurely renounce the promises of happiness received in early childhood easily enters the gravitational pull of the "death drive." It is therefore, above all, contact with women that arouses fear and hatred—behind which lies hatred of the mother, who has been unable to continue her work of benevolence and protection of the child from the "masculine" reality principle.[28]

In short, violence, even in its extreme forms, is simply a consequence of a society based on the commodity:

> More than ever before, there is a danger that a dreadful thesis already formulated by Horkheimer and Adorno in *Dialectic of Enlightenment* will become true: reason reduced to economic and instrumental rationality and a utilitarian morality allows for "the impossibility of deriving from reason a fundamental argument against murder."[29] . . . Within the development of capitalist society, the "cold stream" (Ernst Bloch) arising from the depths of bourgeois society—in the last instance, from the abstraction of exchange—makes its way through all the levels of the social edifice, engulfing social and moral traditions and finally penetrating into the inner world of human beings, transforming it into an icy landscape of frozen feelings and psychic processes. "Bourgeois coldness" (Adorno) abolishes the pity that for long periods of modernity welded the principle of individuation to the capacity of feeling empathy for others and their suffering, thus setting some limits to the "war of all against all." The "flexible man" demanded by the economy must abandon all inhibitions in order to become capable of anything. The results of these processes in the individual subject are recorded by criminal psychiatry as an "emotional defect" and attributed as a "flaw" in the offender in question.[30]

Francesco Berardi, known as "Bifo," is a veteran of the Italian social movements of the seventies. He is known for his analysis of "semio-capitalism," often inspired by Gilles Deleuze and Félix Guattari. He is also one of the few authors to have examined the link between *running amok* and capitalism, in his book *Heroes: Mass Murder and Suicide* (2015). His starting point is clear: "I came to the realization that the current becoming of the world could be better understood if observed through this kind of horrible madness, rather than through the polite madness of economists and politicians. I saw the agony of capitalism and the dismantling of social civilization from a very peculiar point of view: crime and suicide."[31] His view of current psychosocial conditions is close to that of Eisenberg: "A paralysis of empathic relations, and an increasing fragility of the common ground of interpersonal understanding, are becoming common features in the psycho-scape of our time."[32] Like Eisenberg, Berardi identifies the major effects of children glued to their screens: "The fact that human beings learn more vocabulary from a machine than from their mothers is undeniably leading to the development of a new kind of sensibility. The new forms of mass psychopathology of our time cannot be investigated without due consideration of the effects of this new environment, in particular the new process of language learning. Two main developments demand consideration: the first is the dissociation of language learning from the bodily affective experience; the second is the virtualization of the experience of the other."[33] As he continues: "There is much evidence to suggest that this mutation in the experience of communication is producing a pathology in the sphere of empathy (an autistic trend) and in the sphere of sensibility (desensitization to the presence of the other). And this mutation of the psychic and linguistic interaction may also be at the root of the contemporary precariousness of life."[34]

Berardi is as interested in the motivations of those *running amok* as he is in the motivations of more "political" killers like Breivik. He emphasizes the role of social Darwinism: at the center of the mental universe of killers lies the acceptance of a society of competition and the elimination of the weakest.[35] However, paradoxical as it may seem, they have already internalized the conviction that they themselves will never be anything but *losers*. "[T]he young man knew very well that he was not going to be a winner in the social game. Instead, he decides that he will be a winner for a moment: I'll kill and I'll win; then I'll die."[36] After recalling that "[o]n the day of the [Columbine] massacre, Eric Harris wore a white T-shirt on which the words 'Natural selection' were printed in black,"[37] and that other mass murderers have employed the same reference, Berardi continues: "The mass murderer is someone who believes in the right of the fittest and the strongest to win in the social game, but he also knows or senses that he is not the fittest nor the strongest. So he opts for the only possible act of retaliation and self-assertion: to kill and be killed."[38]

These considerations about the role of competition can be taken a step further. It is the universalization of competition that has transformed the whole of life—and not only economic life—into a perpetual war in which each person, if they want to survive, must isolate themselves and look with cold indifference, and then with savage aggression, at anything that stands in the way of "success" in the market, including themselves. Ultimately, the market, the eternal war, and the death drive basically designate the same thing. Universal competition was never as peaceful or beneficial as bourgeois ideology claimed—violence was always lurking close behind. In crisis situations, violence explodes and the veneer of civilization is shattered. Untethered violence can thus become detached from any relationship between ends and means. It can also turn against the subject itself. The subject of the commodity first had to grow accustomed to seeing other subjects as executioners capable of "running over corpses" in economic competition; now he has to resign himself to seeing them as potential assassins in the literal sense, without in any way allowing him to anticipate their aggression according to the usual criteria or by relying on any predetermined calculation. Just as one can be frisked everywhere and at any moment like a criminal, one has had to get used to being a potential victim of crime at any moment, simply by being in the wrong place at the wrong time, without any recourse for protection. Any "crime prevention" strategy can only fail when faced with individuals who no longer apply the minimum of rationality as the calculation between means and ends, which in some sense would make it possible to anticipate violent behavior.

No Reason to Be Found

Today, mass killings defy all common explanation. The "paradigm of self-interest" cannot be applied to these acts of "madness." To understand these phenomena, one must consider the *irrationality* of capitalism, the consequence of its tautological ends and its fundamental emptiness. Murderous ideologies—racism, ethnocentrism, antisemitism, religious fundamentalism—are not incompatible with capitalist rationality. They constitute one side of the same coin. Nihilism—a concept much abused—is at the foundation of a socialization based on value and is therefore found in all subjects carrying out this socialization, who are formed by it in turn. In most cases, what prevented—and still prevents—subjects from carrying out such destructive actions are the aspects of life not determined by the form of value, which are essentially inherited from the past. The more triumphant a society based on value and commodities, on labor and money, the more it destroys these remnants of the past, and with them what prevents it from unleashing the madness that has been inscribed in its heart for centuries.

In a way, the first great expression of this death drive of capitalism, where destruction and self-destruction became a goal in itself, was *Nazism*. Hitler could be considered the greatest *amok runner* in history, a case of "absolute narcissism," whose own end was to coincide with the end of the world. "If the German people lose the war, they have not shown themselves worthy of me," Hitler said a few days before his death. However, to follow this line of inquiry, promising as it is, would lead us into a debate too vast to be addressed here. We will therefore limit ourselves to quoting two stanzas from a song entitled "The Rotten Bones are Trembling," often sung by Nazis and in particular by the Hitler Youth:

> We will continue to march,
> Even if everything shatters;
> Because today Germany hears us,
> And tomorrow, the whole World.
>
> And because of the Great War
> The World lies in ruins,

But devil may care;
We build it up again.[39]

The education that produced Nazi subjects has been replaced by new forms of education that have not avoided creating new types of monsters. Today, the manifestations of the destructive and self-destructive impulses have become individualized. Above all, what we observe is an objectless "hate," "*generalized* hatred."[40]

Jean Baudrillard was perhaps a better observer than a theoretician. Long before the surge of *running amok* and jihadism in Europe, and even before the great banlieue revolts of 2005, he wrote:

> Born of indifference—particularly the indifference radiated by the media – hate is a cool, discontinuous form, which can switch instantly to any object. It is not heated and it lacks conviction; it is consumed in the process of its acting-out – and often in its image and the immediate repercussions – as can be seen from the current outbursts of delinquency on the big city estates. If traditional violence reflected the level of oppression and conflict, hate reflects the level of consensus and conviviality. . . . In a sense, we use hate to protect ourselves from this lack of the other, the enemy or opposition – with hate mobilizing a kind of artificial, objectless oppositionality. In this way, hate is a kind of 'fatal strategy' against the pacification of existence. In its very ambiguity, it is a desperate protest against the indifference of our world and doubtless, for that reason, a much more intense mode of relation than consensus or conviviality. . . . The contemporary transition from violence to hate is characteristic of the shift from an object passion to an objectless passion. . . . Hate is more unreal, more elusive in its manifestations than straight violence. You can see this clearly in racism and delinquency. This is why it is so difficult to counter it, either by prevention or police crackdowns. You cannot de-motivate it, since it has no explicit motivation. You can't demobilize it, since it has no clear mobilizing factor. And it is none too easy to punish it, since most of the time it takes itself as the target: it is, pre-eminently, a passion at odds with itself. We seem doomed to reproduce the Same in an endless identification, in a universal culture of identity, and this gives rise to an enormous resentment: self-hatred. Not hatred of the other, as a superficial interpretation of racism would have it, but the loss of the other and resentment of that loss. . . . This is a culture of *Ressentiment*, then, but one in which, behind the resentment of the other, one cannot but sense a resentment of self, of the dictatorship of the self and the selfsame, which may extend as far as self-destruction.[41]

What appears in this form of hatred is the contemporary subject's certainty of his own nothingness and superfluousness. This is the opposite of a situation of the exploited, who knew that their exploiters needed them, and was therefore obliged to "recognize" them.[42] The result is a characteristic feeling of our time, which can be found in all those *running amok*: the impression of "not existing in the world." It is not due to an individual failure or to a guilty "inability to adapt to a changing society." The crisis of capitalist forms of socialization renders more and more human beings "unprofitable" and thus "superfluous." Hence the rage of such human "debris" can assume barbaric traits, far removed from the "class struggles" of yesteryear, which were centered around "interests."

Today, one state of mind prevails over all others: *resentment*. Quite similar to envy, this feeling has a connection with narcissism that has been little examined until now.[43] Some forms of resentment, and in particular aversion to entire categories of people, are directed towards objects that in truth have done no harm to the resentful subject or with whom these people have no real connection, as is often the case in racism, antisemitism, homophobia, or detesting the "corrupt." It is a *displacement*: a feeling of rage or spite whose origin can be quite justified—although not necessarily—and is directed towards an object of *substitution*. In other words, the feeling is true; it is the target which is false.[44] There is thus a kind of confusion between objects: the subject attributes to an object the characteristics of *another* object. It releases on this substitute object the rage that cannot be exerted on the real object of its hate, consequently erasing the differences between objects.

This revolves around the *reductio ad unum* already evoked, which is at the heart of the fetish-narcissistic constitution: the narcissist has never established real relations to the object and has unconsciously remained in its originary condition of omnipotence and fusion with the environment. For the narcissist, the external world dissolves into a unitary state of "non-self." There is the self and there is "the world." A parent with whom the child is angry and a toy, a boss the subject cannot oppose and his family when he returns home, a desirable woman who repels the macho subject and all women, a

pickpocket with the face of an immigrant and "all immigrants"—
for the narcissist, these are nothing but interchangeable figures, momentary embodiments of the "world," of the "non-self." On the
basis of what has been established in the earlier chapters, we can
now say that resentment, as the quintessence of narcissism, is an
emotion specific to capitalist society; not only for the rather obvious reason that consumer society permanently arouses feelings of
frustration and inadequacy in subjects, as well as desires that remain
never really satisfied, but also because value operates everywhere in
this *reductio ad unum*, this annihilation of the concrete particularities
of the world in favor of the quantified abstraction that renders all
"objects" (in the broad sense) finally one and the same and perfectly
interchangeable.

Resentment is undoubtedly one of the most powerful human
emotions, and also one of the most harmful—unlike rage, which
is consciously directed at the object that provoked it. To mobilize
resentment for anti-capitalist struggle, as Slavoj Žižek proposes, is to
play with fire and to pave the way for populist movements, the embodiment of resentment.[45] If we really want to know where resentment leads, and what relation it has with a critical understanding of
the world, we should look at the works and career of Louis-Ferdi-
nand Céline. Nazism, on the other hand, had taken resentment as
a basic passion of a collective psychology to unprecedented heights,
after modern antisemitism paved the way. Nazism proved that the
ultimate consequence of resentment is not the conquest, however
violent, of what seems to be lacking in order to find happiness—in
the case of Nazism, world domination—but an orgy of destruction
that only ends when the subject has completed its own destruction.

The narcissist's feelings of impotence lead to feelings of omnipotence, whether at the individual level, consumed by the idea
of being—even if for just fifteen minutes—the supreme judge, the
one who dispenses life and death, a quasi-god, or, at the collective
level, feeling strength in belonging to a "superior" people, "race,"
social category, or religion. It is often the failed confirmation of the
"normal" desire for recognition—"benign narcissism," some would
say—that can lead to extreme actions.

The valorization of capital and the social life that results are not only empty, but above all senseless. Nothing counts for itself, and every human being must subordinate its real personality, its inclinations, and its tastes to the demands of valorization—to the point of becoming a *quantified self* constantly measuring and "sharing" its personal and especially physical "data" with the help of "mobile apps." Life is subject to total rationalization in which even the smallest activity must be useful and productive, and managed by technologies.[46] The total commodification of life, even its most intimate moments, does not necessarily mean that everything is for sale, but that everything is subject to the demands of efficiency and time-saving, performance, and guaranteed output: from looking for sexual partners *via* mobile apps and "managing one's health capital," to taking meditation classes to better cope with the working day, and filling up on amphetamines to pass the entrance exams for prestigious universities . . .

Today, the most common way of responding to this painful feeling of emptiness is media narcissism in all its forms, from the poorly named "social media" to reality television. The narcissism of the media is in no way an alternative to crime; on the contrary, it is its perfect complement. Examples of this collusion are innumerable: from instances of rape filmed and posted online, allowing the perpetrators to be quickly identified and arrested, to the "livestreamed" murder of two police officers in Magnanville, France in June 2016; from the infamous leader of the Mexican "narcos," "El Chapo," who unwittingly put investigators on his trail by wanting to meet famous actors while in hiding, to the killers of a priest in a small church in Normandy in August 2016, who forced an elderly couple at the scene to video record the events, as well as the Italian teenage girls who posted a video online—in which you can hear their laughter—of their friend being raped in front of their eyes at a nightclub. To describe these phenomena, the media speak of a kind of "malignant media narcissism," suggesting that to publicize the entirety of one's private life on social media and to measure it by the yardstick of "likes" collected on one's "page," "account," or "channel," would be a matter of "benign media narcissism," easily remedied by more moderate usage.[47]

In the contemporary "attention economy,"[48] *running amok* and suicide killings are the most extreme form: dying in order to exist in the eyes of others for just one fleeting moment. Provided that they are ready to sacrifice their lives, anyone, even those to whom no one had ever paid the slightest attention, can decide that tomorrow everyone will be talking about them; and if the target is well chosen, the most powerful people in the world will attend the funeral of the victims. The proletarians and lumpen-proletarians of the attention economy, to whom no *American Idol* would ever open its doors, can fall back on this form of 'guerrilla marketing' that costs nothing—except their lives. Whoever finds no form of recognition through the usual channels can always go down in history as an anti-hero, and the media will certainly share in the complicity.[49]

Capitalism and Violence

Among most of the critics of capitalism discussed in this book, including Franco Berardi, there is some confusion as to whether they are talking about capitalism in general, or only about its neoliberal phase, suggesting that a restoration of a "healthier" capitalism is possible. Berardi, despite his emergence from the radical movements of the seventies and his seemingly sincere disgust for today's society, nonetheless indulges in a kind of praise for the capitalism of yesteryear, a eulogy that is as curious as it is characteristic of much of today's left. He thus writes: "The conflictive alliance between industrious bourgeois and industrial workers—which had left the public education system, health care, transportation, and welfare as the material legacy of the modern age—was sacrificed to the religious dogma of the Market-God." This sacrifice is said to have occurred in 1977 precisely (the year of the last great wave of revolt in Italy): "That year was a watershed: from the age of human evolution the world shifted to the age of de-evolution, or de-civilization. What had been produced by labour and social solidarity in the centuries of modernity started to fall under finance's predatory process of de-realization."[50] This alliance between "productive" capital and the workers, an alliance that allegedly benefits everyone, is all too well-known. Writing that "[c]risis, therefore, presents a situation in which the natural law is out of joint, and crime spreads,"[51] Berardi clearly considers pre-crisis capitalism—Fordism—as the expression of a "natural law." Furthermore, when he writes that "the 'elsewhere class' [new "absentee owners" who easily move their capital everywhere without being attached to any particular place] has re-established the economic rationale of the rentier, as profit is no longer linked to the mere possession of an invisible asset: money, or, more accurately, credit," he regresses to the populist denunciation of the "rentier" who does not use capital to "increase social wealth." The capitalist who would do so is then clearly deserving in his capital. In fact, Berardi's glorification of "social" capitalism is present throughout the book: "In the context of a long-term anthropological evolution, contemporary capitalism can be understood as the turning point beyond the age of Humanism. The modern bourgeoisie embodied the values of Humanist freedom from theological destiny, and bourgeois capitalism was a product of the Humanist revolution."[52]

Although Berardi refers to Marx's notion of abstract labor, he links it to the "de-materialization of value" that would be "part of the general process of abstraction," which leads to the emergence of "semiocapitalism, the contemporary regime of production in which capital valorization is based on the constant emanation of information flows," as the "emancipation of signs" (a notion borrowed from Jean Baudrillard).[53] Similarly, he believes that "language, imagination, information and immaterial flows become the force of production and the general space of exchange" par excellence.[54] If he rejects the term "cognitive capitalism," it is only to insist that it is labor that is now cognitive: "Capital is not the subject of cognitive activity: it is only its exploiter. The bearer of knowledge, creativity and skills is the cognitive worker."[55] Berardi thus remains within the framework of Negri's theories, which are based on an erroneous interpretation of the concept of value.[56] He also asserts, in a bizarre shortcut, that the difficulty of measuring the value of immaterial—"cognitive"—labor is at the origin of the current rise of corruption and mafia activity![57]

This goes hand in hand with a positive vision of modernity, except for its most recent developments, which according to him are in complete contradiction with what preceded them: "As a result of these progressive developments, modernity culminated in the creation of a form of social civilization, a civilization in which common needs prevailed over the affirmation of individual interests. This social civilization was forged with the intention of preventing interminable wars of every man against the other. Yet, over the last thirty years, the social civilization has been crumbling, under the blows of a philosophy of social Darwinism, which has acted as the ideological precursor to the affirmation of Neoliberal politics on a global scale."[58] He thus seems to be saying that if we could return to the seventies, civilization would be saved. However, at the time, a position like Berardi's would have been considered "social-democratic" and not at all revolutionary.

Although Götz Eisenberg does not fall into this trap, he does not fail to attribute great weight to the dismantling of the welfare state as a source of anxiety, loneliness, and dissociation that can lead to blind violence. For him, social security would have formed a barrier against the excesses of competition and would have partially removed certain spheres of life from the terrorism of the economy. The abolition of these protected islands by neoliberalism also destroyed the social safety nets. He thus writes: "My 'definition of vandalism' is social disintegration (that is, a shrinking labor market, multiple exclusions, ghettoization) plus psychic de-structuring (diminished superego, widespread ego weakness, lack of social bonds, archaic and unintegrated rage), equaling the likelihood of increased outbursts of uncontrollable violence."[59]

This analysis is empirically correct, but one should not believe that "capitalism with a human face" could have been maintained indefinitely as a "class compromise." Capitalism is regressive by its very nature, and the capitalist subject inevitably ends up entangled by its darker side. Eisenberg makes this clear elsewhere when he speaks about the "expanded suicide of capital." It is money itself that *runs amok*. Financial capital, which is a "production of nothing from nothing," is not the perversion of what would otherwise have been a "reasonable" capitalism, but constitutes the logical outcome of value and its emptiness. The destruction of the capacity of subjects to replace outbursts by the imagination—what is called "symbolization"—is an element of the self-destruction of the capitalist system itself. The subject, far from being the counterweight of the system, declines alongside the system that contains it:

> The contemporary subject self-decomposes. A part of it becomes an interior extension of the machinery of social production; the remainder becomes the primary material for publicity, consumption, and the culture industry, as a development of its own dynamism. The derivatives of the death drive, aggression, and the desire for destruction are less and less forced to bind themselves to libidinal object investments that could place them at the service of Eros. The current tendencies to the disassociation of the drives demonstrate that aggression, when it is not linked to the libido, can hardly be sublimated. If it is aggression that commands the libido, and no longer the other way around, and if more and more people are governed by aggressive and destructive emotions, we can confidently predict a continuous increase in blind violence.[60]

Additionally, Eisenberg always emphasizes the fact that the destructive and suicidal behavior of individuals corresponds to that of the "decision-makers" and business leaders. This fact has indeed become obvious, even to the general public. Life at both ends of the chain is similar, from the favelas to the upper echelons of the economy and politics: one lives only in the present, the only morality is success, and others exist merely as instruments.[61]

A fundamental contribution to this investigation was made by Robert Kurz, notably in the aforementioned essay, "The Death Drive of Competition," and in its re-elaboration in his book *Weltordnungskrieg* (2003).[62] Above all, Kurz emphasizes what is common between the various forms of violence: "The lines separating the mafia, the cult, ethic separatism, the Nazi and criminal gangs, the guerrilla, etc., have long since faded. As for the phenotype of the massacres, it is the same everywhere: it is the 'young man,' aged between fifteen and thirty-five, morally and culturally disconnected and unattached, a veritable 'self-entrepreneur' with a laptop and Reebok or Adidas sneakers, casually slinging his machine gun across his shoulder as an accessory and instrument of murder, and reveling in his immediate physical power and in the fear he inspires in his human prey, because he has nothing else left." The reigning madness of these situations is just another stage of "ordinary capitalist madness" in times of crisis. These murderous behaviors are not independent of a "certain economic rationality," but they have "abandoned the regulation and legal form of capitalist conditions and the corresponding form of consciousness to return to forms of immediate violence"—although the verb "return" is inappropriate, Kurz adds, because "the historical passage through the capitalist form is naturally irreversible."[63] This barbarization is never a genuine return to archaic social forms, but a postmodern barbarism that combines the worst of modernity with the worst of past societies.

The crisis of capitalism is a crisis of the subject-form, which refers to the very origins of capitalism itself: in the beginning as in the end, there is plunder and direct violence.

> When global competition in times of crisis becomes savage at all levels, subjects themselves also become savage. The subject-form disintegrates, revealing in a new way its violent core. Violence, blood, and fear are therefore not phenomena that are added to economic reductionism from without, but integral parts of it. It is revealing that today, at the end of capitalism, the post-modern plunder economy and its atrocities repeat the foundational crimes of its own beginnings. Contrary to the legends that are supposed to legitimize it, the modern money machine did not emerge from peaceful commerce but from the firearm economy of the early modern era and its military despotisms.[64]

Ordinary "economic horrors" (Rimbaud) have not in truth "replaced" direct violence, thus constituting a kind of "lesser evil": they have always accompanied it as its shadow.

Kurz also highlights that gang violence—especially in areas where capitalist normality has already collapsed and the "illegal" economy is the only one still functioning—is not a revolt of the poor: "The 'lost generation' is not only the long-term unemployed and the 'superfluous,' but also the (male) youth who are not directly (or not yet) affected by the climate of social crisis and who became morally untamed. Most of the militias and gangs in the areas where the crisis and collapse have struck thus represent a bizarre mix of barbarized unemployed and an equally barbarized 'affluent youth' (whose fathers often act as 'godfathers' and 'sub-godfathers')."[65] This not only concerns the areas where open civil wars are raging, but also everyday violence: "A molecular civil war is also, and above all, taking place among the youth of the confined pseudo-normality, that of the 'big earners,' the crisis profiteers, and the fanatics of respectability, whose souls are no less deserted and lost to themselves than those of the young killers of the slums. The cult of murder and rape as sport and staged suicide are also rampant in the residential areas of Rio de Janeiro, New York, and Tokyo."[66] Even less should one see in it a revolt of the "wretched of the earth": the perpetrators of suicide attacks, "in Palestine as in Sri Lanka," often come from well-off families. They are ready to organize their life according to insane ideas and finally "throw their life away like a dirty Kleenex."[67] The subject-form has become universal, Kurz insists, and the differences between cultures and religions of the world do not explain such killings, but rather are merely different "shades" of this universal form. This is why the jihadist suicide bomber and the suburban school shooter have more in common than they have differences.

The self-destructive character of these behaviors seems, at first glance, to contradict the utilitarianism that dominates the competitive economy. However, Kurz insists on their continuity:

> In the global crisis, competition is transformed into economic competition of annihilation and thus into existential social competition, which in turn transforms into immediate violent and "masculinist" competition. If, in this context, the risk of dying a violent death becomes a daily occurrence—which now exists at the micro level of everyday life, as it once did on the fronts of world wars—this is not necessarily in contradiction with "selfish interest" and the covetousness aroused by the consumption of commodities. The self-contradictory, literally murderous character of the subject of competition spreads to such an extent that, aggravated by the crisis, the self-contradiction of capitalist logic is also reproduced within individuals, and especially in men because of their socialization.

The capitalist social form offers no way out, and in the face of its "increasingly idiotic and destructive contents," the subject of competition finally goes beyond "risk" and "interest": "indifference towards others is transformed into indifference towards oneself."[68]

This "coldness" towards oneself had already emerged during other great crises of capitalism, especially during the interwar period. Kurz recalls that Hannah Arendt, in *The Origins of Totalitarianism* (1951), offered the same diagnosis about the 1920s, a time when the rise of totalitarian regimes left many young men feeling superfluous and worthless. They were thus ready to sacrifice their lives, which they considered useless, without this attitude having any relation with "idealism" in the traditional sense. But Arendt, Kurz objects, attributed to "totalitarian" regimes (in the political sense) features that in truth characterize all modern commodity-producing societies. Their violent core lies in the total submission of individuals "to the abstract and contentless principle of capital valorization, of which the modern state (the principle of sovereignty) is but a secondary expression."[69] Behind the self-affirmation of individuals as the supreme law of survival in the regime of competition stands "equally abstract self-negation, or more precisely: self-affirmation and self-negation are identical in their complete separation from any social community, and this identity becomes visible in the course of the great catastrophes of capitalist society." From an originally temporary situation, the "loss of self" becomes permanent when capitalism reaches its absolute limits. Every individual, whether of the "superfluous" masses or among the financiers, knows that they can at any moment be replaced by someone else who counts as little as themselves. "It is one and the same 'loss of self' that characterizes the gangs of thugs, goons, and rapists as well as the self-exploiters of the new economy or the investment bankers behind their computer screens."

If Kurz agrees with German essayist Hans Magnus Enzenberger when he states in *Die Große Wanderung* (1993)[70] that contemporary civil wars "are about nothing," he also adds:

> The nothingness at question here is the complete emptiness of the modern, self-valorizing "automatic subject" (Marx). . . . This self-sufficiency, this necessary movement of exteriorization and, in the end, this self-referentiality of the empty metaphysical

form of "value" and the "subject establishes a potential for the destruction of the world, because it is only in nothingness and thus in annihilation that the contradiction between the metaphysical emptiness and the imperative necessity for value to incarnate itself in the sensible world can be resolved. The emptiness of value, money, and the state must be externalized in all things of the world, without exception, in order to be represented as real: from the toothbrush to the most subtle psychic emotions.

The tautological movement of capital that reduces every object to a simple quantity of what Marx called "jelly," of the value created by abstract labor, includes a "double potential of annihilation: a 'normal,' everyday potential that has always arisen from the process of the reproduction of capital, and a 'final' potential, when the 'process of exteriorization' comes up against its absolute limits. The real metaphysics of the modern commodity-producing system partially destroys the world as 'collateral damage' from the success of its 'exteriorization.' It then becomes an absolute will to destroy the world when it can no longer be embodied in the things of the world."[71] In the first case, it is a question of destruction and death caused by the "ordinary" functioning of the economy, while in the second, the death drive can be directed against the subject itself since the subject is part of the concrete and sensible world.

Self-preservation coincides with what appears to be its opposite, self-annihilation:

The abstract character of this will to annihilate reflects the self-contradiction of the capitalist relation in a double manner: on the one hand, this will aims at the annihilation of the 'other' in order to ensure its own self-preservation at any cost; on the other hand, it is a will to self-annihilation that realizes the absurdity of the subject's own existence as a subject of the market. In other words, the difference between suicide and homicide blurs. Beyond the "risk" linked to competition, what is at stake is a will to unlimited destruction developed to such an extent that the distinction between one's own self and that of others begins to disappear.[72]

The disposition to destroy the other in competition ends in a generalized hatred towards the entire world; a world that this competition has reduced to nothing, including the subject itself. He thinks he is following his "interests," but in truth, without knowing it clearly, he hates himself as much as he hates other subjects.

The metaphysics of value, its emptiness and its necessity to realize itself in the world, as described by Descartes, Kant, and Hegel, is thus linked by Kurz to the anomie reigning over the contemporary world in a dazzling summation, which, in a certain manner, encapsulates the very meaning of this book.

EPILOGUE
WHAT IS TO BE DONE WITH THIS
BAD SUBJECT?

Throughout the course of this book, the "subject" of capitalist society has been examined in various ways: as a subject-form, that is, as an *a priori* that predetermines ("preforms") individual behavior, but an *a priori* that is the product of history; as a psyche in the psychoanalytic sense, but a psyche which is subject to historical change; as an object of empirical observation and critique with respect to recent developments. The investigation has not presupposed an ontological and eternal relation between subject and object in general. Rather, we have indicated in the subject-form a specific way of life, individually and collectively, whose origins go back at least to the late Middle Ages and whose form today is in many respects that which took shape during the Enlightenment. The emergence of this form was briefly examined, followed by a more detailed account of its period of crisis, including its most extreme dimensions. Is it possible to draw conclusions from this analysis in order to answer the most urgent question: how to get rid of capitalism and with what to replace it?

It will have to be understood that the discourse developed here is far from any search for a "revolutionary subject" in the classical sense, or for any subject situated outside capitalist logic, forced or manipulated into participating, and which, in essence, remains undamaged by this logic and thus carries within it the potential of a non-capitalist world.[1] In other words, the history of capitalism is not the history of a colonization of the subject by an oppressive and manipulative exteriority called "capital" or even "capitalist," but the history of the subject itself. The subject-form is not what is oppressed by the commodity-form and must therefore be liberated: the two forms have in fact become almost identical. On the other hand, it is obvious that the capital relation does not encompass all aspects of life and consciousness. Otherwise it could not be subject to critique, and people would be as much part of society as ants are part of an ant colony.

Social constraints have been internalized in tandem with the internalization of capitalist logic, or, to be more precise, a parallel and joint development of the subject-form and commodity-form has taken place. If someone had told a revolutionary at the beginning of the twentieth century that a hundred years later there would be no more military conscription, that the Church would be almost completely absent from public debate, that the authoritarian family would have almost disappeared, that the old class distinctions would no longer be visible, and that a Black man or a woman would be able to manage a school or a state, but that, in spite of all this, we would still be governed by the capitalist system and that there would be much less radical protest than before, it would appear unbelievable. What is at stake is not merely a psychological internalization obtained through brainwashing, that is to say, the internalization of the cop into our heads. It is rather the fact that commodity value has effectively become the universal form of social synthesis and that everyone is *really following* their "own interests," at least in the short-term, when they are exploiting themselves as "self-entrepreneurs" instead of fortifying barricades. Whoever has devoted themselves body and soul to "self-valorization" will police themselves better than any supervisor and will believe in the religion of the market more strongly than the fetishes of any faithful Christian. Of course, the old forms of authoritarianism have not completely disappeared; they even seem to be making a comeback as of late. But the persistence of capitalism is not due to their residual survival, and their definitive abolition would by no means amount to the final step of moving beyond capitalism itself.

It is therefore necessary to critique theories that attribute a central role to forms of personal domination, as well as adherents of "self-management" and "real" (or "direct") democracy, in all their variants. One must also underline the limits of a large part of traditional anarchist discourse, excessively preoccupied with the political and organizational aspects of alienation. The history of failed revolutions is not just about the betrayal of the honest revolutionary masses by leaders corrupted by power—although this aspect obviously might play a role. Rather, people and their leaders often share the same fetishistic forms. In a fetishistic society, even the purest form of self-management does no good. There is no point in worrying about the thousand and one details of a direct democracy guaranteed to be "anti-manipulative"—about the modalities of the "mandates" that will exist in a direct democracy, or about the right size of the political units—if everything that is decided in the most democratic manner imaginable always remains based on the execution of unconsciously presupposed systemic imperatives. Power is not the creation of those who exercise it, nor can it be understood by studying its functionaries alone.[2] Nor will shifting the gaze towards a "microphysics of power" (so dear to Foucault and Deleuze) touch what is essential: if these approaches have been valuable in showing that capitalist society reproduces itself less through what is decided by government ministers or the board of directors than through the daily repetition of everyday attitudes, they nevertheless maintain a fundamental dichotomy between the dominant and the dominated, the oppressors and the oppressed, between those who are in the system and those who are outside it and merely subjected to it. The form of social mediation common to all subjects remains outside the scope of any such considerations. Whether one identifies what is oppressed with flesh-and-blood individuals (homosexuals, women, immigrants), or with elements inscribed within the very substance of individuals (non-oedipal sexuality, the "will to live"), nothing essential really changes.

On the other hand, in other historical periods—especially during the transition from traditional societies to industrial society, which occurred at different times and in different ways in different places—those who were still considered "outside" the system must have felt, in their entire being, the shock of the interval between the new capitalist logic and the old ways of life. Many revolutionary movements, and perhaps, more than any other, the Spanish revolutionary movement between the end of the nineteenth century and 1939, drew their strength and their horizon from this shock. But it would be a mistake to apply this perspective to the contemporary situation. To oppose the "one percent" to the remaining 99 percent of the population is an aberration. This understanding of the role of the "subject" almost necessarily leads to theories of manipulation, seduction, secrecy, and conspiracy.

At the deepest level, the principle of capitalism does not reside in the fact that some individuals impose their will on others. *Capital is a social relation and not a group of human beings.* Of course, this system benefits some actors much more than others, but this means that rather than speaking of a "ruling class," we should speak of a "profiteering class"—as one that "profits" from circumstances. As André Gorz wrote in his last book: "It's not 'I' who acts, but the automated logic of social systems that works through me as Other, that makes me participate in the production and reproduction of the social megamachine. That logic is the real subject. The dominant social strata suffer its domination, as much as do the dominated. The dominant dominate only insofar as they serve it as loyal functionaries."[3]

If fetishism is not external to subjects and if the fetish-form is the subject-form itself, then one cannot mobilize subjects as subjects against the very economic and political order that constitutes them. Everyone executes the laws of competition and, in the context of a capitalist society, even the workers of the self-managed factory could not help but execute the laws of the market. Rather, what is necessary is emancipation from automatized and fetishistic social forms, starting with one's own narcissistic psychic constitution. The affirmation that human emancipation means first to emancipate oneself from the structures that dominate us has also been advanced by authors like Cornelius Castoriadis. According to him, the autonomy claimed by the ecological movement, to which he adhered, "puts the primary question of autonomy in relation to a technical productive system which is supposedly inevitable and claims to be optimal, that of the technical and productive system which exists in the present society."[4]

It is important to be wary of certain "subjective" forms that appear within current and future challenges to capitalism. They must *at minimum* be subjected to a harsh critique. Thus, a critique limited to financial capitalism alone, and thus falling under a "truncated anti-capitalism," often fuels current populisms which, rather than being right-wing or left-wing, are beginning to converge into a "transversal populism." The role of "identity" can clearly be seen here and has become the main version of the subject-form and its dark side. The pseudo-concrete, in the form of a people or "race," religion or "sovereign state," has the upper hand when the abstraction of the commodity passes like a steamroller over social life, especially when no one, including the most shameless demagogues of the political circus, can any longer claim to have blueprints for getting out of the crisis. That is when the flags start rolling out.

Even the gradual disappearance of a society based on labor, which is rapidly advancing because of the introduction of new technologies that are now also replacing managers and technical jobs, is not necessarily positive when subjects have no idea what to do with their free time and devote it either to mind-numbing "leisure" or to the search for a few scraps of market value at any price, even if it means robbing one's neighbor or giving oneself up to unspeakable trades.

The vast panorama of self-destructive phenomena undeniably demonstrates that there is no generalized biological "survival instinct" as the ultimate foundation of life. Many have been captivated by this ruse, from Karl Kautsky—who, like many socialists of his generation, wanted to base the advent of socialism on Darwinian evolutionism—to Serge Latouche and many ecologists who believe in the "pedagogy of catastrophes."[5] Historical materialism as well as bourgeois economic thought consider immediate individual self-preservation to be an evident and primary human preoccupation—which is obviously not always the case, neither individually nor collectively, neither today nor in the past. Quite the contrary, a "death drive" seems to lead an independent existence alongside self-preservation. It is difficult to know whether it exists as a universal, even cosmic, inescapable phenomenon, or whether, on the contrary, it is only the result of conditions of existence in which life has largely lost the reasons for which it deserves to be lived, or whether, if present in all human cultures, it has undergone an infinitely greater diffusion in the capitalist era. The third possibility seems most probable, as has already been mentioned. In any case, it seems very risky to base political strategies on the presumption that humanity is endowed with a survival instinct and that, in the face of extreme danger, it will always be able to find and pull the emergency brake.

The crisis of the subject-form is thus not a crisis like others; it is not the passage from one stage of social life to another fairly similar stage. It is rather part of what increasingly appears as a real *anthropological rupture*. Until just a few years ago, this notion was almost unheard of. It is now beginning to spread widely. Indeed, the digitalization of the world and permanent connectivity, genetic manipulation and artificial procreation, the arrival of the "Anthropocene" or the "Capitalocene," where humanity has become a geological force, as well as the application of computer technology to almost all aspects of life—all are phenomena that have appeared in only a few decades, with risks of incalculable and probably irreversible consequence. What is emerging is a transformation of the human condition itself, of what defines humanity and its relationship to the world.

An evaluation of the different aspects of this transformation would obviously far exceed the scope of this book. But it can still nevertheless be asked whether, beyond an "anthropological mutation," it is a question of an "anthropological *regression*" or a "regressive anthropogenesis" (Adorno). Is it possible that this regression, as Adorno suspected, is not necessarily linked to the darkest moments of modern history, such as Nazism? Is it even possible to talk about without first defining "progress," whether in positive or negative terms? To know whether humanity has "regressed" in the capitalist era relative to certain earlier forms of social organization is a complex task, especially if one wants to make comparisons "en bloc," without examining the particulars. There is, however, one sphere in which the concept of "regression" seems to have a precise meaning: does the life of fetish-narcissistic society allow individuals to emerge from childhood and develop some form of maturity, or does it ossify individuals at infantile stages, such as narcissism and the desire for fusion, or the "paranoid position" and splitting, rendering this fixation a condition for the survival of the system? Is contemporary capitalism based on what is an irresistible promise for many human beings: to "save" them from the efforts required for becoming an adult? Or, as a matter of speculation, does it draw its strength from its alliance with the regressive desire that has always accompanied human beings: to remain a child for the entirety of one's life?

A brief excursus on *ways of seeing* helps to better grasp the "infantilizing" power of capitalism, already mentioned several times. Let us add the following consideration: whoever criticizes the "spectacle," television, or the power of audiovisual media is almost always quick to emphasize that they are not "against the image as such."[6] However, the extreme dominance of the image in current culture is itself a sign of infantilization. English essayist and art critic John Berger begins *Ways of Seeing* as follows: "Seeing comes before words. The child looks and recognizes before it can speak."[7] So it may be, but the preference for images should diminish over the course of life, as should the taste for sweet foods. Humanization is realized precisely through the appropriation of language. And this appropriation, especially in its written form, is less encouraged in contemporary culture than in past cultures. No other culture has known this hypertrophic significance of *seeing* like Western culture. Cultures without "written language" were not based on the image, but on orality, much closer to writing than to the image. In such cultures, speaking well was not necessarily an aristocratic privilege, as shown, for example, by the importance attached to improvising poems and songs on metrical models. In many traditional cultures, this was an important aspect of social life, and significant contests would be held in front of large audiences. This is demonstrated, for example, even today by the *Bertsolaritza* in the Basque country.

Highly developed cultures, such as the Hebrew and Islamic cultures, were suspicious of images to the point of banning them. In fact, before the nineteenth century, most people rarely saw images at all. Churches, with their stained-glass windows, frescoes, paintings, and statues, are not a counterexample: when each image is a handi-craft, a unique object, it remains rare and does not constitute a main source of the individual's relationship to the world. But modern cul-ture has reversed the relationship between word and image to the point of "humiliating" the word, as Jacques Ellul has emphasized.[8] The 2002 report "Reading at Risk" by the National Endowment for the Arts, concludes that "[f]or the first time in modern history, less than half the adult population now reads literature."[9] If any-thing like real historical progress existed, it may have been with the spread of active reading amongst the popular classes between 1850 and 1950. Two million people attended the funeral of Victor Hugo. This massive diffusion of literacy, and thus of reason, undoubted-ly represented a danger for the established powers. Its decline is a serious setback for humanity. It is obviously a consequence of the diffusion of the image. Reading can hardly resist when the possibil-ity of watching a film or cinematographic adaptation of a book is on offer. However, images, and especially their incessant circulation, are much more manipulable than the written word; they contain more hidden contradictions and are much less nuanced and com-plex. Moreover, an image is never "false"; only the context in which it is situated.[10] Images are more difficult to authenticate since, rather than appealing to reason (the common ground of humanity, which is open to discussion), they instead appeal to feelings and tastes, which are as such personal and unquestionable.

Many might object that today a radical social change that abol-ishes money and labor is "unrealistic" or "utopian." We are told to be content with avoiding the worst, especially ecological disasters, and instead to strive for more social justice. "The world will never be perfect, let's just improve it a little, which is already a lot . . ." We re-fuse such a perspective. And yet this book has referred throughout to the search for "realistic compromises" as the goal of psychoanalysis. It is not a question of establishing eternal happiness, but of accept-ing the limits and of settling in them to acquire realistic satisfactions. The contradiction is evident: it is precisely capitalism that destroys these "realistic compromises" and drives the world beyond all limits. Money, labor, the state, and the market cannot be overcome in the name of a "maximalist" program or an unprecedented break in human history, or in the name of a "new human being," but precisely in the name of a modest realism. It can be seen every day: even the humblest reforms have become impossible within a capitalist framework. When the ship can no longer sail without burning the boards of its own deck, then even the most urgent measures to limit the destruction of nature are as impossible as a simple "redistribution of wealth" which would allow the ship to keep sail just a little longer. It is thus in the name of "realism" that we must leave commodity society, and therefore abandon ship. And as much as we may hold the impression that money, labor, the state, and competition are part of the human condition itself, they are in truth only very recent phenomena, much less rooted in the structure of the individual than our "need for consolation". . .[11]

There is certainly no general agreement on how to move beyond present society, but there will be very strong resistance which will undoubtedly proceed through violent confrontations. But the fractures will not be established simply between the "dominant" who defend the system and the "dominated" who seek its destruction. It is quite possible that the precarious worker who is finally able to purchase a car on credit will seek to defend their right to travel around with the same ardor as their exploiter. The critique of value is sometimes wrongly accused of being "deterministic." In truth, it anticipates that individual decisions will become much more important in times of severe crisis.

It is now possible to return to the myth of Erysichthon. As described at the outset, the hubris that irresistibly drives the king of Thessaly emerges as a profound prefiguration of the narcissism of the contemporary period. Are we condemned to the same fate and to follow the path of Erysichthon, to devour ourselves after having destroyed nature? In the myth, the king is the culprit, whereas the serfs are frightened by the sacrilegious act and hesitate. Yet, when faced with the violence of the king—who does not hesitate to decapitate one of them—they give in. Although they are obviously in a position to oppose the king, they fail to use their strength and end up his accomplices.

In all of these considerations on the modern subject, we have rejected the idea that capitalist society is clearly divided between dominant and dominated, guilty and innocent. No project of social emancipation can ignore the great question posed almost five hundred years ago by Étienne de La Boétie, that of "voluntary servitude." If we are to seriously consider a way out of this world, we must succeed, in theory as well as in practice, in untangling the infinite threads that force individuals to collaborate—to varying degrees—with the system that oppresses them. The subject-form is one of the most important threads. As such, one of the main objectives of this book was to have made a contribution to solving the mystery of the contemporary *homo homini ovis*.

To conclude, let us give the final word to a contemporary of La Boétie, the poet Pierre de Ronsard. In his elegy "Elegy Against the Woodcutters of Gâtine," he evokes the myth of Erysichthon and draws from it an incredibly prescient lesson:

> Whoever will first have busied himself
> By striking you down, forest, with a hardened axe,
> May he strike himself with his own staff,
> And feel in his stomach the hunger of Erysichthon,
> He who cut down Ceres' venerable oak,
> And who, hungry for everything, insatiable,
> Slaughtered his mother's cattle and sheep,
> Then, spurred by hunger, ate himself alive:
> Thus swallowed up his rents and his land,
> To be devoured himself thereafter by the teeth of war.
>
> That he may, in order to exchange the blood of our forests,
> Always forever new loans on new interests
> Owe to the usurer, and that in the end it consumes
> All that is his to pay the principal sum.
>
> Never shall his mind be at rest,
> Than to plot some new design,
> Worn away with impatience and diverse fury,
> And of bad council that overturns men.
>
> Stay, woodsman, stay thy hand awhile, and hark,
> It is not trees that thou art laying low,
> Dost thou not see the dripping life-blood flow
> From Nymphs that lived beneath the rigid bark?
> Unholy murderer of our Goddesses,

If for some petty theft a varlet hangs,
What deaths hast thou deserved, what bitter pangs,
What brandings, burnings, tortures, dire distress?

O lofty wood, grove-dwelling birds' retreat,
No more shall stag and doe, with light-foot tread,
Feed in thy shadow, for thy leafy head
No more shall break the sun's midsummer heat.

The loving shepherd on his four-holed flute
Piping the praises of his fair Janette,
His mastiff near, his crook beside him set,
No more shall sing of love, but all be mute:
Silence shall fall where Echo spoke of yore,
And where soft-waving lay uncertain shade,
Coulter and plough shall pass with cutting blade,
And frightened Pans and Satyrs come no more.

Farewell, thou ancient forest, Zephyr's toy,
Where first I taught my seven-tongued lyre to sing,
Where first I heard Apollo's arrows ring
Against my heart, and strike it through with joy:
Where first I worshipped fair Calliope
And loved her noble company of nine
Who showered their roses on this brow of mine,
Where with her milk Euterpe nurtured me.

Farewell, ye ancient oaks, ye sacred heads,
With images and flower-gifts worshipped erst,
But now the scorn of passers-by athirst,
Who, parched with heat the gleaming ether sheds,
And robbed of your cool verdure at their need,
Accuse your murderers, and speak them scathe.

Farewell, ye oaks, the valiant patriot's wreath,
Ye trees Jove himself, Dodona's seed,
'Twas you, great oaks, that gave their earliest food,
To men, ungrateful and degenerate race,
Forgetful of your favors, recreant, base,
And quick to shed their foster-fathers' blood.

Wretched is he who sets his trust upon the world!
How truly speaks philosophy,
Saying that each thing in the end must die,
Must change its form and take another on:
Fair Tempé's vale shall be in hills uptossed,
And Athos' peak become a level plain;
Old Neptune's fields shall some day wave with grain.
Matter abides forever, form is lost.

APPENDIX
SOME ESSENTIAL POINTS OF THE
CRITIQUE OF VALUE

The capitalist system has now entered a serious crisis. This crisis is not only cyclical, but final: not in the sense of an imminent collapse, but as the disintegration of a centuries-old system. This is not a prophecy of a future event, but the observation of a process that became visible in the early seventies and whose roots go back to the very origin of capitalism.

We witness today not the transition from one regime of accumulation to another (as was the case with Fordism), nor simply the advent of new technologies (such as the automobile), nor a shift in the center of gravity of society towards other regions of the world. Rather, this crisis is the complete exhaustion of the very source of capitalism itself: the transformation of living labor into value.

The fundamental categories of capitalism, as analyzed by Karl Marx in his critique of political economy, are abstract labor, value, the commodity, and money, which are abridged in the concept of "the fetish-character of the commodity." A moral critique, based on a denunciation of "greed," misses the point entirely.

It is not a question of being Marxist or post-Marxist, or interpreting Marx's work or supplementing it with new theoretical contributions. Rather, it is a matter of recognizing the difference between the "exoteric" Marx and the "esoteric" Marx, between the conceptual core and the historical development, between the essence and the appearance. Marx is not "outdated," as bourgeois critics relish in repeating. Even if we were only to retain from him the critique of political economy, and within that above all the theory of value and abstract labor, this would still constitute the most important contribution to understanding the world in which we live. An emancipatory use of Marx's theory does not mean "going beyond" it, nor combining it with other theories, or trying to re-establish the "real Marx." Nor does it even mean always appropriating his analysis at face value. Instead, it means thinking about the world of today with the instruments he placed at our disposal. We must develop his fundamental intuitions, sometimes against the letter of his word.

The basic categories of capitalism are neither neutral nor transhistorical. Their consequences are disastrous: the supremacy of the abstract over the concrete (thus their inversion), the fetishism of the commodity, the autonomization of social processes from conscious human will, the domination of human beings by their own creations. Capitalism is inseparable from big industry while value and technology go hand in hand—they are two forms of determinism and fetishism.

Moreover, these categories are subject to a historical dynamic that makes them all the more destructive, but which also opens the possibility of their overcoming. Indeed, value is exhausted. Since its beginning, more than two hundred years ago, capitalist logic has tended to "saw off the branch on which it sits," since competition drives each individual capital to employ technologies that replace living labor. This entails an immediate advantage for the individual capital in question, but it also diminishes the production of value, surplus-value, and profit on a global scale, thus endangering the reproduction of the system as a whole. The various compensatory mechanisms, the last of which was Fordism, are also definitively exhausted. Nor will the "tertiary" sector be adequate to save capitalism, since it remains necessary to distinguish between productive and unproductive labor (which is always of course a question of the productivity of *capital*).

The beginning of the seventies witnessed a triple, or even quadruple, point of rupture: economic (visible in the abandonment of the gold standard), ecological (visible in the report of the Club of Rome), and energy (visible in the "first oil shock")—to which should be added the changes in mentality and lifestyles of the post-1968 period ("liquid modernity," "the third spirit of capitalism"). Thus, capitalist society begun to come up against both its external and internal constraints.

In this permanent crisis of accumulation—designating an increasing difficulty in making profits—the financial markets (fictitious capital) have become the main source of profit by allowing the consumption of unrealized future gains. The global boom in finance is the effect, not the cause, of the crisis of capital valorization.

High profit levels of some economic actors do not demonstrate that the system as such is in good health. The cake is always getting smaller, regardless of whether it is cut into larger pieces. Neither China nor other "emerging markets" will save capitalism, despite the savage exploitation persisting there.

The centrality of the concept of "class struggle" in the analysis of capitalism must also be criticized. The role of classes is a consequence of their place in the accumulation of value as an anonymous process—classes are not at its origin. Social injustice is not what makes capitalism historically unique; it has existed long before. It is abstract labor and money that represent the particularity of capitalism, and they have created an entirely new society, where actors, even the "dominant" ones, are essentially the executors of a logic that is outside of their control (a fact that need not exonerate certain figures from the consequences of their activities).

Above all, the historical role of the workers' movement consisted, beyond its proclaimed intentions, in promoting the integration of the proletariat. This was indeed possible during the long phase of ascension of capitalist society, but is no longer possible today. It is necessary to resume a critique of *production*, and not simply struggle for a more equitable *distribution* of that mode of production's basic categories (money, value, labor). Today, the question of abstract labor is no longer "abstract," but directly perceivable.

The Soviet Union was essentially a form of "catch-up modernization" (through autarky). This is also true for the revolutionary movements of the "periphery" and the countries they were able to govern, whose failure after 1980 lies at the origin of many current conflicts.

The triumph of capitalism is also its failure. Value does not create a sustainable or just society, but destroys its own foundations across all domains.

Rather than continuing to seek out a "revolutionary subject," the "automatic subject" (Marx) on which capitalist society is based must be overcome.

Alongside exploitation—which continues to exist, even in gigantic proportions—it is the creation of a "superfluous" humanity, even as "waste," that has become the main problem posed by capitalism. Capital no longer has any need of humanity and ends up devouring itself. This situation constitutes a terrain favorable to emancipation, but also to barbarism. Rather than a North-South dichotomy, we are now faced with a "global apartheid," with walls surrounding small islands of wealth in every country and city.

The powerlessness of states in the face of global capital is not only a problem of unwillingness, but results from the structural subordination of the state and politics to the domain of value.

The ecological crisis is impossible to overcome within the framework of capitalism, even if we aim at "degrowth" or, much worse, "green capitalism" and "sustainable development." As long as capitalist society persists, productivity gains mean that an ever-increasing mass of material objects—whose production consumes real resources—represents an ever-smaller mass of value, which is the expression of the abstract side of labor. Within the logic of capital, it is only the production of value that matters. Capitalism is therefore essentially and inevitably productivist, oriented towards production for production's sake.

At the same time, we are also experiencing an anthropological crisis, a crisis of civilization, and a crisis of subjectivity. There is a loss of imagination, especially that which emerges in childhood. Narcissism has become the dominant psychic form. It is a worldwide phenomenon: a PlayStation can just as easily be found in a hut in the middle of the jungle as in a New York loft. Faced with the regression and de-civilization promoted by capital, we must decolonize the imagination and reinvent happiness.

Capitalist society, based on labor and value, is also a *patriarchal* society, in essence and not just by accident. Historically, the production of value has been a masculine affair. Indeed, not all activities create the value that appears within market exchange. So-called "reproductive" activities, which take place mainly in the domestic sphere, are generally assigned to women. These activities are essential to the production of value, but they do not produce value. They play an indispensable but auxiliary role in the society of value. This society consists as much of the sphere of value as of the sphere of non-value, that is to say, of the whole of these two spheres. Yet the realm of non-value is not a "free" or "non-alienated" sphere—quite the contrary. This sphere of non-value contains the status of "non-subject" (even for a long time at the legal level), since these activities are not considered "labor" (however useful they may be) and do not appear on the market.

Capitalism did not invent the separation between the private, domestic sphere and the public sphere of labor. But it has greatly accentuated that separation. Despite its universalist pretensions, expressed through the Enlightenment, it emerged in the form of a domination by white, Western men, and it has continued to base itself on a logic of exclusion: separation between, on the one hand, the production of value, the labor that creates it, and the human qualities that contribute to it (in particular, internalized discipline and the spirit of individual competition), and, on the other hand, everything that is not part of it. Some of those excluded, especially women, have been partially "integrated" into market logic over the last few decades and have been able to achieve "subject" status—but only when they have demonstrated that they have acquired and internalized the "qualities" of white, Western men. Generally, the price of this integration consists of a double alienation (women must work *and* raise a family). At the same time, new forms of exclusion are created, especially in times of crisis. However, it is not a question of demanding "inclusion" within the sphere of labor, money, and subject status, but of putting an end to a society where only participation in the market bestows the right to "subjecthood." Neither patriarchy nor racism are anachronistic residues in the framework of a capitalism that tends towards equality under the gaze of money.

Contemporary populism is a great danger. Its mere critique of the financial sphere, a mixture of elements of both left and right, sometimes evokes the perverted "anti-capitalism" of fascists. Capitalism must be fought as a whole, not just its neoliberal phase. A return to Keynesianism and the welfare state is neither desirable nor possible. Is the struggle for greater "integration" into dominant society worthwhile (to obtain rights, to improve one's material conditions)—or is it simply impossible?

It is important to avoid the misleading enthusiasm of those who add up all the current forms of protest to deduce that revolution is already in motion. Some of these protests risk being recuperated by a defense of the established order, while others can lead to barbarism. Capitalism actualizes its own abolition, of money, work, etc., but it depends on the conscious activity of people—the only force that can ensure what follows is not worse.

It is necessary to overcome the dichotomy between reform and revolution—but in the name of radicalism, since reformism is in no way "realistic." Too much attention is often paid to the *form* of protest (violence/non-violence, etc.) instead of to its content.

The abolition of money and value, of commodities and labor, of the state and the market, must take place immediately—neither as a "maximalist" program nor as a utopia, but as the only form of "realism." It is not enough to free ourselves from the "capitalist class." We must emancipate ourselves from the capitalist social relation, a relation that involves everyone, regardless of social roles. It is therefore difficult to draw a clear line between "us and them," or to even say "we are the 99 percent," as the "square movements" have so often done. However, this problem might present itself in very different ways in different parts of the world.

Neither is it a question of realizing some form of self-management of capitalist alienation. The abolition of the private ownership of the means of production is not enough. The subordination of the content of social life to the value-form and its accumulation could, at most, operate without a "ruling class" and take place "democratically," without being any less destructive. The fault lies neither with the technical structure as such, nor with an unsurpassable modernity, but rather with the "automatic subject" that is value.

There are different ways of understanding the "abolition of work." Conceiving its abolition through the use of new technologies risks reinforcing the prevailing technophilia. Rather than simply reducing working time or praising "the right to be lazy," it is a question of going beyond the very distinction between "work" and other activities. On this point, non-capitalist cultures have an abundance of lessons to teach.

There is no model from the past to emulate and reproduce, no ancestral wisdom to offer guidance, no spontaneity of the people that will save us with certainty. But the very fact that all of humanity—for very long periods of time, and still a large part of it until recently—has lived without capitalist categories, demonstrates at the very least that they can hardly be considered natural, and that it is possible to live without them.

Endnotes

Prologue

1 The translator would like to acknowledge the work of Peter Dunn, whose previous work on a separate English translation was kindly shared.—Trans.

2 Callimachus, *Hymn to Demeter* and Ovid, *Metamorphoses* Book 8, lines 738–878. The myth is even older: a fragment of the *Catalogue of Women*, attributed to Hesiod (seventh or eighth century BCE), already mentions it. Later, Dante briefly describes Erysichthon in "Purgatorio" of his *Divine Comedy* (canto XXIII, lines 25-27).

3 Ovid, *Metamorphoses* (Indianapolis: Hackett Publishing Company, 2010), 234.

4 The Greeks knew only the beginning of this logic, and as such the myth does not refer to it. But there are many cases in which stories can represent something very different from the original meaning in the eyes of subsequent generations—not to mention the fact that *hubris*, which is the subject of this myth, constitutes one of the psychological presuppositions of the future development of capitalism.

5 Ovid, *Metamorphoses*, 232.

6 Anselm Jappe, "Degrowthers, One More Effort If You Want to Be Revolutionaries!," in *The Writing on the Wall: On The Decomposition of Capitalism and Its Critics*, trans. Alastair Hemmens (Washington: Zero Books, 2017), 130.

7 Which, apart from any metaphor, is true in the case of the island of Nauru. The inhabitants of this tiny Pacific island, a formally independent state resting on phosphate deposits, have literally let their island be destroyed by mining companies seeking to gain, for some decades, access to commodity abundance. They now live in absolute poverty. Luc Folliet, *Nauru, l'île dévastée. Comment la civilisation capitaliste a détruit le pays le plus riche du monde* (Paris: La Découverte, 2010).

8 As German philosophers Theodor W. Adorno and Max Horkheimer, two of the earliest observers of this phenomenon, already wrote in 1944. *Dialectic of Enlightenment: Philosophical Fragments* (Stanford: Stanford University Press, 2002), 28.

9 Anselm Jappe, *The Adventures of the Commodity* (London: Bloomsbury, 2023).

Chapter 1

1 Karl Marx, "Economic Manuscripts of 1857–58 [*Grundrisse*]," in *Karl Marx/Frederick Engels Collected Works, Vol. 28* (New York: Progress Publishers, 1986), 94.

2 Moishe Postone, *Time, Labor, and Social Domination: A Reinterpretation of Marx's Critical Theory* (Cambridge: Cambridge University Press, 1993).

3 Marx returns to fetishism in a fragment intended for the third volume of *Capital*, which Engels, when preparing the volume for publication after Marx's death, placed almost at the end, again as a conclusion. This fragment, called the "Trinity Formula," effectively presents fetishism as a kind of disguise for the fact that the true origin of surplus-value lies in labor alone. He thus seems to vindicate traditional Marxists, who tend to interpret fetishism as simply a "veil" or deception. However, the place of the two analyses of fetishism, one at the very beginning and another at the very end of the twenty-five hundred pages of *Capital*, allows us to say that the two levels of reading are not mutually exclusive: the fetishism of the first chapter corresponds to the invisible *essence* of capitalism (value), while

that of the "Trinity Formula" corresponds, like many of the developments in the third volume, to the phenomenal level, to the "surface appearance." This demonstrates once again the importance of the Hegelian distinction between essence and appearance.

4 Karl Marx, "Capital: A Critique of Political Economy, Volume I," in *Karl Marx/ Frederick Engels Collected Works, Vol. 35* (New York: Progress Publishers, 1996), 94.

5 See, for example, Ernst Cassirer in *Philosophy of Symbolic Forms* (1923).

6 To this must be added the work of Durkheim, whose "collective representations" are also an attempt to describe a social *a priori*.

7 A small number of other authors have contributed to the discussion of "constitutive subjectivity," especially in relation to Kant. Here we are thinking of Theodor W. Adorno; his first mentor, Alfred Sohn-Rethel; and his student, Hans-Jürgen Krahl.

8 The term "subject-form" indicates an *a priori* form—but one that is limited to a historical period—into which all behavior and consciousness must be molded in order for the individual to be recognized as a "subject." The term "subject" also indicates the living, empirically present subjects that correspond to this form, just as the values of different commodities are always expressions of the value-form.

9 Marx, Karl, *Capital: A Critique of Political Economy, Volume I* (London: Penguin Books, 1976), 255.

10 For more detailed considerations on the "automatic subject," as well as other issues dealt with in this introductory part of the present work, see Anselm Jappe, *The Adventures of the Commodity* (London: Bloomsbury, 2023).

11 "Oedipus's answer to the riddle of the Sphinx—"That being is man"—is repeated indiscriminately as enlightenment's stereotyped message." Adorno and Horkheimer, *Dialectic of Enlightenment*, 4.

12 Rene Descartes, *Discourse on Method and Meditations on First Philosophy* (Indianapolis: Hackett Publishing, 1988), 9. Unfortunately, here Descartes does not mention about whom he is thinking.

13 Descartes, *Discourse*, 13–14.

14 Descartes, *Discourse*, 34.

15 Descartes, *Discourse*, 34.

16 Descartes, *Discourse*, 8, 17.

17 The *reductio ad unum* as a fundamental principle of his thought is also demonstrated in his aversion to historically "improved" cities, to which he contrasts buildings and cities built according to plans and by engineers with straight and right-angled streets (Descartes, *Discourse*, 7). He expresses the same hostility towards anything that is not a uniform creation in the realm of legislation, religion, or natural reason.

18 The "dualistic" conception of man, which devalues the body in favor of those parts of man which communicate with the transcendent, is much less characteristic of medieval Christianity than is usually thought and only really begins with Descartes. In this respect, see Jérôme Baschet, *Corps et âmes. Une histoire de la personne au Moyen Âge* (Paris: Flammarion, 2016).

19 Descartes, *Discourse*, 18–19.

20 Descartes, *Discourse*, 21.

21 Descartes, *Discourse*, 21.

22 Descartes, *Discourse*, 55.

23 Descartes, *Discourse*, 28.

24 It is somewhat surprising that in the eyes of Descartes, the construction of a robot that even utters a few words does not seem to be a major technical difficulty.

25 Descartes, *Discourse*, 63.

26 Descartes, *Discourse*, 65.

27 Descartes, *Discourse*, 73.

28 Descartes, *Discourse*, 94–95.

29 Whereas Christianity recognized that the most important possession—an immor-

tal soul—is given to every human being.

30 Even regarding his character, Descartes' writings demonstrate a permanent oscillation between proclamations—probably insincere—of modesty and submission to authorities, along with expressions of great contempt for all past and contemporary scholars.

31 This causal relationship to death and the dead is one of the features that allow us to speak of a real "break within civilization" (or *Zivilisationbruch: Denken nach Auschwitz*, the title of the German publication in which Postone's essay about antisemitism appeared: Dan Diner and Seyla Benhabib, eds., *Zivilisationbruch: Denken nach Auschwitz* (Frankfurt: Fischer, 1988). In all civilizations, the burial of the dead was one of the elements that made it possible to distinguish between situations of anomie and total barbarism, as they can arise particularly during war. The story of Hector in the *Iliad* illustrates that the honors bestowed to the dead were just as important as those reserved for the living.

32 See Jonathan Crary, *24/7: Late Capitalism and the Ends of Sleep* (London: Verso, 2013). While the roots of this attitude in Christian asceticism seem fairly obvious, it remains to be seen what place the ancient and oriental "techniques of the self" have in this framework.

33 Which, of course, in the practice of pre-modern societies, did not exclude very strong antagonisms.

34 Edmund Husserl, *Ideas Pertaining to a Pure Phenomenology and to a Phenomenological Philosophy, First Book: General Introduction to a Pure Phenomenology* (Boston: Martinus Nijhoff Publishers, 1983), 109. In his 1950 French translation of the book, Paul Ricœur commented, with regard to §49 ("Absolute Consciousness as the Residuum After the Annihilation of the World), that Husserl "draws the radical consequence: consciousness does not need things to exist; it is the absolute affirmed in §44 and §46."

35 Eske Bockelmann, *Im Takt des Geldes. Zur Genese modernen Denkens* (Springe: Zu Klampen, 2004).

36 Eske Bockelmann, "Die Synthese am Geld: Natur der Neuzeit," *Exit!*, no. 5 (2008).

37 Descartes, *Discourse*, 69.

38 In many ways, Leibniz was one of the major ideologues of capitalist modernity, and of its worst aspects in particular. For example, he dreamed of a "universal language," a simple system of unambiguous signs, which would eliminate all ambiguity from social life. This can be seen as an anticipation of cybernetics and binary logic, where structures of domination disappear behind mathematical structures.

39 In the words of Canadian philosopher and anthropologist Charles Taylor, an author rather distant from the critical approach developed here: "Instrumental reason has also grown along with a disengaged model of the human subject, which has a great hold on our imagination. It offers an ideal picture of a human thinking that has disengaged from its messy embedding in our bodily constitution, our dialogical situation, our emotions, and our traditional life forms in order to be pure, self-verifying rationality. This is one of the most prestigious forms of reason in our culture, exemplified by mathematical thinking, or other types of formal calculation." Charles Taylor, *The Malaise of Modernity* (Toronto: House of Anansi Press, 1992), 101–102.

40 To cite just a few studies: Louis Dumont, *From Mandeville to Marx: The Genesis and Triumph of Economic Ideology* (Chicago: University of Chicago Press, 1977); Serge Latouche, *L'Invention de l'économie* (Paris: Albin Michel, 2005); Dany-Robert Dufour, *La Cité perverse. Libéralisme et pornographie* (Paris: Denoël, 2009), especially with regard to Mandeville.

41 Access to the "right to vote" has long been the main battleground of this struggle, even if its scope has always been rather symbolic. Today, access to the labor market through quotas and representation in the media are other fields of

the same struggle. For Kant, it was obvious that the right to vote could not apply to women or servants: "Anyone who has the right to vote on this legislation is a *citizen*. . . . The only qualification required by a citizen (apart, of course, from being an adult male) is that he must be his *own master (sui juris)*, and must have some *property*." Immanuel Kant, "On the Common Saying: 'This May Be True in Theory, But It Does Not Apply in Practice'," *Kant: Political Writings* (Cambridge: Cambridge University Press, 1991), 77–78.

42 We also say "to be subject to," which is the opposite of the usual sense of the word "subject."

43 Marxists have made a wide variety of judgments about Kant, although Marx himself almost completely ignored him. Later, Marxists who were more committed to Marx's Hegelian roots, such as Lukács, subscribed to Hegel's critique of Kant. Certain "revisionist" currents, such as the early twentieth-century "Austro-Marxism," pointed to Kantian ethics as a possible basis for socialist engagement. Even without direct reference to these antecedents, there are many Marxists (such as André Tosel, *Kant révolutionnaire*, (Paris: Presses universitaires de France, 1998)) or critics of neoliberalism (such as Dany-Robert Dufour, *The Art of Shrinking Heads* (London: Polity, 2008)) who see Kant as a theorist of human freedom and dignity: the one who proclaimed that the autonomy of the subject present today—especially by a social critique reduced to discourses on "civil society," democracy, and human rights—is the last bulwark against neoliberal onslaught and barbarism. Even when it seems difficult to turn Kant into a thinker of revolution, efforts are often made to turn him into a potential critic of capitalist society. Others, such as Lucio Colletti in Italy, have called upon Kant as a witness for their condemnation of Marx and Hegel, and especially of the "Hegelian" aspects of Marx (*Marxism and Hegel* (London: Verso, 1979)). Obviously, the discourse on such an important thinker as Kant cannot be fully resolved in the few pages here. There are other developments in his thinking, notably on "dignity," which is "above all superior" and "admits of no equivalent," and which correspond to the fact that the Enlightenment was at once both the passage to a "disciplinary society," with its internalization of new constraints, and the opening of new horizons of emancipation.

44 For example, regarding non-Western populations: "The Negroes of Africa have by nature no feeling that rises above the ridiculous." Immanuel Kant, *Observations on the Feeling of the Beautiful and Sublime* (Cambridge: Cambridge University Press, 2011), 58.

45 Immanuel Kant, *Critique of Practical Reason* (Indianapolis: Hackett Publishing, 2002), 34.

46 In this context, it is significant that "[a]ll respect for a person is properly only respect for the law" (Immanuel Kant, *Groundwork for the Metaphysics of Morals* (New Haven: Yale University Press, 2002), 17). Kantian morality is not concerned with real human beings, but only with "general laws." A person exists only as a representative of the law, the concrete as representative of the abstract: it is the same logic of inversion that, in commodity society, permeates all spheres of life, starting from the relationship between use-value and commodity value.

47 For example, Bertrand Russell, *Human Society in Ethics and Politics* (London: George Allen & Unwin, 1954).

48 In order to explain the "categorical imperative," Kant provides the following example: if a person holds a cash deposit from someone, and the latter dies without their heir knowing anything about it, and even if the depositor is very poor, with a family to support, and is moreover virtuous and charitable, while the heir is rich, and moreover, cold-hearted and a spendthrift, the depositor is still morally obligated to return the money. This is dictated by the principle of the possible universalization of one's own behavior: if everyone, in such a case, appropriated the deposit, there would no longer be any confidence and the very institution of the deposit would disappear (Kant, "On the Common Saying," 70, as well

as Kant, *Critique of Practical Reason*, 40–41). Hegel already criticized the "empty formalism" of the categorical imperative: a thief who denies private property and accepts being robbed in turn applies the Kantian categorical imperative just as rigorously. In his supposedly non-empirical example, Kant has already sneaked in a particular presupposition: property is a moral institution.

49 See Hartmut Böhme and Gernot Böhme, *Das Andere der Vernunft. Zur Entwicklung von Rationalitätsstrukturen am Beispiel Kants* (Frankfurt am Main: Suhrkamp, 1983), final chapter.

50 Kant, *Critique of Practical Reason*, 149.

51 Kant, *Critique of Practical Reason*, 113.

52 Robert Kurz, "Der Kampf um die Wahrheit," *Exit!*, no. 12, 72–73.

53 The beginnings of industrialization in England went hand in hand with the emergence of a generation of poets who developed a new sensibility for beauty, nature, and the irrational, from William Blake to Thomas De Quincey. It was above all the latter who expressed the dual nature of the modern subject then emerging: on the one hand extreme rationality, classical culture, studies in political economy, great lucidity; on the other, drug addiction (which De Quincey describes in his *Confessions of an English Opium-Eater* [1822], translated into French by Baudelaire), a ravaged spirit, disordered life, family disasters, self-destructive tendencies, Nero-like behavior. De Quincey's admiration for Kant (*The Last Days of Immanuel Kant*, 1827) and praise for murder (*On Murder Considered as One of the Fine Arts*, 1827, precursor to the aestheticization of disaster and violence) fit perfectly well together. The division into two parts, one of which coldly observes the craziest and most terrifying dreams of the other, is indeed a very modern split.

54 The first to notice this parallelism were Max Horkheimer and Theodor W. Adorno, who devote a chapter to Sade in their *Dialectic of Enlightenment*. See also Jacques Lacan's 1963 essay "Kant with Sade," *October* 51, 1989, 55–75, and his critical analysis in Dufour, *La Cité perverse*, 240–276. Our critique of the cult of Sade is similar to that proposed by Dufour, although we do not at all share his praise for Kant as a thinker of the strong subject, which he opposes to the liberalism embodied by Sade.

55 "Sade's ethics radically transcend any form of hedonism. All sensuous experience must be subdued, not unleashed. And sensuality must be entirely surrendered to the directives of reason and the empire of the will. Drawing Sade towards Stoicism or Kant rallies him on the side of reason and to the demands of a severe philosophy that cannot turn pleasure into a principle" (Claire Margat, "Une horrible liberté"). The author quotes Simone de Beauvoir's *Must We Burn Sade?*: "With a severity similar to Kant's, and which has its source in the same puritan tradition, Sade conceives the free act only as an act free of all feeling. If it were to obey emotional motives, it would make us Nature's slaves again and not autonomous subjects."

56 Rationality of means is accompanied by excessiveness and irrationality in ends. Robert Kurz quotes the disturbing Captain Ahab in *Moby Dick*, that "great parable about the modern age," who states: "all my means are sane, my motive and object mad." Robert Kurz, "Totalitarian Economy and Paranoia of Terror: The Death Wish of Capitalist Reason," *Krisis: Contributions to the Critique of Commodity Society* (London: Chronos Publications, 2002), 29.

57 Marquis de Sade, *Philosophy in the Bedroom* (New York: Grove Press, 1965), 320.

58 Georges Bataille, "De Sade's Sovereign Man," in *Erotism: Death and Sensuality* (San Francisco: City Lights Books, 1986), 166.

59 "[T]he only crime possible would be in resisting her: all the criminals on earth are nothing but the agents of her caprices" (Sade, *Philosophy in the Bedroom*, 361). He returns several times to this idea, two hundred years before the atomic bomb: nature itself could order man to set the universe on fire. The absolute determinism professed by Sade is thus reminiscent of social fetishism and its blind laws.

60 As observed clearly by Denis de Rougemont in *Love in the Western World* (Prince-

ton: Princeton University Press, [1938] 1983), 260.

61 "The aspiration to integral monstrosity is in Sade the frenzied aspiration to try out all the imaginable forms of pleasure, to become the subject capable of exhausting the totality of the possible (whereas this totality of the possible can never be attained, the possible in fact being what is impossible to exhaust, being the inexhaustible)." Pierre Klossowski, *Sade My Neighbor* (Evanston: Northwestern University Press, 1991), 137.

62 Bataille, "De Sade's Sovereign Man," 167.

63 Bataille, "De Sade's Sovereign Man," 174–175.

64 Sade, *Philosophy in the Bedroom*, 230.

65 Ernst Lohoff, "Die Verzauberung der Welt. Die Subjektform und ihre Konstitutionsgeschichte," *Krisis*, no. 29 (2005), 13–60.

66 In reality, this concreteness is a pseudo-concreteness, since the very process of consolidating the most diverse things under the real abstraction of "use-value" or "concrete labor" already constitutes an abstraction.

67 Lohoff, "Die Verzauberung der Welt," 36–37.

68 Lohoff, "Die Verzauberung der Welt," 47.

69 Lohoff, "Die Verzauberung der Welt," 49.

70 For the labor movement, anyone who does not work is necessarily a parasite that does not deserve to eat. The exploiting class is by definition a class of non-workers. Faced with populations that are not exploitative at all, but remain faithful to traditional forms of activity that do not follow the rules of "work"—from gypsies to Native Americans, from the descendants of slaves to Mediterranean populations, from nomadic tribes to Russian peasants—the workers' movement has shown great desire to put them to work and to make them give up their taste for unproductive activities such as partying, drinking, and love. Antonio Gramsci and Lenin were great admirers of Taylorism, that is, the "scientific management of the labor force," as well as Fordism. Gramsci, so frequently presented as the "good Leninist," was particularly pleased that assembly-line work would free workers from their unfortunate penchant for drink and sex. Antonio Gramsci, "Americanism and Fordism," in *Selections from the Prison Notebooks* (New York: International Publishers, 1971), 277–318.

71 Let us offer the floor to Schopenhauer, who, it must be admitted, had more than one arrow in his quiver: "Every miserable fool who has nothing at all of which he can be proud, adopts as a last resource pride in the nation to which he belongs" Arthur Schopenhauer, *Parerga and Paralipomena: A Collection of Philosophical Essays* (New York: Cosimo Classics, 2007), 60.

72 The new religious fundamentalisms do not fit into these two mega-subjects of classical modernity and will be discussed towards the end of this book.

73 This is one of the causes of the great difficulty in adopting even the most elementary measures to safeguard the environment: the rationality for the subject—self-assertion at all costs, identification with "winning" values such as speed or efficiency—is in almost absolute contrast with ecological concerns, and therefore also with the continuation of industrial society in the medium-term.

74 Lohoff, "Die Verzauberung der Welt," 60.

75 Arthur Schopenhauer, *The World as Will and Representation, Volume 1* (Cambridge: Cambridge University Press, 2010), §2, 25.

76 In fact, many of his letters end with the phrase: "And what are the police doing about it?"

77 According to traditional Marxism—for example, Lukács—the success of these two thinkers, both of whom propose a form of withdrawal, among the German bourgeoisie of the nineteenth century (obviously in quite different registers), is explained by the frustration of this bourgeoisie, which sees itself excluded from political power and relegated to private life. Although this explanation is not wrong, it is too partial. Schopenhauer and Stirner expressed a typically modern form of existence that goes far beyond the specific conditions of nineteenth-cen-

tury Germany—which explains why both are still read today.

78 Max Stirner, *The Unique and Its Property* (Baltimore: Underworld Amusements, Paris, 2017), 180, 109.

79 However, there is a point of convergence with the "libertarians" and their defense of "anarcho-capitalism." Portuguese writer Fernando Pessoa had already exploited the paradox of the absolute freedom of the individual, advocated by individualist anarchists in *The Anarchist Banker* (1922).

Chapter 2

1 Bela Grunberger, *Narcissism: Psychoanalytic Essays* (New York: International Universities Press, 1979), 2. In *The Language of Psychoanalysis*, Jean Laplanche and J. B. Pontalis note that the terms primary and secondary narcissism have "such varied uses in psycho-analytic literature—and even within Freud's own work— that it is impossible to give a more precise yet consistent definition than the one offered above" and that "[t]he notion of primary narcissism undergoes extreme variations in sense from one author to the next," with some even doubting its very existence. Jean Laplanche and J. B. Pontalis, *The Language of Psychoanalysis* (London: Karnac Books, 1988), 337.

2 Albert Eiguer, *Le Pervers narcissique et son complice* (Paris: Dunod, 2003).

3 Marie-France Hirigoyen, *Stalking the Soul: Emotional Abuse and the Erosion of Identity* (New York: Helen Marx Books, 2005).

4 Pascale Chapaux-Morelli and Pascal Couderc, *La Manipulation affective dans le couple. Faire face à un pervers narcissique* (Paris: Albin Michel, 2010).

5 It should be remembered that for Freud, at least in principle, the term "perversion" does not imply a moral judgment, but qualifies "[d]eviation from the 'normal' sexual act when this is defined as coitus with a person of the opposite sex directed towards the achievement of orgasm by means of genital penetration" (Laplanche and Pontalis, *The Language of Psychoanalysis*, 306). This amounts to identifying the non-perverse act essentially with the biological purpose of sexuality, i.e. procreation. Strictly speaking, even kissing would therefore constitute a perverse act.

6 "Narcissism in this sense would not be a perversion, but the libidinal complement to the egoism of the instinct of self-preservation, a measure of which may justifiably be attributed to every living creature." Sigmund Freud, "On Narcissism: An Introduction," *The Standard Edition of the Complete Psychological Works of Sigmund Freud*, Vol. XIV (London: The Hogarth Press, 2001), 73–74.

7 This statement falls under the "economic" conception of psychoanalysis, as Freud himself called it, while others, such as Erich Fromm, have qualified it as a "hydraulic" conception. It deserves separate consideration: did Freud develop his conception of the drives and the unconscious by taking as a model the capitalist economy, and more precisely value, that quantity without quality which can easily be converted from one form to another while remaining itself? This would be a good example of the fact that even Freud's unconscious, unbeknownst to him, was inadvertently formed by "real abstractions" and the social synthesis governed by value, and that he too took them for granted. At the same time, it must be stressed that the term "investment" (cathexis) can be misleading with regard to the Freudian "psychic economy": it corresponds to the German term *Besetzung*, which literally means "occupation" and has no economic significance.

8 "Finally, as regards the differentiation of psychical energies, we are led to the conclusion that to begin with, during the state of narcissism, they exist together and that our analysis is too coarse to distinguish between them; not until there is object-cathexis is it possible to discriminate a sexual energy – the libido – from an energy of the ego-instincts." Freud, "On Narcissism," 76.

9 "This leads us to look upon the narcissism which arises through the drawing in of

object-cathexes as a secondary one, superimposed upon a primary narcissism that is obscured by a number of different influences." Freud, "On Narcissism," 75.

10 To be more precise, in the 1914 essay, narcissism is supposed to supersede auto-erotism, whereas in Freud's subsequent writings, narcissism characterizes the very beginning of life and is confused with auto-erotism.

11 This constitutes the core of the future Freudian conception of the superego (which is, however, in its complete form the result of the end of the Oedipal complex and the internalization of the paternal prohibition).

12 "What [the adult] projects before him as his ideal is the substitute for the lost narcissism of his childhood in which he was his own ideal." Freud, "On Narcissism," 94.

13 Freud, "On Narcissism," 100.

14 Freud, "On Narcissism," 94.

15 Sigmund Freud, "Group Psychology and the Analysis of the Ego," *The Standard Edition of the Complete Psychological Works of Sigmund Freud*, Vol. XVIII (London: The Hogarth Press, 1981), 130.

16 Freud, "Group Psychology," 131.

17 Laplanche and Pontalis, *The Language of Psychoanalysis*, 338.

18 Patrick Juignet, *Manuel de psychopathologie générale* (Grenoble: Presses universitaires de Grenoble, 2015), 72.

19 Juignet, *Manuel*, 65.

20 Juignet, *Manuel*, 72. In fact, Freud expressed doubts, especially at the beginning of *Civilization and its Discontents*, about the relevance of the concept of "oceanic feeling," which the writer Romain Rolland mentioned to him in a letter as the source of all religious sentiment.

21 Juignet, *Manuel*, 70.

22 Pierre Dessuant, *Le Narcissisme* (Paris: Presses universitaires de France, 2007), 65–66 and elsewhere.

23 Dessuant, *Le Narcissisme*, 91–92.

24 Heinz Kohut, *The Analysis of the Self: A Systematic Approach to the Psychoanalytic Treatment of Narcissistic Personality Disorders* (Chicago: University of Chicago Press, [1971] 2009).

25 Cited in Paul Denis, *Le Narcissisme* (Paris: Presses universitaires de France, 2012), 100.

26 Denis, *Le Narcissisme*, 76–77.

27 This is not a reference to Heidegger (although perhaps to The Doors' song "Riders on the Storm"!). The term is already found in a passage of Freud's *Inhibitions, Symptoms and Anxiety* (1926), quoted in Laplanche and Pontalis, *The Language of Psychoanalysis*, 190.

28 Here, as throughout this book, we obviously do not necessarily mean biological mother, nor necessarily a woman, but the person who primarily cares for the child—the "maternal figure."

29 The term proposed by Laplanche and Pontalis, *The Language of Psychoanalysis*, 190.

30 Recently, Dany-Robert Dufour has taken up this conception under the name of "neoteny," making it the basis of vast considerations on the relationship between nature and culture. Dany-Robert Dufour, *On achève bien les hommes* (Paris: Denoël, 2005). Before him, biologists Louis Bolk and Desmond Morris, as well as Jacques Lacan, had already made mention of it.

31 It is possible that the death drive—that much contested Freudian concept to which we shall return—is less a desire for death than for a return to this primary state. It is rather the "Nirvana principle," an expression that Freud introduced in 1920 in *Beyond the Pleasure Principle*, and which he borrowed from English psychoanalyst Barbara Low. In the same essay, Freud also defines the "principle of constancy" as the organism's tendency to reduce tensions and excitations as much as possible. According to his own admission, the relationship between the death

drive, the Nirvana principle, and the principle of constancy is not very clear and is part of the most speculative aspect of his thinking.

32 See note 28.

33 For more recent psychoanalytic theories, it is of little importance how the Oedipus complex actually unfolds, such as whether there is a father, whether it is two men, or two women, etc. It is like an equation that can be filled with different variables without the equation itself changing. It should also be noted that this conflict does not necessarily occur all at once; rather, it seems to be a constellation that repeats itself several times, perhaps as early as the first year.

34 Sigmund Freud, "The Libido Theory and Narcissism," in *Introductory Lectures on Psycho-Analysis (Part III)*, *The Standard Edition of the Complete Psychological Works of Sigmund Freud*, Vol. XVI (London: The Hogarth Press, 1981), 421.

35 The child may even openly deny the reality of separation—but in this case, very serious and visible disorders in the sense of child psychosis might follow.

36 Freud, "On Narcissism," 99–100.

37 This drowning evokes a return to the amniotic fluid, as Lasch notes, citing Grunberger (Christopher Lasch, *The Minimal Self: Psychic Survival in Troubled Times* (New York: W.W. Norton & Company, 1984), 184).

38 A version of the following analysis was first published in English as Anselm Jappe, "Narcissus or Orpheus? Notes on Freud, Fromm, Marcuse and Lasch," *Cured Quail Vol. 2*, 2020, 190–215.

39 Valentin Voloshinov, *Freudianism: A Marxist Critique* (London: Verso, 2013).

40 This idea of an almost infinite plasticity of the human being then returns, in a certain manner, to postmodern discourse: everything is construction, even biological sex.

41 In *Civilization and Its Discontents*, Freud accepts as self-evident Hobbes' theory that *bellum omnium contra omnes* [the war of all against all] constitutes the original human condition and remains at the root of all possible variations.

42 It is possible to speak of a Freudian left (as with the Hegelian left). See, for example, Paul Robinson, *The Freudian Left: Wilhelm Reich, Geza Roheim, Herbert Marcuse* (New York: Harper & Row, 1969) and Helmut Dahmer, *Libido und Gesellschaft. Studien über Freud und die Freudsche Linke* (Frankfurt: Suhrkamp, 1973). Lasch also uses this term in *The Minimal Self*. But the distinction between a "left wing" and "right wing" of psychoanalysis can already be found in Marcuse. Herbert Marcuse, *Eros and Civilization: A Philosophical Inquiry into Freud* (Boston: Beacon Press, 1966), 239. One cannot really talk about a Freudian right in explicit terms (Marcuse refers to Jung when he speaks about the right wing of Freudianism): those who only wanted to be therapists and heal individuals, were "naturally" led to accept capitalist society as an unsurpassable horizon and to push their patients to adapt to the world as it is. In the United States, this occurred from the very beginning with the spread of Freud's ideas, and almost everywhere after the Second World War. Outside the field of professional analysts, French surrealism, to which Marcuse also refers, was the first major attempt to utilize the results of psychoanalysis in order to "change life."

43 Norman O. Brown, *Life Against Death: The Psychoanalytical Meaning of History* (Middletown: Wesleyan University Press), 1959.

44 "My friend Marcuse and I: Romulus and Remus quarreling; which of them is the *real* 'revolutionary.'" Thus begins the reply of Norman Brown to Marcuse's rather critical review of the former's 1967 *Love's Body*. Norman O. Brown, "A Reply to Herbert Marcuse," *Commentary*, no. 43 (1967), 83.

45 The term "neo-Freudian revisionism" used by Adorno and Marcuse is obviously pejorative and refers to the Marxist "revisionism" of the beginning of the century (i.e., Bernstein). The members of this current instead describe themselves as belonging to the "culturalist" or "interpersonal" school.

46 For a brief summary of the relationship between Fromm and the Institute for Social Research, see Jacques Le Rider, *L'Allié incommode* (Paris: L'Olivier, 2007); The-

odor W. Adorno, "Revisionist Psychoanalysis," *Philosophy & Social Criticism* 40, no. 3 (2014), 326–338; Jordi Maiso, "Soggettività offesa e falsa coscienza. La psicodinamica del risentimento nella teoria critica della società," *Costruzioni psicoanalitiche* no. 23 (2012); John Rickert, "The Fromm-Marcuse Debate Revisited," *Theory and Society*, no. 15 (1986), 351–400. Also worth mentioning are the classic works on the history of the Frankfurt School: Rolf Wiggerhaus, *The Frankfurt School: Its History, Theories and Political Significance* (Cambridge: Polity Press, 1995) and Martin Jay, *The Dialectical Imagination: A History of the Frankfurt School and the Institute of Social Research, 1923–1950* (Berkeley: University of California Press, 1973).

47 Fromm's criticism claimed to be based on the categories of Marx. However, it was formulated mainly in terms of "class" rather than by analyzing the fetishistic forms of life and consciousness that concern all members of society. This is why it seems quite dated today: for Fromm, psychological traits correspond closely to the socio-economic position of individuals. This also constitutes a limitation of the Institute's first attempts in the 1930s to utilize together the categories of Freud and Marx. Even in this respect, Marcuse's perspective seems more relevant today than Fromm's.

48 John Rickert, "The Fromm-Marcuse Debate," 361.

49 First published in German in 1952 and in English in 2014. Adorno repeats fairly similar observations on psychoanalysis in §§36–40 of *Minima Moralia*, published in 1951, but written beginning in the late 1930s.

50 Adorno, "Revisionist Psychoanalysis," 335.

51 Marcuse, *Eros and Civilization*, 241.

52 Marcuse, *Eros and Civilization*, 238–239.

53 Marcuse, *Eros and Civilization*, 240.

54 Marcuse, *Eros and Civilization*, 240–241. The *Standard Edition* of Freud's works in English translates the German *Trieb* as "instinct." As a result, English translations of Marcuse and other English-speaking authors often employ the same term. However, scholarly argument exists for the rendition of *Trieb* as "drive" (e.g., Ben Y. Fong, *Death and Mastery: Psychoanalytic Drive Theory and the Subject of Late Capitalism* (New York: Columbia University Press, 2016), 139–141). The present work does not alter existing translations but predominantly employs the category of "drive."—Trans.

55 Marcuse, *Eros and Civilization*, 242.

56 Marcuse, *Eros and Civilization*, 243.

57 Marcuse, *Eros and Civilization*, 253.

58 Marcuse, *Eros and Civilization*, 254.

59 Marcuse, *Eros and Civilization*, 254.

60 Marcuse, *Eros and Civilization*, 260.

61 Marcuse, *Eros and Civilization*, xxviii.

62 Adorno's essay "Sociology and Psychology" strongly affirms this point. Theodor W. Adorno, "Sociology and Psychology," *New Left Review*, 46, (Nov/Dec 1967), 67–97.

63 For a detailed critique of the Marcusian interpretation of Fromm, see Rickert, "The Fromm-Marcuse Debate."

64 See Erich Fromm, "The Human Implications of Instinctivistic 'Radicalism,' A Reply to Herbert Marcuse," *Dissent*, vol. II (1955), 342.

65 This critique seems fairly accurate, and even more so today. But Marcuse certainly did not advocate for this kind of liberated sexuality, which on the contrary corresponds to what he calls "repressive desublimation."

66 Fromm, "The Human Implications," 349.

67 Herbert Marcuse, "A Reply to Erich Fromm" and Erich Fromm, "A Counter-Rebuttal," *Dissent*, vol. III (1956), 81.

68 Four years later, philologist Norman O. Brown published *Life against Death*. In his introduction, Brown recalls the proximity of his study to that of Marcuse. Additionally, the two authors were often brought together during the sixties. It

is remarkable that the United States of the fifties, whose puritan and philistine spirit were depicted in the paintings of Edward Hopper and the novel *Lolita* by Nabokov, should have produced at the same time such radical challenges to puritan culture in the name of a kind of cosmic eroticism.

69 Marcuse interprets the death drive not only as a desire for destruction, but also, and above all, as an extreme form of the pleasure principle, as the "Nirvana principle" and as a search for absolute calm and the appeasement of all tensions. For him, it is not the death drive that paralyzes efforts for a better future (as Karen Horney puts it), but it is social conditions that prevent the instincts of life from developing and "bind[ing]" aggression. Marcuse, *Eros and Civilization*, 272.

70 The power of the universal over individuals appears with particular force in these surviving archaic processes deep within each individual. But this indicates, even in Freud, a *historical* point of origin for the unconscious.

71 However, Daniel Cohn-Bendit claims in *Le Grand Bazar* that until 1968, no more than forty copies of the French translation were ever sold.

72 "The more complete the alienation of labor, the greater the potential of freedom: total automation would be the optimum. It is the sphere outside labor which defines freedom and fulfillment." Marcuse, *Eros and Civilization*, 156.

73 Although this is a translation popularized by Ernest Mandel's 1964 *An Introduction to Marxist Economic Theory*, Marx's original formulation, found within the *Grundrisse*, is "der große zivilisierende Einfluß des Kapitals," more accurately translated as "the great civilizing influence of capital." See Karl Marx, "Economic Manuscripts of 1857-1861," in *Karl Marx/Frederick Engels Collected Works, Volume 28* (London: Progress Publishers, 1986), 336.—Trans.

74 Marcuse, *Eros and Civilization*, 268.

75 "Possession and procurement of the necessities of life are the prerequisite, rather than the content, of a free society." Marcuse, *Eros and Civilization*, 195.

76 Marcuse, *Eros and Civilization*, 153.

77 See, for example, Asger Jorn's article "The Situationists and Automation" in the first issue of *Situationist International* (1958), where he says, among other things: "Automation can develop rapidly only once it has established as a goal a perspective contrary to its own establishment, and only if it is known how to realize such a general perspective in the process of the development of automation." For Jorn, it is necessary to seize the opportunities offered by automation: "Depending on the outcome, we may arrive at a total degradation of human life or at the possibility of perpetually discovering new desires." Asger Jorn, "The Situationists and Automation," *Situationist International Anthology* (Berkeley: Bureau of Public Secrets, 2006), 57.

78 By the sixties, Debord had maintained a relationship of mutual esteem with Jacques Ellul.

79 To cite but one: Marshall Sahlins, *Stone Age Economics* (Hawthorne: Aldine de Gruyter, 1972).

80 As someone once said: "In the sixties, sexuality seemed like a roaring tiger locked in a closet. But when the closet was finally opened, only a meowing kitten emerged."

81 Marcuse, *Eros and Civilization*, 239.

82 Marcuse, *Eros and Civilization*, 213.

83 Moreover, Marcuse wanted to value the primary "narcissistic" relationship with the mother, instead of celebrating the father as a savior in the face of the threat of overwhelming absorption into the womb. (Marcuse, *Eros and Civilization*, 229–230) Already in his 1946 lecture, Adorno considered narcissism as a defense of the individual against a repressive society: it constitutes a desperate attempt by the individual to compensate for the injustice suffered in the society of universal exchange. In addition, the individual must direct the impulsive energies towards itself when other people have become inaccessible. Adorno, "Revisionist Psychoanalysis," 333.

84 See Herbert Marcuse, "Obsolescence of the Freudian Concept of Man," *Five Lectures: Psychoanalysis, Politics and Utopia* (Boston: Beacon Press, 1970).

85 Marcuse, "Obsolescence," 47–52.

86 Alexander Mitscherlich, *Society Without the Father: A Contribution to Social Psychology* (London: Tavistock, 1969).

87 Christopher Lasch, *The Culture of Narcissism: American Life in An Age of Diminishing Expectations* (New York: W.W. Norton, 1979) and Lasch, *The Minimal Self: Psychic Survival in Troubled Times* (New York: W.W. Norton, 1984). Of Lasch's work, only these two titles will be considered here.

88 Other aspects of his thinking are more questionable: his populism, the absence of any critique of political economy, his nostalgia for nineteenth century America, the apology for sport and especially for work, etc.

89 Commentators on Lasch generally pay much more attention to his descriptive side than to his theoretical foundations and reading of Freud. He has aroused little interest among psychoanalysts themselves, as is generally the case for any perspective opened by non-analysts.

90 Lasch, *The Culture of Narcissism*, 240.

91 Lasch, *The Culture of Narcissism*, 231.

92 Lasch, *The Culture of Narcissism*, xv.

93 Lasch, *The Culture of Narcissism*, 178–179.

94 This is well described, without any particular use of psychoanalytical categories, in the works of Zygmunt Bauman.

95 Michela Marzano, *Extension du domaine de la manipulation: De l'entreprise à la vie privée* (Paris: Grasset, 2008).

96 For Lasch, this term signifies a kind of "cultural left" that includes the "New Left," feminism, ecological thought, the self-help movement, and other forms of protest emergent around 1968.

97 Lasch, *The Minimal Self*, 170.

98 Lasch, *The Minimal Self*, 171.

99 Lasch, *The Minimal Self*, 172.

100 Lasch, *The Minimal Self*, 172–173.

101 Lasch, *The Minimal Self*, 167–168.

102 Lasch, *The Minimal Self*, 185.

103 Lasch, *The Minimal Self*, 193.

104 Donald Winnicott, *Playing and Reality* (London: Tavistock, 1971).

105 Lasch, *The Minimal Self*, 195–196.

106 Lasch, *The Minimal Self*, 224–260.

107 Lasch, *The Minimal Self*, 228.

108 Lasch criticizes Fromm for identifying narcissism, in *The Heart of Man: Its Genius for Good and Evil*, with simple anti-social and individualistic behavior. Lasch, *The Culture of Narcissism*, 31.

109 Lasch, *The Minimal Self*, 232.

110 Lasch, *The Minimal Self*, 232–233.

111 Lasch, *The Minimal Self*, 233.

112 Lasch, *The Minimal Self*, 233–234.

113 Lasch, *The Minimal Self*, 234.

114 Lasch, *The Minimal Self*, 293.

115 Lasch, *The Minimal Self*, 236.

116 Lasch, *The Minimal Self*, 247.

117 Lasch, *The Minimal Self*, 240.

118 Lasch, *The Minimal Self*, 175–176.

119 In his own way, Slavoj Žižek also noticed this in his preface to the Croatian edition of *The Culture of Narcissism*, published in 1986: "In addition to the inherent incompleteness of his analytical conceptual apparatus, Lasch's weak point lies in the fact that he does not supply a sufficient theoretical definition of that turning point in the socio-economic reality of late capitalism which corresponds to

the transition of 'organisation man' to 'pathological Narcissus.' At the level of discourse, this turning point is not difficult to determine: it is the transformation of the bureaucratic capitalist society of the 1940s and 50s into a society described as 'permissive.' It entails a 'post-industrial' process which, at this level, has been described in terms of the 'Third Wave' theory of writers such as Toffler." Slavoj Žižek, "'Pathological Narcissus' as a Socially Mandatory Form of Subjectivity," *Manifesta* (European Biennial of Contemporary Art, 2000), 250.

120 In the 1946 lecture on revisionist psychoanalysis, Adorno addressed this surprising criticism to Karen Horney: that she puts too much emphasis on competition. "In the epoch of the concentration camps, castration is more characteristic of social reality than competition." Adorno, "Revisionist Psychoanalysis," 333. According to Adorno, to speak of "competition" is a euphemism for omnipresent violence. Indeed, at the same time, he had developed with Horkheimer the concept of "rackets," which would have replaced the sphere of circulation. This is, however, one of the weakest aspects of his theoretical path.

121 Marcuse, *Eros and Civilization*, 96–97.

122 Even if this term, as Henri Lefebvre had already noticed in the sixties, means nothing. He instead proposed "bureaucratic society of directed consumption."

123 Remarkably, this passage was written in 2017, unknowingly prophetic of the turbulent geopolitical events of 2022 and their economic implications, which have included a Europe-wide heating crisis.—Trans.

124 See Robert Kurz, *Geld ohne Wert. Grundrisse zu einer Transformation der Kritik der politischen Ökonomie* (Bad Honnef: Horlemann, 2012).

125 Marx, *Capital, Vol. I*, 10.

126 These illuminating pages should be reread in their entirety. (Karl Marx, *Economic and Philosophic Manuscripts of 1844*, in *Marx and Engels Collected Works*, Vol. 3 (London: Progress Publishers, 1975), 322–326.

127 Charles Baudelaire, *The Flowers of Evil* (Oxford: Oxford University Press, 1993), 289.

128 What can be made of the impression that high-tech consumer capitalism corresponds to a fundamental human aspiration, given that it is often (but not always!) welcomed with open arms by "post-communist" societies, as if its arrival had long been expected? How can it be explained that the abolition of Coca-Cola would certainly cause worldwide outcry, even among those who never stop denouncing "American imperialism" and "Western crusades"? Why is it so easy to find three-year-olds who immediately prefer to play with their "tablet" rather than with other children? It may be tempting to describe all these phenomena as "regression," but is it possible to speak of "regression," another eternal dilemma, without at the same time idealizing earlier, "traditional" societies?

129 See, for example, the works of Swiss psychoanalysts Paul Parin and Fritz Morgenthaler, notably *The Whites Think Too Much: Psychoanalytic Investigations Among the Dogon in West Africa* (New Haven: Human Relations Area Files), 1986.

130 In this context, mention should be made of the important book by Rudolf Wolfgang Müller, *Geld und Geist. Zur Entstehungsgeschichte von Identitätsbewußtsein und Rationalität seit der Antike* (Frankfurt am Main: Campus, 1977), unfortunately still without an English translation and, moreover, without thematic continuation in the author's later work. Müller links the birth of the subject-form to the birth of the money-form among the Greeks, taking up the ideas of Alfred Sohn-Rethel. See Anselm Jappe, "Sohn-Rethel and the Origin of 'Real Abstraction': A Critique of Production or a Critique of Circulation?" *Historical Materialism*, 21(1), 2013, 3–14.

131 Notably in in Pierre Clastres, *Society Against the State: Essays in Political Anthropology* (New York: Zone Books, 1987).

132 Sahlins, *Stone Age Economics*, 162.

133 Lasch, *The Minimal Self*, 34. It is notable that this was written fifteen to twenty years before Richard Sennett's *The Corrosion of Character* and Zygmunt Bauman's

Liquid Modernity.

134 A parallel could be drawn with the distinction that Ivan Illich created a few years earlier between "convivial objects" and "industrial objects."

135 Perhaps humanity as a whole has grown weary of its millennial efforts to become adult and has finally given in to the Sirens of infantilism?

Chapter 3

1 Their approach has some affinities with the critique elaborated at the same time by Jean-Claude Michéa, which has been examined in Anselm Jappe, "Common Decency or Corporatism?" in *The Writing on the Wall: On the Decomposition of Capitalism and its Critics* (Winchester: Zero Books, 2017).

2 Jean-Pierre Lebrun, *Un Monde sans limites, essai pour une clinique psychanalytique du social* (Toulouse: Érès, 1997).

3 Charles Melman, *L'Homme sans gravité. Jouir à tout prix* (Paris: Denoël, 2002).

4 The Lacanian term *jouissance* is not easily rendered into English (the most common correlates appear as "enjoyment" or "pleasure"). In the present work, the term has been retained in its original form when the context clearly elicits its Lacanian discursive significance.—Trans.

5 As Dufour himself summarizes in an interview: Dany-Robert Dufour, "Le Divin Marché," *Psychasoc* Dec. 31, 2006, http://www.psychasoc.com/Kiosque/Le-Divin-Marche.

6 Dany-Robert Dufour, *Le Divin Marché. La révolution culturelle libérale* (Paris: Denoël, 2007), 304.

7 The three authors examined here—Dufour, Lebrun, and Melman—do not agree on everything; moreover, the latter two tend to confine themselves to the clinical field. However, for the sake of the present discussion, we take into account what these authors have in common, therewith simply calling them "neo-Lacanians," without wanting to define a school of thought or anything of the sort.

8 Rather than speaking of "narcissism," or "individualism," Dufour prefers the term "egoism," and especially "gregarious egoism." He reproaches Lasch for forgetting that current society entails a *lack* of primary narcissism, that is, love of the self. See Dufour, *Le Divin Marché*, 24.

9 It is rather curious that the concept of neoteny was already used in 1963 by sociologist Georges Lapassade, in his book *L'Entrée dans la vie. Essai sur l'inachèvement de l'homme* (Paris: Minuit, 1963), with an aim diametrically opposed to that of Dufour: while for the latter neoteny explains the necessity that young human beings be guided and "completed" over a long time by an adult, Lapassade drew from it the justification of a permanent youth revolt against the dangers of social sclerosis.

10 Dany-Robert Dufour, *Le Délire occidental et ses effets actuels dans la vie quotidienne : travail, loisir, amour* (Paris: Les Liens qui libèrent, 2014), 169.

11 Dufour, *Le Divin Marché*, 99.

12 Dufour, *Le Divin Marché*, 100.

13 Dufour, *Le Divin Marché*, 188.

14 Dufour, *Le Divin Marché*, 309.

15 Dufour, *Le Divin Marché*, 318.

16 *Le Divin marché* offers, in its very title, a parallel between the words of the "divine Marquis de Sade" and capitalist logic, echoing the considerations developed in the first chapter.

17 Dufour, *Le Divin Marché*, 187.

18 Dufour, *Le Divin Marché*, 191.

19 We are not abandoning religion and transcendence, but the transcendental of Kant and Freud, that is to say, reason and the Enlightenment. Dufour, *Le Divin Marché*, 118.

20 Dufour, *Le Divin Marché*, 191.

21 Dufour, *Le Divin Marché*, 337.

22 Dufour, *Le Divin Marché*, 103.

23 Dufour, *Le Divin Marché*, 134.

24 Dufour, *Le Divin Marché*, 127. Dufour cites François Ewald and Blandine Kriegel as "right-wing" interpreters of Foucault.

25 Dufour, *Le Divin Marché*, 109.

26 Dufour, *Le Divin Marché*, 171–172.

27 Dufour, *Le Divin Marché*, 175.

28 Even Slavoj Žižek, generally an admirer of Deleuze, notes the "impersonal imitation of affects . . . the communication of affective intensities beneath the level of meaning . . . exploding the limits of self-contained subjectivity and directly coupling man to a machine . . . the need to reinvent oneself permanently, opening oneself up to a multitude of desires that push us to the limit." "There are, effectively," he concludes, "features that justify calling Deleuze the ideologist of late capitalism." Slavoj Žižek, *Organs without Bodies: On Deleuze and Consequences* (London: Routledge, 2004), 163.

29 Dufour, *Le Divin Marché*, 85.

30 Melman, for his part, observes that the law—which proposes today to "follow the evolution of morals"—now refuses to recognize sexual difference and wants to impose perfect equality everywhere. Thus society prolongs the childish denial of sexual difference. Melman, *L'Homme sans gravité*, 202.

31 Melman, *L'Homme sans gravité*, 117.

32 Melman, *L'Homme sans gravité*, 224.

33 Melman, *L'Homme sans gravité*, 69–70.

34 Melman, *L'Homme sans gravité*, 24.

35 Melman, *L'Homme sans gravité*, 34.

36 Melman, *L'Homme sans gravité*, 68. It is thus an inversion of the critique of the spectacle, according to which representation has replaced reality.

37 Melman, *L'Homme sans gravité*, 80.

38 Melman, *L'Homme sans gravité*, 146.

39 Melman, *L'Homme sans gravité*, 150.

40 Dufour, *Le Délire occidental*, 160.

41 Dufour, *Le Délire occidental*, 228.

42 Dufour, *Le Délire occidental*, 312.

43 Lebrun judges that "it is at this precise point that *the subjectivity of our time* binds together what Freud called pre-oedipal—henceforth extended to both sexes—and neoliberalism," even before speaking of "neoliberal subjectivity, that which psychically internalizes the model of the market." Lebrun, *Un monde sans limites*, 16–17.

44 Melman, *L'Homme sans gravité*, 92.

45 Melman, *L'Homme sans gravité*, 135.

46 Melman, *L'Homme sans gravité*, 80.

47 Lebrun, *Un monde sans limites*, 11.

48 Dufour, *Le Divin Marché*, 325.

49 Melman argues that the right of each person to the full satisfaction of their desires does not make the subject stronger, but weaker, by depriving them of any position "from which they could stand in opposition." Melman, *L'Homme sans gravité*, 47.

50 Melman, *L'Homme sans gravité*, 35.

51 Melman, *L'Homme sans gravité*, 141.

52 According to Melman, it is necessary to "consider a change of great magnitude with incalculable anthropological consequences," which testifies to the link between an unbridled liberal economy and a subjectivity believing itself to be free of any debt to previous generations—in other words, "'producing' a subject that believes it can wipe the slate clean of its past." He then quotes Marcel Gauchet

who wrote in *La Religion dans la démocratie* (1998): "It is a real internalization of the model of the market that we are witnessing—an event with incalculable anthropological consequences, which we are only beginning to glimpse." Melman, *L'Homme sans gravité*, 13.

53 We have already made the same reproach to Christopher Lasch.

54 Melman, *L'Homme sans gravité*, 10 (introduction by Jean-Pierre Lebrun).

55 Whether matriarchy existed historically is not a question they discuss. They rather speak of a matriarchy linked to early childhood.

56 See also Michel Schneider, *Big Mother* (Paris: Odile Jacob, 2003).

57 Melman, *L'Homme sans gravité*, 265.

58 Dufour cites six of them: "the market economy, the political economy, the economy of the living, the symbolic economy, the semiotic economy, and the psychic economy." Dufour, *Le Divin Marché*, 299.

59 He thus agrees with one of Marcuse's key concepts (but without citing him), as well as the idea of distinguishing between unavoidable repression (to maintain culture) and avoidable surplus repression (as it only serves to maintain a specific form of social domination).

60 Melman, *L'Homme sans gravité*, 167.

61 "Felicity is a continual progress of the desire, from one object to another; the attaining of the former, being still but the way to the latter. . . . So that in the first place, I put for a general inclination of all mankind, a perpetual and restless desire of power after power, that ceaseth only in death." Thomas Hobbes, *Leviathan* (Oxford: Oxford University Press, 1996), 66.

62 Also the title of a recent book by Dufour. Dany-Robert Dufour, *Pléonexie* (Lormont: Le Bord de l'eau, 2015).

63 Aristotle, *Politics* (London: Longmans, Green, and Co., 1877), Book I, chap. 2, lines 31–39.

64 Dufour, *Le Divin Marché*, 177.

65 In the same way, Dufour's denunciation of the degradation of labor by capitalism (especially in *Le Délire occidental*) is fairly accurate (particularly with regard to the blindness of Marxists in the face of the dehumanization produced by Taylorism), but does not recognize the link between the double nature of labor and the loss of control of the worker over their work.

66 Michel de Montaigne, *The Complete Essays of Montaigne*, (Stanford: Stanford University Press, 1966), Book I, chap. XIV, 46. Montaigne's source is Xenophon, *Cyropaedia*, VII, 3.

67 Montaigne, *The Complete Essays*, Book III, chap. XIII, 857.

68 "The demon of our age was like that legendary African king who mounted his highest tower with twelve women, twelve singers, and twenty-four goatskins of wine. He was as tall as a steeple, fat as butter, and covered with hair. The entire city shook with dancing and song; the oldest huts collapsed to the ground. At first the king danced. Then, growing tired, he sat down on a stone and began to laugh. Then he grew tired of laughing and began to yawn, and in order to pass the time he hurled from the tower first the women, then the singers, and finally the empty wineskins. But his heart felt no relief, and he began to bewail the inconsolable suffering of kings. . . ." Nikos Kazantzakis, *Report to Greco* (New York: Simon and Schuster, 1964), 330–331.

69 Marx, *Capital, Vol. I*, 143–144. Marx speaks about this at greater length in *A Contribution to the Critique of Political Economy, Marx and Engels Collected Works, Vol. 29* (London: Progress Publishers, 1987), 362–365. See Jappe, *Les Aventures de la marchandise*, 139–140; English translation forthcoming from Bloomsbury.

70 Marx, *A Contribution*, 366–367.

71 Cornelius Castoriadis, *The Imaginary Institution of Society* (Cambridge: MIT Press, 1997).

72 Thus, with regard to them, one could quote the old line: "What these gentlemen all lack is dialectic," as Friedrich Engels said in a letter to German socialist

Conrad Schmidt in 1890 about certain authors of his time—a sentence taken up again on the cover of issue eight of *The Surrealist Revolution* and then, in a modified manner, in the work of Man Ray and in an article by Guy Debord in the bulletin *Potlatch*.

73 Dufour, *Le Divin Marché*, 13.

74 Drawn from the philosopher Gilbert Simondon, indicating the possibility that the logics of certain orders of reality have influence over others.

75 Dufour, *Le Divin Marché*, 213.

76 Which, moreover, already have their limits at the level of understanding. He misquotes a passage from *Capital* on the "automatic subject," which he cites as "automatic substance." Dufour, *Le Divin Marché*, 295. Similarly, to speak of "the share of abstract labor decreasing in the production of wealth in proportion to the increase of wealth produced by science and technology" (Dufour, *Le Délire occidental*, 144), makes no sense: it is *living* labor that decreases, not abstract labor. Abstract labor, as we have repeatedly emphasized, can neither decrease nor increase, as the other side of labor. Elsewhere, Dufour's discourse on the different "economies" leads him to indulge in inconsistent shortcuts based merely on analogy. He thus asserts that capitalism responds to the tendency of the rate of profit to fall by the proletarianization of consumers, resulting in a "tendency of the rate of subjectivation to fall." Dufour, *Le Divin Marché*, 328.

77 He quotes a passage from *Value, Price and Profit* (1865)—which belongs to Marx's so-called "economist" phase—where Marx denounces the reduction of the worker to a "beast of burden" when he is deprived of leisure. Dufour, *Le Délire occidental*, 175. In spite of this, Dufour asserts that since 1847, Marx was "ready to consent to alienated labor in the hope that it could be put into the service of the revolution." Dufour, *Le Délire occidental*, 179.

78 Dufour, *Le Délire occidental*, 143.

79 The confusion increases when Dufour writes that "this critique of value gave rise to another current developed by André Gorz in France at the end of his life, then by Hardt and Negri, and then by certain authors of the journal *Multitude*." Dufour, *Le Délire occidental*, 147. The theories of Negri and *Multitude* (in the face of which Dufour admits his great perplexity) have origins completely independent from the critique of value. André Gorz, after having been close to Negri's views, came very close to the critique of value within the last years of his life. See Anselm Jappe, "André Gorz et la critique de la Valeur," in *Sortir du capitalisme. Le scénario Gorz* (Lormont: Le Bord de L'eau, 2013), 161-170.

80 Dufour, *Le Délire occidental*, 146.

81 See Anselm Jappe and Robert Kurz, *Les Habits neufs de l'Empire. Remarques sur Negri, Hardt et Rufin* (Paris: Lignes, 2003).

82 Dufour, *Le Délire occidental*, 144.

83 Dufour, *Le Délire occidental*, 145.

84 Dufour, *Le Délire occidental*, 146.

85 Dufour, *Le Délire occidental*, 186.

86 Maine de Biran, *L'Homme public au temps de "la" légitimité 1815-1824*, Œuvres XII/2 (Paris: Vrin, 1999), 469.

87 Boltanski and Chiapello evoke the role of Lacanianism in freeing managers [*cadres*], in the name of "realism," from the moral constraints that limited the possibilities of profit. Luc Boltanski and Eve Chiapello, *The New Spirit of Capitalism* (London: Verso, 2018), 498.

88 Boltanski and Chiapello, *The New Spirit*, 7. The authors themselves subscribe to the critique of the unlimited: "This detachment of capital from material forms of wealth gives it a genuinely abstract character, which helps make accumulation an interminable process. In so far as enrichment is assessed in accounting terms, the profit accumulated in a span of time being calculated as the difference between the balance-sheets of two different periods, there exists no limit, no possible satiation, contrary to when wealth is directed towards consumer needs, including lux-

uries." Boltanski and Chiapello, *The New Spirit*, 5. The authors add in a note: "As Georg Simmel observes, in effect money alone never holds any disappointment in store, on condition that it is not intended for expenditure but for accumulation as an end in itself."

89 Boltanski and Chiapello, *The New Spirit*, 9.

90 Boltanski and Chiapello, *The New Spirit*, 109.

91 They thus refer to the distinction, introduced by Karl Polanyi and Fernand Braudel, between the *market*, which is considered a very vast historical category and subject to numerous regulations, and *capitalism*, which is considered the specific and recent case of an *unregulated market*. For obvious reasons, it seems impossible to speak of a "market" before capitalism and the autonomization of money.

92 Boltanski and Chiapello, *The New Spirit*, 27.

93 Boltanski and Chiapello, *The New Spirit*, 27.

94 Boltanski and Chiapello, *The New Spirit*, 35.

95 Boltanski and Chiapello demonstrate this through a detailed reading of the management literature of the period.

96 Boltanski and Chiapello, *The New Spirit*, 97.

97 Boltanski and Chiapello, *The New Spirit*, 319.

98 Boltanski and Chiapello, *The New Spirit*, 97. In this regard, the authors cite passages from Raoul Vaneigem's *The Revolution of Everyday Life*, which "could feature in the corpus of neo-management." Boltanski and Chiapello, *The New Spirit*, 101.

99 We have already mentioned this diffuse obstinacy in considering postmodern capitalism as if it were still characterized by older forms. See Anselm Jappe, "The Princess of Clèves Today," in *The Writing on the Wall: On the Decomposition of Capitalism and its Critics* (Winchester: Zero Books, 2017).

100 Boltanski and Chiapello, *The New Spirit*, 327.

101 Boltanski and Chiapello, *The New Spirit*, 450–455.

102 Boltanski and Chiapello, *The New Spirit*, 481.

103 Boltanski and Chiapello, *The New Spirit*, 433.

104 Boltanski and Chiapello, *The New Spirit*, 433–434.

105 Boltanski and Chiapello, *The New Spirit*, 422.

106 Boltanski and Chiapello, *The New Spirit*, 126.

107 Boltanski and Chiapello, *The New Spirit*, 429.

108 Boltanski and Chiapello, *The New Spirit*, 432.

109 Boltanski and Chiapello, *The New Spirit*, 535.

110 Boltanski and Chiapello, *The New Spirit*, xliii.

111 Naomi Klein, *No Logo: Taking Aim at the Brand Bullies* (New York: Knopf Canada, 2000). In the following pages, several studies are mentioned. They have been chosen because they are, in our opinion, those with which a critical dialogue is possible.

112 Thomas Frank, *The Conquest of Cool. Business Culture, Counterculture, and the Rise of Hip Consumerism* (Chicago: University of Chicago Press, 1997).

113 Annie Le Brun, "Du trop de théorie," in *Ailleurs et autrement* (Paris: Gallimard, 2011), 241.

114 Annie Le Brun, "Une maison pour la tête," in *Ailleurs et autrement* (Paris: Gallimard, 2011), 73.

115 Anselm Jappe, "What are the Children Lacking?," *Cured Quail Vol. 2* (2020), 230–240.

116 Theodor W. Adorno and Max Horkheimer, *Dialectic of Enlightenment: Philosophical Fragments* (Stanford: Stanford University Press, 2002), 26.

117 Neil Postman, *The Disappearance of Childhood* (New York: Random House, 1982). The analyses of Postman on the functioning of the media, notably in *Amusing Ourselves to Death* (New York: Viking Penguin, 1985), are among the best.

118 Guy Debord, "Critique of Separation," in *Complete Cinematic Works: Scripts, Stills, Documents* (Oakland: AK Press, 2003), 30.

119 Benjamin Barber, *Consumed: How Markets Corrupt Children, Infantilize Adults, and Swallow Citizens Whole* (New York: W.W. Norton, 2007). Jean-Pierre Lebrun refers to Barber and his denunciation of the spirit of infantilization, which corresponds to a psychic function "organized by the priority of sensation, mere presence, the prevalence of the immediate." Consumerist capitalism, "by discrediting any loss of jouissance, perpetuates in the adult the polymorphic perversion of the child." Lebrun, *Un monde sans limites*, 17.

120 Two recent analyses can be found in Richard Sennett, *The Craftsman* (New Haven: Yale University Press, 2008) and Nicolas Carr, *The Glass Cage: Automation and Us* (New York: W.W. Norton, 2014).

121 See Jonathan Crary, *24/7: Late Capitalism and the Ends of Sleep* (London: Verso, 2013).

122 Lothar Baier, *No Time: 18 Attempts on Acceleration* (Munich: Antje Kunstmann, 2000) and Hartmut Rosa, *Acceleration: A New Theory of Modernity* (New York: Columbia University Press, 2013). We have published a review of this book, which has received wide press coverage in France: "Où sont les freins? Sur l'accélération de l'accélération du temps social," available in French at http://www.palim-psao. fr.

123 As Walter Benjamin had already noted in his important essays "Experience and Poverty" (1933) and "The Storyteller: Tales Out of Loneliness" (1936).

124 Indeed, Hegel's *Phenomenology of Spirit* constitutes a vision of the world conceived as experience, as a turbulent journey of alienation concluding with the integration of episodes that could pass for moments of loss. In the introduction, Hegel writes: "*Inasmuch as the new true object issues from it*, this *dialectical* movement which consciousness exercises on itself and which affects both its knowledge and its object, is precisely what is called *experience* [*Erfahrung*]. . . . Because of this necessity, the way to Science is itself already *Science*, and hence, in virtue of its content, is the Science of the *experience of consciousness*." G.W.F. Hegel, *Phenomenology of Spirit* (Oxford: Oxford University Press, 1977), 55–56.

125 As for the *experience economy* discussed here, it must be remembered that in English "experience" covers a semantic field that includes what we here *oppose* to experience *stricto sensu*, that is to say, *Erlebnis*.

126 In their book *Experience Economy: Work Is Theatre & Every Business a Stage* (1999), Joseph Pine and James H. Gilmore argue that the consumer economy has reached a new stage where the key to economic success is in providing experiences. This new stage, they argue, is the successor to earlier stages that focused first on goods themselves and later on services. Pine and Gilmore argue that a successful business today "must learn to stage a rich, compelling experience." "The aesthetisation . . . of hardware design and user interfaces of information products which took place throughout the industry in the following decade fits very well with the idea of 'experience economy.' Like any other interaction, *interaction with information devices became a designed experience*. In fact, we can say that the three stages in the development of user interfaces of computers—command-line interfaces, classical GUI of 1970s-1990s, and the new sensual and entertaining interfaces of post OS X era can be correlated to the three stages of consumer economy as a whole: goods, services, and experiences. Command-line interfaces 'deliver the goods,' that is, they focus on pure functionality and utility. GUI adds 'service' to interfaces. And at next stage, interfaces become 'experiences.'" This is what Lev Manovich, a "world-renowned" researcher in the field of new information technologies, said in his 2007 *Tate Lecture* (available at http://manovich.net/ content/04-projects/056-information-as-an-aesthetic-event/53_article_2007. pdf). This demonstrates once again that sometimes uncritical aims unintentionally reveal truths that one would rather conceal. What to think of a society where even the "interface" of a cell phone becomes a purchasable "experience," and where researchers in renowned art institutions analyze the renewal of computer operating system icons with the same seriousness with which we used to analyze

the transition from Mannerist to Baroque painting?

127 In *L'Esthétisation du monde. Vivre à l'âge du capitalisme artiste* (Paris: Gallimard, 2013), Gilles Lipovetsky and Jean Serroy provided a detailed description of this stage of capitalism. Lipovetsky's work would deserve a thorough examination. He began with books praising narcissism (*L'Ère du vide. Essais sur l'individualisme contemporain* (Paris: Gallimard, 1983)) and fashion (*The Empire of Fashion: Dressing Modern Democracy* (Princeton: Princeton University Press, 1994)). However, his arguments can be read in reverse: by exalting consumer narcissism, and specifically fashion, because they constitute for him the accomplished expression of the modern spirit, the self-determination of individuals, and democracy, Lipovetsky unwittingly confesses the truth about what democracy and individualism really are within commodity society: nothing but variations on the surface of a fetishistic system, where freedom ultimately consists in choosing between two different cellphone models. Later, Lipovetsky seems to have begun having some doubts about whether he really lived in the best of all possible worlds, and whether the aestheticization of capitalism was indeed creating mature, post-ideological individuals.

128 Annie Le Brun, *The Reality Overload: The Modern World's Assault on the Imaginal Realm* (Rochester: Inner Traditions, 2008); Mona Cholet, *La Tyrannie de la réalité* (Paris: Gallimard, 2006).

129 Two studies seem particularly useful in this context: Nicholas Carr, *The Shallows: What the Internet is Doing to Our Brains* (New York: W.W. Norton, 2010) and Sherry Turkle, *Alone Together: Why We Expect More from Technology and Less from Each Other* (New York: Basic Books, 2011).

130 One of the first authors to talk about this in France was Pierre Lévy in *Collective Intelligence: Mankind's Emerging World in Cyberspace* (Cambridge: Perseus Books, 1999).

131 See, for example, Ippolita, *The Dark Side of Google* (Amsterdam: Institute of Network Cultures, 2013).

132 Alain Ehrenberg, *L'Individu incertain* (Paris: Calmann-Lévy, 1995), 14–15. See also Andrew Wood's 2004 dissertation "The Uncertain Individual: A Critical Translation of Alain Ehrenberg's *L'Individu incertain*" (University of Pittsburgh). Ehrenberg extended his thoughts in *The Weariness of the Self* (Montreal: McGill-Queens University Press, 2016).

133 Ehrenberg, *L'Individu incertain*, 18.

134 Ehrenberg, *L'Individu incertain*, 149.

135 See Richard Sennett's already classic analysis in *The Corrosion of Character: The Personal Consequences of Work in the New Capitalism* (New York: W.W. Norton, 1998).

136 Ehrenberg, *L'Individu incertain*, 257.

137 Ehrenberg, *L'Individu incertain*, 18–19.

138 Ehrenberg, *L'Individu incertain*, 305.

139 As early as 1974, one in five high school students in France used psychotropic drugs to cope with difficulties. Ehrenberg, *L'Individu incertain*, 95. Today, "one out of four people in France have taken a psychotropic drug in the last twelve months" (*Le Monde*, 9 September 2008—but this type of information continually appears).

140 Ehrenberg, *L'Individu incertain*, 125.

141 Ehrenberg, *L'Individu incertain*, 127–128.

142 Ehrenberg, *L'Individu incertain*, 150.

143 Ehrenberg, *L'Individu incertain*, 147.

144 Ehrenberg, *L'Individu incertain*, 159.

Chapter 4

1 Baruch Spinoza, *Ethics* (Oxford: Oxford University Press, 2000), Part IV, Proposi-

tion 22.

2 This phrase of Spinoza "contains the true maxim of all Western civilization, in which the religious and philosophical differences of the bourgeoisie are laid to rest." Adorno and Horkheimer, *Dialectic of Enlightenment*, 22.

3 In this regard, see Anselm Jappe, "The 'Dark Side' of Value and the Gift," in *The Writing on the Wall: On the Decomposition of Capitalism and its Critics* (Washington: Zero Books, 2017), in particular the references in it to the work of Roswitha Scholz.

4 "[A]utotelic violence is about destroying the body. . . . Of the three forms of violence, autotelic violence disturbs us most, for it's the one that most escapes understanding and explanation." (Jan Reemtsma, *Trust and Violence: An Essay on a Modern Relationship* (Princeton: Princeton University Press, 2012), 62.

5 Family massacres have always existed (see the famous case of Pierre Rivière). It is not a question of knowing if they are really more frequent today than in the past. The important point is that their forms are changing. They are very eloquent: if, in a petty-bourgeois family without particular problems, described by the "psychiatric expert" as "extraordinarily ordinary," one day the fifteen-year-old son, considered until that point an "angel," spontaneously decides, but calmly and in full possession of his mental faculties (according to the expert), to exterminate his entire family, shoots down the father, the mother, and his siblings one after the other as soon as they arrive home, then returning to his *Shrek* cartoon between each act, without explaining himself or expressing any emotion or regret, answering questions from the judge during his trial calmly, and simply shaking his head at the sound of his eighteen-year prison sentence (as in the case of Pierre F. in Ancourteville-sur-Héricourt), one is led to believe in a more general logic—which explains the strong impression that this kind of misdeed arouses. While it would be consoling to explain these acts by insanity or the social environment, or by a long series of previous disputes, the facts escape this kind of causality. In "traditional" family dramas, from Greek tragedy to Nepalese royalty, there was always an *excess* of emotion discharged during the crime. What is striking in contemporary dramas, as in many psychological disorders, is the *absence* of emotion and the lack of "motive." What deserves psychosocial explanation is not the relatively frequent idea of killing of one's parents, but the absence of inhibition mechanisms and the ease with which they take place.

6 Götz Eisenberg (see below) himself admits that he often uses the word *amok* in a vague and rather associative manner. See Götz Eisenberg, ... *damit mich kein Mensch mehr vergisst! Warum Amok und Gewalt kein Zufall sind* (Munich: Pattloch, 2010), 50.

7 Which led him to go as far as to consider himself an adherent of the pre-Socratic philosopher Empedocles.

8 Jean Laplanche and J. B. Pontalis, *The Language of Psychoanalysis*, (London: Karnac Books, 1988), 324.

9 It is André Green who studied this possible link in his book *Life Narcissism, Death Narcissism* (London: Free Association Books, 2001).

10 Erich Fromm, *The Anatomy of Human Destructiveness* (London: Pimlico, 1973).

11 This, even in Europe and even for teenagers, never seems difficult. It is therefore a mistake to attribute the main responsibility for *running amok* to the free circulation of weapons in the United States, as Michael Moore does in his film *Bowling for Columbine* (2002). The large number of weapons in circulation would instead explain the ease with which trivial quarrels spontaneously degenerate into murders. The facts can sometimes resemble *running amok*—as when a drunk man who thinks he is being cheated in a bar during a game of cards runs home, grabs a gun, returns to the bar, and mows down everyone there. The psychosocial dynamics, however, are very different.

12 These journals, after being kept secret for a long time, were made public in 2011 and can be accessed on the internet. On the other hand, videos shot by the killers were destroyed by local police under the pretext of preventing their diffusion on the internet.

13 There certainly are some places chosen at random, but they are much rarer.

14 Robert Kurz, "Der Todestrieb der Konkurrenz," *Exit! Krise und Kritik der Warenge-sellschaft*, https://www.exit-online.org/link.php?tabelle=autoren&posnr=136.

15 Thus far, not all groups are participating to the same extent. However, the increase in the number of girls and converts in the ranks of radical Islam is quite significant.

16 This also explains why there are so few books published in France on the subject. *Tueurs de masse. Un nouveau type de tueurs est né* by Olivier Hassid and Julien Marcel (Paris: Eyrolles, 2012) deals with the topic mostly with statistics and tries to explain it by narrow sociological factors (unemployment, harassment, etc.).

17 Since "pure" *running amok* and "jihadist acts" are becoming increasingly similar, both occur as much in Germany (the 2016 Christmas market killing in Berlin) as in France (the Grasse shooting).

18 *Garde-fous* refers to the guardrails or barriers atop very high structures that deter people from jumping off and plummeting to their death. *La levée des garde-fous* means their removal.—Trans.

19 Götz Eisenberg, "Die Innenseite der Globalisierung," *Aus Politik und Zeitgeschichte*, no. 44 (2002).

20 An extreme form of lack of empathy has been identified in "alexithymia," the inability to recognize and express feelings. This symptom is similar to autism— and it is known that cases of autism have at least tripled in recent decades. Even if one cannot ignore that this increase is partly due to enlarged diagnostic criteria, and as far as the genesis of autism remains bitterly debated, one cannot but notice this coincidence between the rise of autism and the anthropological mutations induced by the total submission of life to commodity value and by the invasion of technologies.

21 The desire to give a (pseudo) concrete face to invisible, untouchable, inconceivable abstractions constitutes one of the main sources of "truncated" anti-capitalism and of populist movements. Thus, the abstraction "value" is embodied, in the eyes of the antisemite, in the figure of the "usurer" or the "Jewish" "speculator"; state violence is embodied for many in the figure of the "corrupt politician"; the globalization of capital in the figure of the immigrant. On the other hand, the (pseudo) concreteness of the people, race, religion, or nation is opposed to abstractions.

22 Eisenberg, ... *damit mich*, 217–218.

23 Götz Eisenberg, *Amok—Kinder der Kälte. Über die Wurzeln von Wut und Hass* (Reinbeck: Rowohlt, 2000), 51.

24 Eisenberg, "Die Innenseite."

25 Eisenberg, "Die Innenseite."

26 Cited in Götz Eisenberg, *Zwischen Arbeitswut und Überfremdungsangst. Zur Sozialpsychologie des entfesselten Kapitalismus. Band 2* (Gießen: Verlag Wolfgang Polkowki, 2016), 113.

27 Today, mourning is sometimes used for the purposes of "corporate restructuring": during the revelations about the wave of suicides at France Telecom between 2008 and 2011—the "suicide craze," as its then CEO Didier Lombard called it—we learned that management used the work of psychologist and "thanatologist" Elisabeth Kübler-Ross on the "five stages of grief" in the face of impending death to better strategically organize pushing its employees to resign—which, for about sixty of them, ended in suicide.

28 In these considerations, Eisenberg relies on the now classic analysis of authoritarian and pre-Nazi education by Klaus Theweleit. He was especially interested in the image of women and the image of the body that it conveyed. His main work has been translated into English: *Male Fantasies* (Minneapolis: University of Minnesota Press, 1987). In it, Theweleit examines, above all, the letters and writings of the members of the German *Freikorps*, composed of veterans and which, after the First World War, constituted the first nucleus of future Nazism.

29 Adorno and Horkheimer, *Dialectic of Enlightenment*, 93.

30 Eisenberg, ... *damit mich*, 215–216.

31 Franco Berardi, *Heroes: Mass Murder and Suicide* (London: Verso, 2015), 2.

32 Berardi, *Heroes*, 66.

33 Berardi, *Heroes*, 48.

34 Berardi, *Heroes*, 49.

35 For Eisenberg, Breivik's political motivation resembles a belated verbalization of hatred that comes from somewhere much deeper: hatred of women, fear of the symbiotic mother (which is expressed in the fear that Europe will be "submerged by Islam"), desire to show that he is a "real man." It is always the hatred of a part of oneself that one represses. Ideology does not explain everything: not all right-wing extremists become mass murderers; just as there are killers who are not right-wing extremists. Breivik's individual pathology has social origins; his manifesto is confused, but no more so than *Mein Kampf*, whose success is well-known. Eisenberg, *Zwischen Amok*, 127.

36 Berardi, *Heroes*, 50.

37 While the shirt of the other killer, Dylan Klebold, had the word "Rage" displayed on it.

38 Berardi, *Heroes*, 50, 52.

39 It is interesting to note that following the war, the author of this song, Hans Baumann, had a big international career as an author of children's books, without his Nazi sympathies troubling his fans too much.

40 Psychoanalyst Jean-Pierre Lebrun has this to say on the subject: "an example of this, and I find that the language captures it very well—I think you have to be very careful about the words that change in language—is the expression 'to have hatred.' You know that this phrase has emerged in the last ten years or so, whereas until then it was 'to have hatred for.' 'Hate for' obviously implies an addressee, an encounter. On the other hand, 'to have hate' comes to indicate a question of having something cumbersome which sticks to the skin, and which one does not really know how to get rid of. It has thus become intransitive, interstitial, without address, unsubscribed to the Other, non-vectorized, because there is no longer a visible Other, which 'embodies' the subtraction of jouissance and gives a concrete body to the name-of-the-father." Jean-Pierre Lebrun, "Les morts pour le dire," *Association des forums du champ lacanien de Wallonie*, proceedings from the colloquium of May 3rd 2003, 5–6. This is an presentation about Richard Durn, the Nanterre killer.

41 Jean Baudrillard, *Screened Out* (London: Verso, 2002), 93–94.

42 The academic debate of the last few years around "recognition," triggered by Axel Honneth, representative of a kind of "third infusion" of critical theory with a touch of citizen's responsibility, constitutes a very distant "recognition" of this problematic.

43 Guy Debord's article "To Abolish" in issue 11 (1987) of the post-situationist journal *Encyclopédie des Nuisances* wittily asserts that envy is the only one of the seven traditionally deadly sins that is still with us today, and that it has now encompassed all the other sins, the exercise of which has been made impossible by capitalist modernity. In obviously different terms, envy plays a role for Melanie Klein and her school of thought. Melanie Klein, *Envy and Gratitude and Other Works 1946–1963* (London: The Hogarth Press, 1984).

44 The short story "Emma Zunz" (1948) by Jorge Luis Borges describes this mechanism of substitution with a kind of black humor. It seems to be inspired by an experience that American anarchist Emma Goldmann describes in her autobiography.

45 See his book *Violence*, where he says he wants to "rehabilitate the notion of resentment." Slavoj Žižek, *Violence: Six Sideways Reflections* (New York: Picador, 2008), 189.

46 "You have to learn to seduce robot recruiters," *Le Monde* assures us on October

16th, 2016: "95% of large enterprises use ATS (Applicant Tracking Systems, job applicant management program) for managerial jobs."

47 Berardi cites Michael Serazio's article "Shooting for Fame. The (Anti-) Social Media of a YouTube Killer" (*Flow*, 2009), which mainly analyzes the case of the Finnish school shooter Pekka-Erik Auvinen, but also notes that the perpetrator of the Virginia High Tech massacre, Seung-Hui Cho, was rather archaic in 2007, as between the first and second shootings he went to the post office to send a package to a TV station containing texts and recordings explaining his actions. (Berardi, *Heroes*, 41–44).

48 On this concept, see Yves Citton, *The Ecology of Attention* (London: Polity, 2017).

49 There has been much discussion about the role of video games in the emergence of mass killings. However, the problem is not only the potentially violent content of these "games," but the virtual form itself. Berardi describes it well: "It is not the content of the game, but the stimulation itself, that produces the effect of desensitization to the bodily experience of suffering and of pleasure. Clearly, not everybody becomes a mass murderer merely because they play video games or engage in digital stimulation. But the mass murderer is only an exceptional manifestation of a general trend in this general mutation of the human mind." He adds: "However, the combined effect of a pre-existing condition of psychic suffering and of an enormous investment of time and mental energy in virtual activity is likely to be, especially for young people, an intensification of the sense of alienation." Berardi, *Heroes*, 47, 116.

50 Berardi, *Heroes*, 6.

51 Berardi, *Heroes*, 75.

52 Berardi, *Heroes*, 89.

53 Berardi, *Heroes*, 24–25.

54 Berardi, *Heroes*, 80.

55 Berardi, *Heroes*, 89.

56 See the critique in Jappe, *Les Habits*.

57 Berardi, *Heroes*, 77.

58 Berardi, *Heroes*, 40.

59 Eisenberg, *Zwischen Amok*, 216.

60 Eisenberg, *Amok*, 220–221.

61 In his late writings, Guy Debord developed the idea that capitalism, in the age of the spectacle, has entered a phase of galloping irrationalism and self-destruction achieved through a lack of thinking, which constitutes a fundamental difference to previous forms of domination. To the well-known passages found in *Comments on the Society of the Spectacle*, let us add this quotation, taken from an unpublished work: "All the ruling classes of the past had at least the intelligence to understand that, within their means, they had *no interest* in spreading plague, leprosy, tuberculosis, etc., because they would also be affected. The present ruling class has spread non-thinking, spectacular *looks*, stupidity, and in so doing affects itself in a terrible way: being seen as the stupidity of the 'decision-makers.'" Unpublished note for an unrealized "Projet de dictionnaire," 1980s, in Laurence Le Bras and Emmanuel Guy, eds., *Lire Debord* (Paris: L'Échappée, 2016), 184–185.

62 Robert Kurz, *Weltordnungskrieg. Das Ende der Souveränität und die Wandlungen des Imperialismus im Zeitalter der Globalisierung* (Bad Honnef: Horlemann, 2003). On certain points, these analyses are similar to those contained in Jaime Semprun, *L'Abîme se repeuple* (Paris: L'Encyclopédie des Nuisances, 1997).

63 Kurz, *Weltordnungskrieg*, 48.

64 Kurz, *Weltordnungskrieg*, 56.

65 Kurz, *Weltordnungskrieg*, 59.

66 Kurz, *Weltordnungskrieg*, 72–73.

67 Kurz, *Weltordnungskrieg*, 73.

68 Kurz, *Weltordnungskrieg*, 60.

69 Kurz, *Weltordnungskrieg*, 61.

70 Hans Magnus Enzensberger, *Die Große Wanderung* (Frankfurt: Suhrkamp, 1993). Kurz, however, criticizes most of Enzensberger's reasoning in this book.

71 Kurz, *Weltordnungskrieg*, 69–70.

72 Kurz, *Weltordnungskrieg*, 71.

Epilogue

1 The arguments presented in the foregoing pages have also been the subject of several of my other works, some of them much more detailed, that have appeared in recent years. In addition to my book *The Writing On the Wall*, I also refer to Anselm Jappe, "Narcissus or Orpheus? Notes on Freud, Fromm, Marcuse and Lasch," *Cured Quail Vol. 2*, 2020, 190–215; Anselm Jappe, "What are the Children Lacking?," *Cured Quail Vol. 2* (2020), 230–240; and most recently, Anselm Jappe, *Sous le soleil noir du capital: Chroniques d'une ère de ténèbres* (Paris: Éditions Crise & Critique, 2022).

2 As Luc Boltanski proposes in his book *On Critique: A Sociology of Emancipation* (Cambridge: Polity Press, 2011). This is also the limit of Pierre Bourdieu's notion of "habitus," which attempts to grasp the impersonal character of "domination," but always through the lens of subjective domination, that is to say, of a "dominant class" over another, subaltern one.

3 André Gorz, *Ecologica* (London: Seagull Books, 2010), 4.

4 Cornelius Castoriadis, "From Ecology to Autonomy," *Thesis Eleven*, 3(1), 1981, 15. Of course, in the case of Castoriadis, one must ask what is meant by "increased autonomy" or the "self-institution of society"?

5 See René Riesel and Jaime Semprun, *Catastrophism, disaster management and sustainable submission* (Roofdruk Edities, 2014).

6 On the other hand, Guy Debord already affirmed in 1967 that "[w]hen the real world changes into simple images, simple images become real beings and effective motivations of a hypnotic behavior. The spectacle as a tendency *to make one see* the world by means of various specialized mediations (it can no longer be grasped directly), naturally finds vision to be the privileged human sense which the sense of touch was for other epochs; the most abstract, the most mystifiable sense corresponds to the generalized abstraction of present-day society." Guy Debord, *The Society of the Spectacle* (Detroit: Black & Red, 1970), §18.

7 John Berger, *Ways of Seeing* (London: Penguin Modern Classics, 2008), cover.

8 See Jacques Ellul, *The Humiliation of the Word* (Grand Rapids: W.B. Eerdmans, 1988).

9 National Endowment for the Arts, "Reading at Risk: A Survey of Literary Reading in America," *National Endowment for the Arts*, October 2002, https://www.arts.gov/sites/default/files/RaRExec.pdf. More recently, the National Assessment of Education Progress in the United States reported that, in tracking student achievement, the last two years have witnessed scores in reading for nine-year-old children drop by the largest margin in more than 30 years. National Assessment of Education Progress, "NAEP Long-Term Trend Assessment Results: Reading and Mathematics," *The Nation's Report Card*, September 2022, https://www.nationsreportcard.gov/highlights/ltt/2022/.—Trans.

10 As Neil Postman puts it simply, but very effectively, in his book *Amusing Ourselves to Death*.

11 This is an allusion to Stig Dagerman's 1952 autobiographical essay "Our Need for Consolation is Insatiable."—Trans.

Bibliography

Adorno, Theodor W., "Sociology and Psychology." *New Left Review* 46 (Nov/Dec 1967): 67–97.

Adorno, Theodor W. *Minima Moralia: Reflections from a Damaged Life*. London: Verso, 2005.

Adorno, Theodor W., "Revisionist Psychoanalysis." *Philosophy & Social Criticism* 40, no. 3 (2014): 326–338.

Adorno, Theodor W., and Max Horkheimer. *Dialectic of Enlightenment: Philosophical Fragments*. Stanford: Stanford University Press, 2002.

Aristotle. *Politics*. Indianapolis: Hackett Publishing, 1998.

Baier, Lothar. *No Time: 18 Attempts on Acceleration*. Munich: Antje Kunstmann, 2000.

Bakhtine Mikhaïl M. *Écrits sur le freudisme* [under the name V. Volochinov]. Lausanne: L'Âge d'homme, 1980.

Barber, Benjamin. *Consumed: How Markets Corrupt Children, Infantilize Adults, and Swallow Citizens Whole*. New York: W. W. Norton, 2007.

Baschet, Jérôme. *Corps et âmes. Une histoire de la personne au Moyen Âge*. Flammarion, Paris, 2016.

Bataille, George, "De Sade's Sovereign Man." In *Erotism: Death and Sensuality*. San Francisco: City Lights Books, 1986: 164–176.

Baudelaire, Charles. *The Flowers of Evil*. Oxford: Oxford University Press, 1993.

Baudrillard, Jean. *Screened Out*. London: Verso, 2002.

Bauman, Zygmunt. *Liquid Modernity*. Cambridge: Polity Press, 2012.

Benjamin, Walter, "Experience and Poverty." In *Selected Writings Volume 2, Part 2, 1931–1934*. Cambridge: The Belknap Press of Harvard University Press, 1999: 731–736.

Benjamin, Walter. *The Storyteller: Tales Out of Loneliness*. London: Verso, 2016.

Berardi, Franco. *Heroes: Mass Murder and Suicide*. London: Verso, 2015.

Berger, John. *Ways of Seeing*. London: Penguin Modern Classics, 2008.

Bockelmann, Eske. *Im Takt des Geldes. Zur Genese modernen Denkens*. Springe: Zu Klampen, 2004.

Bockelmann, Eske, "Die Synthese am Geld : Natur der Neuzeit." *Exit!* no. 5 (2008).

Böhme, Hartmut and Gernot Böhme. *Das Andere der Vernunft. Zur Entwicklung von Rationalitätsstrukturen am Beispiel Kants*. Frankfurt am Main: Suhrkamp, 1983.

Boltanski, Luc. *On Critique: A Sociology of Emancipation*. Cambridge: Polity Press, 2011.

Boltanski, Luc and Eve Chiapello. *The New Spirit of Capitalism*. London: Verso, 2018.

Brown, Norman O. *Life Against Death: The Psychoanalytical Meaning of History*. Middletown: Wesleyan University Press, 1959.

Brown, Norman O. "A Reply to Herbert Marcuse." *Commentary* no. 43 (1967): 83–84.

Caillé, Alain. *Anthropologie du don. Le tiers paradigm*. Paris: La Découverte, 2007.

Carr, Nicholas. *The Shallows: What the Internet is Doing to Our Brains*. New York: Norton, 2010.

Carr, Nicolas. *The Glass Cage: Automation and Us*. New York: W. W. Norton, 2014.

Cassirer Ernst. *Philosophy of Symbolic Forms, Volume 4: The Metaphysics of Symbolic Forms*. New Haven: Yale University Press, 1998.

Castoriadis, Cornelius. "From Ecology to Autonomy," *Thesis Eleven* 1, no. 3 (1981): 8–22.

Castoriadis, Cornelius. *The Imaginary Institution of Society*. Cambridge: The MIT Press, 1997.

Chapaux-Morelli, Pascale and Pascal Couderc. *La Manipulation affective dans le couple. Faire face à un pervers narcissique*. Paris: Albin Michel, 2010.

Cholet, Mona. *La Tyrannie de la réalité*. Paris: Gallimard, 2006.

Citton, Yves. *The Ecology of Attention*. London: Polity, 2017.

Clastres. Pierre. *Society Against the State: Essays in Political Anthropology*. New York:

Zone Books, 1987.

Colletti, Lucio. *Marxism and Hegel*. London: Verso, 1979.

Crary, Jonathan. *24/7: Late Capitalism and the Ends of Sleep*. London: Verso, 2013.

Dahmer, Helmut. *Libido und Gesellschaft. Studien über Freud und die Freudische Linke.* Frankfurt am Main: Suhrkamp, 1973.

Davies, William. *The Happiness Industry: How the Government and Big Business Sold Us Wellbeing*. London: Verso, 2015.

Debord, Guy. *The Society of the Spectacle*. Detroit: Black & Red, 1970.

Debord, Guy, "Critique of Separation." In *Complete Cinematic Works: Scripts, Stills, Documents*. Oakland: AK Press, 2003.

Denis, Paul. *Le Narcissisme*. Paris: Presses Universitaires de France, 2012.

Descartes, Rene. *Discourse on Method and Meditations on First Philosophy.* Indianapolis: Hackett Publishing, 1988.

Dessuant, Pierre. *Le Narcissisme*, Paris: Presses Universitaires de France, 2007.

Diner, Dan and Seyla Benhabib, eds. *Zivilisationbruch: Denken nach Auschwitz*. Frankfurt am Main: Fischer, 1988.

Dufour, Dany-Robert. *On achève bien les hommes*. Paris: Denoël, 2005.

Dufour, Dany-Robert. "Le Divin Marché." *Psychasoc*, December 31, 2006, http://www.psychasoc.com.

Dufour, Dany-Robert, "Entretien avec Joseph Rouzel." *Psychasoc*, December 31, 2006, http://www.psychasoc.com.

Dufour, Dany-Robert. *Le Divin Marché. La révolution culturelle libérale*. Paris: Denoël, 2007.

Dufour, Dany-Robert. *The Art of Shrinking Heads*. London: Polity, 2008.

Dufour, Dany-Robert. *La Cité perverse. Libéralisme et pornographie*, Paris: Denoël, 2009.

Dufour, Dany-Robert. *Le Délire occidental et ses effets actuels dans la vie quotidienne: travail, loisir, amour*. Paris: Les Liens qui libèrent, 2014.

Dufour, Dany-Robert. *Pléonexie*. Lormont: Le Bord de l'eau, 2015.

Dumont, Louis. *From Mandeville to Marx: The Genesis and Triumph of Economic Ideology*. Chicago: University of Chicago Press, 1977.

Ehrenberg, Alain. *L'Individu incertain*. Paris: Calmann-Lévy, 1995.

Ehrenberg, Alain. *The Weariness of the Self*. Montreal: McGill-Queens University Press, 2016.

Eiguer, Albert. *Le Pervers narcissique et son complice*. Paris: Dunod, 2003.

Eisenberg, Götz. *Amok – Kinder der Kälte. Über die Wurzeln von Wut und Hass*. Reinbeck: Rowohlt, 2000.

Eisenberg, Götz, "Die Innenseite der Globalisierung," *Aus Politik und Zeitgeschichte* no. 44, (2002): 21–28.

Eisenberg, Götz. *... damit mich kein Mensch mehr vergisst! Warum Amok und Gewalt kein Zufall sind*. Munich: Pattloch, 2010.

Eisenberg, Götz. *Zwischen Amok und Alzheimer. Zur Sozialpsychologie des entfesselten Kapitalismus*. Frankfurt: Brandes und Apsel, 2015

Eisenberg, Götz. *Zwischen Arbeitswut und Überfremdungsangst. Zur Sozialpsychologie des entfesselten Kapitalismus. Band 2*. Gießen: Verlag Wolfgang Polkowki, 2016.

Ellul, Jacques. *The Humiliation of the Word*. Grand Rapids: W. B. Eerdmans, 1988.

Enzensberger, Hans Magnus. *Die Große Wanderung*. Frankfurt am Main: Suhrkamp, 1993.

Folliet, Luc. *Nauru, l'île dévastée. Comment la civilisation capitaliste a détruit le pays le plus riche du monde*. Paris: La Découverte, 2010

Fong, Ben Y. *Death and Mastery: Psychoanalytic Drive Theory and the Subject of Late Capitalism*. New York: Columbia University Press, 2016.

Frank, Thomas. *The Conquest of Cool. Business Culture, Counterculture, and the Rise of Hip Consumerism*. Chicago: University of Chicago Press, 1997.

Freud, Sigmund, "Introductory Lectures on Psycho-analysis (Parts I and II)." In *The Standard Edition of the Complete Psychological Works of Sigmund Freud, Vol. XV*. London: The Hogarth Press, 1963.

Freud, Sigmund, "Group Psychology and the Analysis of the Ego." In *The Standard Edition of the Complete Psychological Works of Sigmund Freud, Vol. XVIII*. London: The Hogarth Press, 1981.

Freud, Sigmund, "The Libido Theory and Narcissism." In *The Standard Edition of the Complete Psychological Works of Sigmund Freud, Vol. XVI*. London: The Hogarth Press, 1981.

Freud, Sigmund, "On Narcissism: An Introduction." In *The Standard Edition of the Complete Psychological Works of Sigmund Freud, Vol. XIV*. London: The Hogarth Press, 2001.

Fromm, Erich, "A Counter-Rebuttal to Herbert Marcuse," *Dissent* 3 (Winter 1956), 1956: 81–83.

Fromm, Erich. *The Anatomy of Human Destructiveness*. London: Pimlico, 1973.

Fromm, Erich. "The Human Implications of Instinctivistic 'Radicalism': A Reply to Herbert Marcuse." *Dissent* 2, no. 4 (1955): 342–349.

Gorz, André. *Ecologica*. London: Seagull Books, 2010.

Gramsci, Antonio. "Americanism and Fordism." In *Selections from the Prison Notebooks*. New York: International Publishers, 1971.

Green, André. *Life Narcissism, Death Narcissism*. London: Free Association Books, 2001.

Grunberger, Bela. *Narcissism: Psychoanalytic Essays*. New York: International Universities Press, 1979.

Hassid, Olivier and Julien Marcel. *Tueurs de masse. Un nouveau type de tueurs est né*. Paris: Eyrolles, 2012.

Hegel, Georg Wilhelm Friedrich. *Phenomenology of Spirit*. Oxford: Oxford University Press, 1977.

Hirigoyen, Marie-France. *Stalking the Soul: Emotional Abuse and the Erosion of Identity*. New York: Helen Marx Books, 2005.

Hobbes, Thomas. *Leviathan*. Oxford: Oxford University Press, 1996.

Husserl Edmund. *Idées directrices pour une phénoménologie pure et une philosophie phénoménologique*. Paris: Gallimard, 1950.

Husserl, Edmund. *Ideas Pertaining to a Pure Phenomenology and to a Phenomenological Philosophy, First Book: General Introduction to a Pure Phenomenology*. Boston: Martinus Nijhoff Publishers, 1983.

Ippolita. *The Dark Side of Google*. Amsterdam: Institute of Network Cultures, 2013.

Jappe, Anselm, "Où sont les freins? Sur l'accélération de l'accélération du temps social." *Palim Psao*, July 10, 2010, www.palim-psao.fr.

Jappe Anselm. *Crédit à mort. La décomposition du capitalisme et ses ennemis*. Paris: Lignes, 2011.

Jappe, Anselm. "Tous contre la finance?" *Le Sarkophage* no. 23 (March 2011).

Jappe, Anselm. "Changer de cheval" *Bruxelles Laïque Échos* no. 78 (October 2012).

Jappe, Anselm. "Être libres pour la libération." *Réfractions* no. 28, 2012.

Jappe, Anselm. "La financiarisation et la spéculation sont des symptômes, non les causes de la crise." *Les Mondes du Travail* no. 12 (November 2012).

Jappe, Anselm. "André Gorz et la critique de la Valeur." In *Sortir du capitalisme. Le scénario Gorz*. Lormont: Le Bord de L'eau, 2013.

Jappe, Anselm. "L'anticapitalisme est-il toujours de gauche?" *Le Sarkophage* no. 35 (March 2013), 2013.

Jappe, Anselm. "Et quand un grand État fera défaut de paiement?" *La Décroissance* no. 99 (May 2013).

Jappe, Anselm. "Sohn-Rethel and the Origin of 'Real Abstraction': A Critique of Production or a Critique of Circulation?" *Historical Materialism* 2, no. 1 (2013): 3–14.

Jappe, Anselm. "Le spread, stade suprême de la politique?" *Lignes* no. 41 (May 2013).

Jappe, Anselm. "De l'aliénation au fétichisme de la marchandise: la continuité des deux concepts." In *La Réification. Histoire et actualité d'un concept critique*. Paris: La Dispute, 2014.

Jappe, Anselm. "Révolution contre le travail? La critique de la valeur et le dépassement du capitalism." *Cités* no. 59 (September 2014).

Jappe, Anselm. *The Writing on the Wall: On The Decomposition of Capitalism and Its Critics.* Washington: Zero Books, 2017.

Jappe, Anselm. "Narcissus or Orpheus? Notes on Freud, Fromm, Marcuse and Lasch." *Cured Quail Vol. 2* (2020).

Jappe, Anselm. "What are the Children Lacking?" *Cured Quail Vol. 2* (2020).

Jappe, Anselm. *Sous le soleil noir du capital: Chroniques d'une ère de ténèbres.* Paris: Éditions Crise & Critique, 2022.

Jappe, Anselm. *The Adventures of the Commodity.* London: Bloomsbury, 2023.

Jappe, Anselm and Robert Kurz. *Les Habits neufs de l'Empire. Remarques sur Negri, Hardt et Rufin.* Paris: Lignes, 2003.

Jay, Martin. *The Dialectical Imagination: A History of the Frankfurt School and the Institute of Social Research, 1923–1950.* Berkeley: University of California Press, 1973.

Jorn, Asger. "The Situationists and Automation." In *Situationist International Anthology.* Berkeley: Bureau of Public Secrets, 2006.

Juignet, Patrick. *Manuel de psychopathologie générale.* Grenoble: Presses Universitaires de Grenoble, 2015.

Kant, Immanuel. "On the Common Saying: 'This May Be True in Theory, But It Does Not Apply in Practice.'" In *Kant: Political Writings.* Cambridge: Cambridge University Press, 1991.

Kant, Immanuel. *Critique of Pure Reason.* Indianapolis: Hackett Publishing, 1996.

Kant, Immanuel. *Critique of Practical Reason.* Indianapolis: Hackett Publishing, 2002.

Kant, Immanuel. *Groundwork for the Metaphysics of Morals.* New Haven: Yale University Press, 2002.

Kant, Immanuel. *Observations on the Feeling of the Beautiful and Sublime.* Cambridge: Cambridge University Press, 2011.

Kazantzakis, Nikos. *Report to Greco.* New York: Simon and Schuster, 1964.

Klein, Melanie. *Envy and Gratitude and Other Works, 1946–1963.* London: The Hogarth Press, 1984.

Klein, Naomi. *No Logo: Taking Aim at the Brand Bullies.* New York: Knopf Canada, 2000.

Klossowski, Pierre. *Sade My Neighbor.* Evanston: Northwestern University Press, 1991.

Kohut, Heinz. *The Analysis of the Self: A Systematic Approach to the Psychoanalytic Treatment of Narcissistic Personality Disorders.* Chicago: University of Chicago Press, 2009.

Kurz, Robert. "Der Todestrieb der Konkurrenz." *Exit! Krise und Kritik der Warengesellschaft,* May 18, 2002.

Kurz, Robert. "Totalitarian Economy and Paranoia of Terror: The Death Wish of Capitalist Reason," *Krisis: Contributions to the Critique of Commodity Society.* London: Chronos Publications, 2002.

Kurz, Robert. *Weltordungskrieg. Das Ende der Souveränität und die Wandlungen des Imperialismus im Zeitalter der Globalisierung.* Bad Honnef: Horlemann, 2003.

Kurz, Robert. *Geld ohne Wert. Grundrisse zu einer Transformation der Kritik der politischen Ökonomie.* Bad Honnef: Horlemann, 2012.

Kurz, Robert. "Der Kampf um die Wahrheit," *Exit! Krise und Kritik der Warengesellschaft* no. 12 (November 2014).

Lacan, Jacques. "Kant with Sade," *October* 51 (1989): 55–75.

Lapassade, Georges. *L'Entrée dans la vie. Essai sur l'inachèvement de l'homme.* Paris: Minuit, 1963.

Laplanche, Jean and J. B. Pontalis. *The Language of Psychoanalysis.* London: Karnac Books, 1988.

Lasch, Christopher. *The Culture of Narcissism: American Life in An Age of Diminishing Expectations.* New York: W. W. Norton & Company, 1979.

Lasch, Christopher. *The Minimal Self: Psychic Survival in Troubled Times,* New York: W.W. Norton & Company, 1984.

Latouche, Serge. *L'Invention de l'économie.* Paris: Albin Michel, 2005.

Latouche Serge. *Sortir de la société de consommation. Voix et voies de la décroissance.* Paris: Les Liens qui libèrent, 2010.

Le Bras, Laurence and Emmanuel Guy, eds. *Lire Debord.* Paris: L'Échappée, 2016.

Le Brun, Annie. *The Reality Overload: The Modern World's Assault on the Imaginal Realm.* Rochester: Inner Traditions, 2008.

Le Brun Annie. "Du trop de théorie." In *Ailleurs et autrement.* Paris: Gallimard, 2011.

Le Brun, Annie. "Une maison pour la tête." In *Ailleurs et autrement.* Paris: Gallimard, 2011.

Lebrun, Jean-Pierre. *Un monde sans limites, essai pour une clinique psychanalytique du social.* Toulouse: Érès, 1997.

Lebrun, Jean-Pierre. "Les morts pour le dire." *Association des forums du champ lacanien de Wallonie* (proceedings from the colloquium of May 3, 2003).

Le Rider, Jacques. *L'Allié incommode.* Paris: L'Olivier, 2007.

Lévy Pierre. *Collective Intelligence: Mankind's Emerging World in Cyberspace.* Cambridge, MA: Perseus Books, 1999.

Liaudet, Jean-Claude. *L'Impasse narcissique du libéralisme.* Paris: Climats, 2007.

Lipovetsky, Gilles. *L'Ère du vide. Essais sur l'individualisme contemporain.* Paris: Gallimard, 1983.

Lipovetsky, Gilles. *The Empire of Fashion: Dressing Modern Democracy.* Princeton: Princeton University Press, 1994.

Lipovetsky, Gilles and Jean Serroy. *L'Esthétisation du monde. Vivre à l'âge du capitalisme artiste.* Paris: Gallimard, 2013.

Lohoff, Ernst. "Die Verzauberung der Welt. Die Subjektform und ihre Konstitutionsgeschichte." *Krisis: Kritik der Warengesellschaft* no. 29 (2005): 13–60.

Maine de Biran, Pierre. "L'Homme public au temps de "la" légitimité 1815–1824." *Œuvres XII/2.* Paris: Vrin, 1999.

Jordi Maiso. "Soggettività offesa e falsa coscienza. La psicodinamica del risentimento nella teoria critica della società." *Costruzioni psicoanalitiche* no. 23 (2012).

Manovich, Lev. "Information as an Aesthetic Event." Tate Lecture, 2007, http://manovich.net.

Marcuse, Herbert. "A Reply to Erich Fromm." *Dissent* 3 (Winter 1956): 79–81.

Marcuse, Herbert. *Eros and Civilization: A Philosophical Inquiry into Freud.* Boston: Beacon Press, 1966.

Marcuse, Herbert. "Obsolescence of the Freudian Concept of Man." In *Five Lectures: Psychoanalysis, Politics and Utopia.* Boston: Beacon Press, 1970.

Margat, Claire. "Une horrible liberté." turandot.ish-lyon.cnrs.fr/essays.

Marx, Karl. *Capital: A Critique of Political Economy, Volume I.* London: Penguin Books, 1976.

Marx, Karl. "Economic and Philosophic Manuscripts of 1844." In *Marx and Engels Collected Works, Vol. 3.* London: Progress Publishers, 1975.

Marx, Karl. "Economic Manuscripts of 1857–58 [*Grundrisse*]." In *Marx and Engels Collected Works, Vol. 28.* New York: Progress Publishers, 1986.

Marx, Karl. "Economic Manuscripts of 1857–1861." In *Marx and Engels Collected Works, Volume 28.* London: Progress Publishers, 1986.

Marx, Karl. "A Contribution to the Critique of Political Economy." In *Marx and Engels Collected Works, Vol. 29.* London: Progress Publishers, 1987.

Marx, Karl. "Capital: A Critique of Political Economy, Volume I." In *Marx and Engels Collected Works, Vol. 35.* New York: Progress Publishers, 1996.

Marzano, Michela. *Extension du domaine de la manipulation: De l'entreprise à la vie privée.* Paris: Grasset, 2008.

Melman, Charles. *L'Homme sans gravité. Jouir à tout prix.* Paris: Denoël, 2002.

Mitscherlich, Alexander. *Society Without the Father: A Contribution to Social Psychology.* London: Tavistock, 1969.

Montaigne, Michel de. *The Complete Essays of Montaigne.* Stanford: Stanford University Press, 1966.

Müller, Rudolf Wolfgang. *Geld und Geist. Zur Entstehungsgeschichte von Identitätsbewußtsein und Rationalität seit der Antike.* Frankfurt am Main: Campus, 1977.

National Assessment of Education Progress. "NAEP Long-Term Trend Assessment Results: Reading and Mathematics." *The Nation's Report Card,* September 2022, https://www.nationsreportcard.gov.

National Endowment for the Arts. "Reading at Risk: A Survey of Literary Reading in America." *National Endowment for the Arts,* October 2002, https://www.arts.gov.

Ouellet, Maxime. "Les 'anneaux du serpent' du libéralisme culturel: pour en finir avec la *bonne conscience.* Un détour par *La Question Juive* de Karl Marx." In *Les deux faces de Janus: Comprendre le libéralisme et le socialisme.* Montreal: Éditions Carré rouge, 2011: 123–144.

Ovid. *Metamorphoses.* Indianapolis: Hackett Publishing Company, 2010.

Parin, Paul and Fritz Morgenthaler. *The Whites Think Too Much: Psychoanalytic Investigations Among the Dogon in West Africa.* New Haven: Human Relations Area Files, 1986.

Pine, Joseph and James H. Gilmore. *Experience Economy: Work Is Theatre & Every Business a Stage.* Boston: [Harvard Business Review Press, 1999.

Postman, Neil. *The Disappearance of Childhood.* New York: Random House, 1982.

Postman, Neil. *Amusing Ourselves to Death.* New York: Viking Penguin, 1985.

Postone, Moishe. *Time, Labor, and Social Domination: A Reinterpretation of Marx's Critical Theory.* Cambridge: Cambridge University Press, 1993.

Postone, Moishe. "Nationalsozialismus und Antisemitismus." In *Zivilisationbruch: Denken nach Auschwitz.* Frankfurt am Main: Fischer, 1988.

Reemtsma, Jan. *Trust and Violence: An Essay on a Modern Relationship.* Princeton: Princeton University Press, 2012.

Rickert, John, "The Fromm-Marcuse Debate Revisited." *Theory and Society* no. 15 (1986): 351–400.

Riesel, René and Jaime Semprun. *Catastrophism, Disaster Management and Sustainable Submission.* Amsterdam: Roofdruk Edities, 2014.

Robinson, Paul. *The Freudian Left: Wilhelm Reich, Geza Roheim, Herbert Marcuse.* New York: Harper & Row, 1969.

Rosa, Hartmut. *Acceleration: A New Theory of Modernity.* New York: Columbia University Press, 2013.

Russell, Bertrand. *Human Society in Ethics and Politics.* London: George Allen & Unwin, 1954.

Rougemont, Denis de. *Love in the Western World.* Princeton: Princeton University Press, 1983.

Sade, Marquis de. *Philosophy in the Bedroom.* New York: Grove Press, 1965.

Sahlins, Marshall. *Stone Age Economics.* Hawthorne: Aldine de Gruyter, 1972.

Schneider, Michel. *Big Mother.* Paris: Odile Jacob, 2003.

Schopenhauer, Arthur. *Parerga and Paralipomena: A Collection of Philosophical Essays.* New York: Cosimo Classics, 2007.

Schopenhauer, Arthur. *The World as Will and Representation, Volume 1.* Cambridge: Cambridge University Press, 2010.

Semprun, Jaime. *L'Abîme se repeuple.* Paris: L'Encyclopédie des Nuisances, 1997.

Sennett, Richard. *The Corrosion of Character: The Personal Consequences of Work in the New Capitalism.* New York: W.W. Norton, 1998.

Sennett, Richard. *The Craftsman.* New Haven: Yale University Press, 2008.

Sohn-Rethel, Alfred. *Warenform und Denkform.* Frankfurt am Main: Europäische Verlagsanstalt Europa Verlag, 1971.

Spinoza, Baruch. *Ethics.* Oxford: Oxford University Press, 2000.

Stirner, Max. *The Unique and Its Property.* Translated by Wolfi Landstreicher. Baltimore: Underworld Amusements, 2017.

Taylor, Charles. *The Malaise of Modernity.* Toronto: House of Anansi Press, 1992.

Theweleit, Klaus. *Male Fantasies.* Minneapolis: University of Minnesota Press, 1987.

Tosel, André. *Kant révolutionnaire.* Paris: Presses Universitaires de France, 1998.

Turkle, Sherry. *Alone Together: Why We Expect More from Technology and Less from*

Each Other. New York: Basic Books, 2011.

Voloshinov, Valentin. *Freudianism: A Marxist Critique*. London: Verso, 2013.

Wiggerhaus, Rolf. *The Frankfurt School: Its History, Theories and Political Significance*. Cambridge: Polity Press, 1995.

Winnicott, Donald. *Playing and Reality*. London: Tavistock, 1971.

Wood, Andrew. "The Uncertain Individual: A Critical Translation of Alain Ehrenberg's *L'Individu incertain*." PhD Dissertation, University of Pittsburgh, 2004.

Žižek, Slavoj. "'Pathological Narcissus' as a Socially Mandatory Form of Subjectivity." *Manifesta* (European Biennial of Contemporary Art, 2000).

Žižek, Slavoj. *Organs without Bodies: On Deleuze and Consequences*. London: Routledge, 2004.

Žižek, Slavoj. *Violence*. New York: Picador, 2008.

ABOUT THE AUTHOR

Anselm Jappe is the author of *Guy Debord* (1993, University of California Press 1999, PM Press 2016), *Les Aventures de la marchandise. Pour une critique de la valeur* (Denoel 2003, La Découverte, 2017, translated as *Adventures of the Commodity*, forthcoming), *L'Avant-garde inacceptable. Réflexions sur Guy Debord* (Lignes, 2004), *Crédit à mort* (Lignes 2011, translated as *The Writing on the Wall*, Zero Books 2016), *La Société autophage* (La Découverte, 2017), and *Béton – Arme de construction massive du capitalisme* (L'Echappée, 2020).

He contributed to the German reviews Krisis and Exit!, founded by Robert Kurz, which developed the "critique of value." He teaches at present at Accademia di Belle Arti in Rome (Italy) and has been visiting professor in various European and Latin American universities. He also lectured at the Ecole des hautes etudes en sciences socials and at the Collège international de philosophie (Paris).